access to religion and philosophy

Social Ethics

Michael Wilcockson

HODDER
EDUCATION
AN HACHETTE UK COMPANY

I am very grateful to Julian Dobson, Philippe Mathieu, Ed Russell and Steve Loxton. But I am especially indebted to Alison Wilcockson for her close critical reading of the whole book.

The Publishers would like to thank the following for permission to reproduce copyright material:

Photo credits
Cover © Justin Guariglia/Corbis; **p.20** © Picture Contact/Alamy; **p.74** © Trevor Smith/Alamy; **p.94** © CSU Archives/Everett Collection/Rex Features; **p.109** © Teun van den Dries/Istock; **p.127** © Pictorial Press Ltd/Alamy; **p.141** © Andrew Fox/Alamy

Acknowledgements
Scripture quotations taken from the Revised Standard Version of the Bible, 2nd edition, copyright © 1971 by the Division of Christian Education of the National Council of the Churches of Christ in the United States of America. Used by permission. All rights reserved; **p.21** *The Times* for the quotes from 'Former lap dancer says that men who think it is harmless are wrong', by Lucy Bannerman, 13 February 2010; **p.74** *The Sunday Express* for the quote from 'We Owe the Arabs Nothing', by Robert Kilroy-Silk, 4 January 2004; **p.173** The Intergovernmental Panel on Climate Change (IPCC) for the graph 'Variations of the Earth's surface temperature: year 1000 to year 2100', SYR – Figure 9-1b

Every effort has been made to trace all copyright holders, but if any have been inadvertently overlooked the Publishers will be pleased to make the necessary arrangements at the first opportunity.

Although every effort has been made to ensure that website addresses are correct at time of going to press, Hodder Education cannot be held responsible for the content of any website mentioned in this book. It is sometimes possible to find a relocated web page by typing in the address of the home page for a website in the URL window of your browser.

Hachette's policy is to use papers that are natural, renewable and recyclable products and made from wood grown in sustainable forests. The logging and manufacturing processes are expected to conform to the environmental regulations of the country of origin.

Orders: please contact Bookpoint Ltd, 130 Milton Park, Abingdon, Oxon OX14 4SB. Telephone: +44 (0)1235 827720. Fax: +44 (0)1235 400454. Lines are open 9.00a.m.–5.00p.m., Monday to Saturday, with a 24-hour message answering service. Visit our website at www.hoddereducation.co.uk

© Michael Wilcockson 2010

First published in 2010
by Hodder Education,
an Hachette UK company
338 Euston Road
London NW1 3BH

Impression number   5 4 3 2 1

Year   2014 2013 2012 2011 2010

Illustrations by Alex Machin and GreenGate Publishing Services

Typeset in Bembo by GreenGate Publishing Services, Tonbridge, Kent

Printed by MPG Books, Bodmin

A catalogue record for this title is available from the British Library

ISBN 978 0340 95774 5

CONTENTS

PREFACE

Access books are written mainly for students studying for examinations at higher level, particularly GCE AS level and A level. A number of features have been included to assist students, such as the study guides at the end of chapters.

To use these books most effectively, you should be aware of the following features:

- At the beginning of each chapter there is a checklist, which is a brief introduction about the key elements that the chapter covers.
- Key questions, words, people, thoughts and quotes in the margin highlight specific points from the main text.
- Profiles of key individuals give information on a philosopher's background and work.
- There are summary diagrams throughout the chapters to aid revision.
- The revision checklist at the end of each chapter summarises the main points.

General advice on answering essay questions

Structured questions will tell you what to include. The following advice is for those questions which leave it to you to work out.

- The most important thing is to read the question carefully and work out what it really means. Make sure you understand all the words in the question (you may need to check some of them in the dictionary or look up technical terms in the glossary at the back of this book).
- Gather the relevant information for answering the question. You will probably not need everything you know on the topic. Keep to what the question is asking.
- Organise your material by drawing up a plan of paragraphs. Make sure that each paragraph is relevant to the question. Include different views within your answer (most questions require arguments for and against).
- Start with an introduction that explains in your own words what the question is asking and defines any technical words. Work through your answer in carefully planned paragraphs. Write a brief conclusion in which you sum up your answer to the question (without repeating everything in the essay).

1 RIGHTS

1 Why rights?

Case study
Torture and the ticking bomb

This well-known example illustrates why many consider that any civilized community must conform to human rights. What was done to the terrorist was inhumane and degrading to society as a whole. All modern human rights agreements consider that torture is wrong, but the paradox is that by refusing to use torture many innocent people will suffer and die and their rights to life and protection violated. The obvious answer is that the rights of the many must count for more than the rights of the one. Yet, this conclusion undermines the very nature of a right which is to protect the individual against the power of the many, but in this scenario the terrorist appears to become the protected victim. So, would it be better to abandon human rights altogether?

Key question

Do we need human rights?

For the past one hundred years moral and legal discussion has increasingly used the language of rights. These rights might include the right to freedom of speech, to movement and travel, to freedom of religious belief, to protest and a right not to be discriminated against because of sex and colour. Rights are at the very heart of contemporary social ethics, which consider the relationship of the individual to society.

The generally accepted view is that rights state something about the dignity and worth of *all* human beings. It is usual, therefore, to refer to them as human rights rather than just rights (which refer to the rights of a particular society). **Civil rights** or **legal rights** on the other hand are granted through law to protect the interests and customs of that society. Rights also fall into two kinds: positive rights give entitlements (such as life and the freedom of speech) and negative rights give protections (such as freedom from cruel punishments and torture).

Key word

Civil rights or **legal rights** are those rights which are based on economic or welfare needs.

But there need not necessarily be a distinction between human rights and civil/legal rights. Increasingly as nation states agree to adopt human rights they are obliged to revise existing laws and rights. However, the distinction between different types of rights is often important when it comes to the relationship between rights and law, especially if their presence enables us to create a more humane, less violent and just world.

2 Rights in theory

Key question

Where do human rights come from, what is their foundation?

If rights are universal and are to establish human dignity and worth then we have to be able to show how a particular right is established. The history of modern rights theory illustrates a significant difference of opinion. For the early rights theorists, rights exist naturally as the foundation of **natural law**. Natural rights are necessary to protect the individual against other humans and the state so that he or she can flourish fully as a human being. But the problem is to determine quite what these natural rights are. The alternative is to argue that certain customs and laws have long been regarded as effective in the governance and welfare of society and these should become the foundation of rights. The problem with this view is that if rights are to have universal application then there are going to be obvious clashes between governments and states as to what constitutes a legitimate right.

Key word

Natural law theorists believe ethics are not derived from human custom but independently from nature.

The quest is to find a rational guiding principle or basis on which human rights can be established.

Key question

What rights are fundamental for human well-being?

Key people

John Locke (1632–1704) was one of the great English philosophers. His philosophy was influenced by his practical study of medicine and chemistry. He was influenced by Descartes but critical of his views. His book *An Essay Concerning Human Understanding* (1690) investigates the origins and limits of reason.

Key quote

'But though this be a state of liberty, yet it is not a state of licence … he has not the liberty to destroy himself.'

JOHN LOCKE, *THE SECOND TREATISE ON CIVIL GOVERNMENT,* IN ERNEST BAKER, *SOCIAL CONTRACT,* 5

Key people

John Finnis (b. 1940) is a legal philosopher at Oxford University. His major work *Natural Law and Natural Rights* (1980) combines the natural law tradition of Aquinas to counter the anti-natural law position of philosophers such as John Austin and H.L.A Hart.

Key thought

Locke's notion of natural rights became the cornerstone on which Thomas Jefferson (1743–1826) based the *American Declaration of Independence* (1776): *'We hold these truths to be self-evident, that all men are created equal, that they are endowed by their Creator with certain unalienable rights, that among these are Life, Liberty and the Pursuit of Happiness.'*

a) Natural rights

The development of modern human rights begins with **John Locke's** essay *The Second Treatise on Civil Government* (1690). Locke argues:

> *The state of nature has a law of nature to govern it, which obliges every one, and reason, which is that law, teaches all mankind, who will but consult is, that being all equal and independent, no one ought to harm another in his life, health, liberty, or possessions: for men being all the workmanship of one omnipotent, and infinitely wise maker; all the servants of one sovereign master, sent into the world by his order, and about his business … there cannot be supposed any such subordination among us, that may authorize us to destroy one another.*
>
> (John Locke, *The Second Treatise on Civil Government* in Ernest Baker, *Social Contract*, pages 5-6)

In summary, Locke proposes the following basic human rights:

- Right of liberty (but that does not mean doing exactly as one wishes).
- Right of self preservation (food, shelter, etc.).
- Right to the protection of life (one's own and others).
- Right of respect for property.
- Right to judge and punish others according to natural law if they violate these rights.

Locke's optimistic view of human nature assumes that at heart humans are co-operative and sympathetic to each other's needs. The underlying principle that reinforces Locke's view is that as life is the generous gift of God then we have a duty not to harm the life, liberty and property of others. Rights therefore remind government that it has no ultimate power over its citizens, for that role is solely God's.

More recently the legal philosopher **John Finnis** has developed an influential natural absolute human rights system based on what he considers to be seven self-evident and equal basic human values (or 'goods') required for human well-being.

- Life (free from mental and physical pain).
- Knowledge (the desire to find out for its own sake).
- Play (physical and mental, alone and social).
- Aesthetic experience (that which gives us pleasure in the appreciation of nature, music, art, etc.).
- Sociability (friendship, harmony in society).
- Practical reasonableness (application of intelligence to one's life and to exercise choice).
- 'Religion' (that which binds us together in collaboration and community).

The rights derived from these basic 'goods' impose absolute duties on governments. This is because the logic of 'practical reasonableness' (the sixth good) indicates that 'to choose directly against any basic values, whether in oneself or in one's fellow human being' would be contradictory and wrong.

b) Contractualism

The natural rights position logically gives no place to government, but for Locke, Rousseau and Hobbes there is a need for government to rule on behalf of the people. In order for this to happen citizens voluntarily give up some of their natural liberties in exchange for protection and the upholding of natural and civil rights and this establishes a **social contract**. So, for example, Locke argued that although we have a natural right to punish those who infringe rights, the administration of punishment is likely to be done in a fairer and more consistent manner by the state. For, as **Rousseau** argues, the state is in a better position to determine what is best for people as a whole:

> *How can the blind multitude, which often does not know what is for its own good, undertake, of itself, an enterprise so extensive and so difficult as the foundation of law? Left to themselves, the People always desire good, but, left to themselves, they do not always know where that good lies.*

> (Jean-Jacques Rousseau, *The Social Contract* quoted in Ernest Baker, *Social Contract*, page 204)

So, as Rousseau argues, natural rights are to be exchanged for **civil rights**, contracting governments to act for the best interests of its citizens. Civil rights fall, as we have already noted, into two kinds: positive rights that place duties on governments to maintain basic standards of living, such as rights to health, housing care and education; and negative rights, such as rights not to be falsely imprisoned, attacked or molested.

However, critics argue that contractual civil rights have completely undermined the original purpose of rights, which were to be universal and independent. Civil rights will inevitably vary greatly from country to country, and from society to society, depending on how affluent a particular society is, and what it considers constitutes a 'basic standard of living'. In some societies people will be able to demand greater goods and services than in others, based on economic conditions rather than basic human dignity. This weakness of the contractual civil rights model has become increasingly more apparent as globalisation has highlighted the unjust inequalities of wealth and living conditions between peoples.

Cross-reference

Read Chapter 8 of *Ethical Theory* by Mel Thompson on contract and rights based ethics.

Key word

A **social contract** is an agreement made between individuals and a governing power, where individual liberties are given up in exchange for general social well-being.

Key people

Jean-Jacques Rousseau (1712–1778) was brought up in Geneva and developed an idea that early human beings were free and happy living instinctive generous lives. It is only once society develops an idea of ownership and power that this original state becomes corrupt. His major works include *Emile* (1762) and *The Social Contract* (1762), both of which were condemned in France.

Cross-reference

See pages 112–114 on globalisation.

Key question

If there are no universal natural rights does it make sense to think in terms of human rights?

Key words

Utilitarianism argues that an action is good if it produces the greatest happiness of the greatest number.

Facts–value distinction considers that the move from saying what something is to what it ought to be is wrong. Fact statements are objective and do not imply value judgements which are subjective and determined by human beliefs or feelings. The distinction is summarised by the phrase: 'is does not imply ought.'

Key people

Jeremy Bentham (1748–1832) was a British philosopher. He used utilitarianism as a rational means of reforming the law.

Key quote

'Natural rights is simple nonsense; natural and imprescriptible rights, rhetorical nonsense, nonsense upon stilts.'

JEREMY BENTHAM, *ANARCHICAL FALLACIES* (1823)

Key word

Positivism is the view that rights are decided by humans on what is observed to work well for society. They are not found in nature or commanded by God.

c) Utilitarianism and rights

Since the nineteenth century the dominant moral system has been **utilitarianism**. Utilitarianism dismisses natural law for two main reasons. First, natural law makes a leap between statements of fact (existing as a human being) to statements of value (what humans ought to do morally). This logical leap is sometimes referred to as the naturalistic fallacy but it establishes the widely held **facts–value distinction**. Second, as natural law ethicists fail to agree on what constitutes basic self-evident rights or duties, it would be irrational to base a whole system on what may be no more than human invented desires.

i) Jeremy Bentham

Utilitarians argue that it is these desires and interests that should be the foundation of morality, which, when fulfilled, lead to general happiness. Happiness should be the only consideration when weighing up how individuals and the state should behave. Such a conclusion would appear to reject natural rights, possibly all rights, out of hand. **Jeremy Bentham** famously said of natural rights that they were 'nonsense upon stilts'. Commenting on Article 2 in the *French Declaration of the Rights of Man and Citizen* (1789) that says rights are 'natural and imprescriptible', Bentham responded, 'More confusion – more nonsense – and the nonsense, as usual, dangerous nonsense'. Natural rights limit government and invite anarchy.

ii) Rights as desires

Nevertheless, Bentham notes that rights are indeed an expression of the things that people desire and would make them happy. But desiring is not enough to make something a right, as he says:

> But reasons for wishing there were such things as rights, are not rights; – a reason for wishing that a certain right were established, is not that right – want is not supply – hunger is not bread.

> (Jeremy Bentham, *Anarchical Fallacies* (1823) quoted in Peter Singer, *Ethics*, page 271)

However, some have argued for a utilitarian basis of rights by developing rights as an expression of interests or preferences. So, if there is a general preference for welfare (for example, health, food and shelter) then these ought to be protected by the state. This argument would suggest a **positivist** version of rights; rights are essentially human inventions based on commonly agreed needs.

The problem with this view is that rights are sometimes designed to override considerations of general welfare, perhaps in favour of a minority or group. This would appear to undermine the flexibility and purpose of utilitarianism which is always to maximise greatest happiness or welfare.

iii) Rights as rules

On the other hand **rule utilitarians** argue that this version of utilitarianism fails to recognise fully that for most of the time individuals and society make their decisions based on well-tried rules. Rules tested and developed over time are designed to save time in moral decision making, distribute goods (such as happiness, preferences and welfare) more fairly, and can have more effective long-term consequences than traditional or act utilitarianism. Rights based on rules can therefore act **instrumentally** as a means of safeguarding these rules and assure people that these rules are given special status.

d) Rights as trumps

Ronald Dworkin is one of the most influential critics of legal positivism and in particular utilitarianism. His argument is that in order for rights to be more than mere preferences, they must have the power, as he puts it, to **trump** or override considerations of general welfare.

The basis for rights, Dworkin argues, is not a general claim to liberty, but rather claims to specific *liberties*. If rights were based on the general principle of liberty, then law would become almost impossible to enact because laws frequently limit individual freedom. Dworkin argues that the foundation of many ethical theories, including utilitarianism, is the principle that people have a basic right to equal consideration and respect when political decisions are being made.

For example, utilitarianism argues that when calculating the 'greatest happiness of the greatest number' each person counts for one, and no more, and no less than one. In other words utilitarianism acknowledges the equal consideration of each individual preference. This is not so very different from Kant's non-utilitarian categorical imperative never to treat people as a means to an end but an end in themselves.

Where Dworkin differs from the utilitarians or Kant is that *only* personal or internal preferences should be considered and external preferences should be discounted. For example, if I wish to live in a large house (internal preference) but I do not want homosexuals to live in large houses (external preference), then the principle of the equality of consideration acknowledges my right to live in a large house but discounts my other preference to exclude others. This is not just a simple calculation of number (I may be supported by the preferences of the local homophobes) but the realisation that by giving someone an internal preference *and* an external preference they effectively count for *two* not for one. Seeing rights in this way does not mean the government is obliged to give me a large house but that I have equal consideration with all others to seek one without hindrance, even if that means revising the law for the sake of a minority.

Nevertheless, Dworkin argues that individual rights may be restricted (through law) if they conflict with another right or can be seen as a serious attack on general welfare (for example, freedom of speech in time of war).

In conclusion, although external preferences exist and are often included in the political process, rights can at least protect those who would be adversely affected by them. This is most clearly seen in the right to practise one's own religion or freedom of speech, which may offend others but would not cause actual harm to society.

3 Rights in practice

a) United Nations Declaration of Human Rights

The Universal Declaration of Human Rights (1948) is the influential document that has helped to establish rights language in everyday Western discourse. Although the *Declaration* is based on the philosophical notion of the 'inherent dignity and equal and inalienable rights of all members of the human family', upholding rights is not just a philosophical idea but a pragmatic one. Rights are *seen* to do good and to have enhanced international law and co-operation.

i) Background

The *Declaration* developed out of the League of Nations and its desire for world justice, fair dealing, protection of minorities and especially ethnic minorities when creating border treaties, workers' rights and the abolition of slavery. Impetus for the *Declaration* was reinforced after the Second World War when the Nuremberg Trials of Nazi genocide atrocities were held to test 'crimes against humanity'. For the first time, crimes could be judged internationally and not domestically and by doing so the notion of legal sovereignty was challenged. 'Crimes against humanity' has expanded to be applicable outside war and to include any systematic violation of human rights.

ii) Aims and Articles of the United Nations Declaration

The preamble to the *Universal Declaration of Human Rights* begins by asserting Locke's and Rousseau's belief in the inherent dignity of all humans. However, it is careful not to state that rights are natural or intrinsic but 'inherent', that is inferred not self-evident.

- Rights are defined as being **inalienable**.
- Rights are therefore the foundation of world freedom, justice and peace.
- The *Declaration* is to act as a 'common standard for all peoples and nations'.

Key word

Inalienable means that rights cannot be transferred or taken away.

Articles 1, 2 and 3 act as the foundation for the 27 articles which follow:

- **Article 1:** 'All humans are born free and equal in dignity and rights. They are endowed with reason and conscience and should act towards one another in a spirit of brotherhood.'
- **Article 2:** 'Everyone is entitled to all the rights and freedoms set forth in this Declaration, without distinction of any kind, such as race, colour, sex, language, religion, political or other opinion, national or social origin, property, birth or other status.' Rights extend beyond political boundaries.
- **Article 3:** 'Everyone has a right to life, liberty and security of person.'

iii) Implementation and development of rights

Since 1948 various **treaties** and **conventions** have developed which have added to and offered variations of the *Declaration*. Treaties establish the terms and conditions in which participating nations subscribe to the notion of international human rights. Conventions have focussed and clarified developing concerns not made explicit in the original *Declaration*. Recent conventions have addressed questions of race (1969), women (1981), torture and inhumane treatment (1987), children (1990), migrant workers (2003), disabilities (2006) and enforced disappearance (2006).

In 1986, the United Nations General Assembly established a system to ensure the integrity of rights' development. They established that rights should be consistent with the existing body of international rights law; rights should always uphold the inherent dignity of humans; rights should be precise, practicable and realistic to implement; and rights should attract broad and international support.

Key words

A **treaty** is a formal contract and agreement.

A **convention** is an agreement which is slightly less formal than a treaty.

Human Rights Act (1998)

In 1998, the United Kingdom 'Humans Rights Act' was passed, coming into full force in October 2000. It enshrines the European Convention on Human Rights by safeguarding these rights in law. The European Convention on Human Rights was passed by the Council of Europe after the Second World War and has its own Court of Human Rights in Strasbourg. It is quite separate from the European Union (EU). The Act does three things:

- It makes it unlawful for a public authority, such as a government, local authority or the police, to breach the Convention rights, unless an Act of Parliament meant it couldn't have acted differently.
- It means that cases can be dealt with in a UK court or tribunal. Until now, anyone who felt that their rights under the Convention had been breached had to go to the European Court of Human Rights in Strasbourg.
- It says that all UK legislation must be given a meaning that fits in with the Convention rights, if that is possible. If a court says that it is not possible it will be up to Parliament to decide what to do.

(Source: *Human Rights Act: An Introduction*
Published by the *Home Office Communication Directorate* (October, 2000))

b) Rights and duties

Article 29 of the *Declaration* makes three important qualifications to the idea of rights and freedoms as expressed in the *Declaration*:

1 'Everyone has duties to the community'.
2 Rights and freedoms may be limited by law in order for the rights and freedoms of others to be possible and importantly in accordance with 'the just requirements of morality, public order and general welfare in a democratic society'.
3 Rights and freedoms must not be exercised contrary to the 'purposes and principles of the United Nations'.

i) What kind of duties correspond to rights?

The *Declaration* states that 'everyone has duties to the community' because a right only operates if it is recognised and protected. Protection implies that relevant duties have been imposed on others. The question is what duties correspond to particular rights.

- If a right is understood morally, then rights imply unconditional duties on the community (that is, the government), which is obliged to protect rights. Therefore, unconditional corresponding moral duties are also imposed on individuals because not to do so would lead to a contradiction; I am obliged to recognise that rights apply to all, not just myself.
- If a right is understood legally then it will depend on what kind of right is implied in law and this will determine what its corresponding or 'correlating' legal duty is.

The last point is dealt with in the influential analysis by the legal philosopher **Wesley N. Hohfeld**. Hohfeld distinguishes four types of right as they are used in law and their correlating 'duties'. The significance of these differences is particularly important in law, because there is a tendency for some people to 'bundle' all rights together as if they are of one kind whereas, in fact, there are different types of right which therefore imply different types of duty.

Hofeld's four types of rights and their correlating or corresponding duties are:

1 **Claim-rights** (or rights) are the moral rights established through a contract in which if x has a claim against y, y has a duty to x. If, for example, x loans y money, then x has a claim-right that obliges y to pay back the loan. The correlating duty to claim-rights is 'moral duty'.
2 **Liberties** (or privileges) give a person the option of doing x but without obligation. For example, if the law allows me to walk across your back garden, you have no right or duty to enforce that I do/do not walk across your back garden. The correlating duty to liberty rights is 'no right'.

3 **Powers** give a person the power of law to set limits on the rights or interests of others. Powers protect rights and enable claims (or 'liabilities' such as costs and repair of damages) to be made against others. For example, in my will I may distribute my possessions to those whom I nominate, even if members of my family think they ought to be included. The correlating duty to power rights is 'liability'.

4 **Immunities** protect a person from the actions of others. For example, if I have the right to join a trade union then I am guaranteed immunity (for example, protection from being sacked) from my employer who might try to stop me from doing this. The correlating duty to immunity rights is 'disability'.

ii) Abortion and the problem of clashing rights

As we have seen, the second condition of Article 29 states that rights may be limited by law in order for the rights and freedoms of others to be possible. Such an idea, however, challenges the absolute nature of rights especially when compromise between clashing duties is particularly problematic. For example, if a woman has been raped, does she have a right to an abortion even if that means violating the rights of the foetus?

- Some argue that rights are only applicable to those creatures capable of making a rational choice. As the status of the foetus is ambiguous, it is doubtful whether it can make any kind of claim-rights which would oblige the woman to keep it. Furthermore, as the woman is the owner of her body and, as Mill expressed it, 'sovereign' over what happens to it, then she has a right to an abortion if she chooses.

- But if, as many argue, the foetus has the basic right to life because it is an innocent human being (and potentially rational) then the question is whether the foetus' rights carry as much weight as the woman's rights. Some have argued that as the woman owns her body then she has *prior* rights; the mother and foetus are not two tenants in the same house rented by both. The foetus is using the mother's body and therefore has tenant's rights not ownership rights. She may choose to acknowledge the rights of the foetus but she is not compelled to do so (immunity rights). Having a right to life does not give one an absolute right to use someone else's body.

- However, although this might give her the right to self-defence and expel the foetus, some argue that it does not give her the right to kill it. In response, some feminists have argued that the overriding right is a woman's right to privacy and reproductive autonomy. In terms made familiar by Dworkin, in this case the particular *internal* liberty trumps any other consideration which might be imposed *externally* by society.

Key question

How absolute are rights?

Cross-reference

For a more detailed discussion of abortion and rights read Michael Wilcockson, *Issues of Life and Death*, pages 43–45.

Key quote

'Over himself, over his own body and mind, the individual is sovereign.'

J.S. MILL, *ON LIBERTY* (1859)

This example illustrates the fact that not all rights carry the same weight and have to be judged according to the underlying principle of most rights, which is the dignity and welfare of all humans. For some, this undermines the very essence of the inviolability of rights, but for others, because rights have instrumental value, circumstance will determine which rights should be prioritised.

iii) Too many rights trivialise the meaning of rights

Finally, Article 29 states that rights and freedoms must not be exercised contrary to the 'purposes and principles of the United Nations'. However, whilst this might imply some constraint on the development of rights outside the moral framework of the UN charter, the tendency has been to proliferate rights and downgrade their moral significance.

Mary Warnock argues that too much rights language can devalue the notion of rights because in many cases a right is unenforceable or it is an ideal which cannot through circumstance be applied. Warnock gives the example of the **UNICEF** Convention on the Rights of the Child which the United Kingdom ratified in 1991. The convention states that children have equally and everywhere: a 'right to life' and a right to a family, not to work, to be educated, a right to play and exercise their minds in the arts and free speech. Admirable as such ideas are, not only are they generally unenforceable, but because they add so many specific enforceable ideas they devalue what is meant by a basic human right:

> *All this is doubtless excellent; but we ought to be clear that the convention is putting forward an ideal of childhood such as is generally enjoyed by children in liberal Western societies, which are prosperous, and where childhood can therefore be prolonged. Even if we embrace this ideal, and attempt to realise it for as many children as possible, it is straining the concept of a right to suggest that for every child whose childhood is not like this there is a positive breach of duty on someone's part, or on the part of society in which the child grows up.*

(Mary Warnock, *An Intelligent Person's Guide to Ethics*, pages 65–66)

c) Waiving and losing rights

How absolute are rights? If rights are inalienable it suggests that they can never be taken away. However, the contractual basis of rights also suggests that although human rights may be universal, it does not mean that someone who has abused their side of the contract is necessarily entitled to their full range of rights. A prisoner who is in jail forfeits many ordinary rights, in particular the right to freedom of movement and travel. But does he lose his right to vote and to be involved in the democratic process of which he is still a part? Could he also commit a crime so heinous that he also loses his right to life?

Key question

Can society have too many rights?

Key people

Dame Mary Warnock (b. 1924) philosopher and Mistress of Girton College, Cambridge (1986–1989). She is widely known through her *Warnock Report* (1984) which became the foundation of the Human Embryology and Fertilisation Act (1990).

Key word

UNICEF stands for United Nations Children's Fund.

Key quote

'The trouble is that if the language of rights is used to describe such ideals, morally excellent though they may be, that language is devalued.'

MARY WARNOCK, *AN INTELLIGENT PERSON'S GUIDE TO ETHICS*, 66

Finally, can one waive or give up certain rights? For example, can a person waive their right to life, if, for example, they are very sick or in pain or they wish to donate an organ to someone that means they will die as a result?

i) Torture and mitigation

Key question

What is inhumane treatment?

In the case study at the start of this chapter we considered the use of torture and the protection of public interests. The *United Nations Convention Against Torture and Other Cruel, Inhumane or Degrading Treatment or Punishment* was adopted in 1984 and established an absolute ban on torture outside war as an individual criminal act (that is, those carrying out torture are liable for punishment). But how is torture to be defined? The United States Justice Department in 2002 stated that torture only included 'agonizing' or 'excruciating' pain'. But public outcry caused by the 'interrogation' of Iraqi prisoners in 2002 led to a modification of the definition to include examples of degrading treatment such as lack of sleep, constant light, loud and incessant noise, loss of a sense of time and so on.

Key quote

'I would suggest that it is over the twin commitments to democracy and human dignity that underlie the continuing prohibition of torture.'

ANDREW CHAPMAN, *HUMAN RIGHTS*, 90

Nevertheless, it is unclear whether degrading treatment also includes insulting or threatening language. More significantly, some argue that at some point the greater aim to protect society and each individual citizen's dignity within it must take priority. As in the case of the terrorist and the ticking bomb, if torture could provide the information needed to avert a major catastrophe then an argument based on **mitigation** acknowledges that in some extreme cases torture is the lesser of two evils.

The problem with this argument is that:

Key word

Mitigation means alleviation and in law is used to refer to factors which can be used to justify a lesser punishment.

- A civilized society should never treat a person in a degrading way.
- Torture undermines the democratic system of law which protects all citizens against the use of violence.
- It is unclear what constitutes the 'lesser of two evils' and if torture is permitted in one extreme case it might lead to a slippery slope whereby it is used in less extreme (but 'vital') situations.
- Evidence produced under torture is unlikely to be reliable.

ii) Euthanasia and criminal law

The issue of euthanasia illustrates the problem that if a person chooses to waive their rights this does not necessarily permit others to behave as if this right did not exist.

Key question

Can a person give up their right to life and ask to be killed?

For example, if, as in the case of assisted suicide, a person waives his or her right to life, this does not permit a doctor or family member to aid in that person's death. In fact, if the person dies because they are assisted by another, according to the Suicide Act (1961) that person will have committed a criminal act. The Act states:

Cross-reference

Read Michael Wilcockson, *Issues of Life and Death* Chapter 4 on euthanasia.

A person who aids, abets, counsels or procures the suicide of another or an attempt by another to commit suicide shall be liable for a term not exceeding fourteen years.

However, there is presently considerable debate regarding whether euthanasia is about waiving one's right to life or the right to die or the right to self-determination. For example, in the case of Diane Pretty (2002), who was paralysed from the neck down with motor neurone disease, her request to the right to self-determination was rejected by the European Court of Human Rights. They ruled that the right to die is not a corollary of the right to life. Furthermore, had she been suffering from a life-threatening condition then the courts might have allowed the doctors to assist in her dying (making it less painful) but not in the termination of her life.

iii) Limitation of freedoms

We have seen that in the case of torture very few would support its use because it is always seen to be a disproportionate means to an end. However, this does not rule out limitations being placed on rights in general. Limitations on human rights are generally judged in proportion to other rights at stake. This is by no means easy and often it is left to judges to determine the balance between competing rights.

For example, does a celebrity have the same right to privacy as an ordinary person? A journalist might argue that the public have a right to know about someone who enjoys the privileges that celebrity brings, providing what he publishes is true.

If we take Dworkin's argument about rights as individual liberties then the role of the judge would be to consider whether the individual right (internal) to privacy applies to everyone equally (externally). Equally, the judge might have to decide between the public's right to know about those in the public sphere who in some way represent them (for example, artistically, politically) as being in 'the public interest' and an individual's right to privacy.

The role of the judge is to determine what is proportionally reasonable. There is no absolute answer because, although the rights in themselves provide a basis or starting point, they are still open to interpretation. Therefore, in practice, limitations placed on rights will depend on the application of existing law, consideration of legal rights and the cultural/moral norms of that society (such as attitudes to sex, language, religion and so on).

iv) Losing rights: capital punishment

Capital punishment raises the question whether criminals who commit heinous crimes forfeit their right to life. The retributivist's argument for capital punishment is that there are some crimes against society so terrible that only the death penalty can adequately

Cross-reference

Read Michael Wilcockson *Issues of Life and Death* on capital punishment as retribution, pages 88–93.

Key question

Is the use of capital punishment necessarily a violation of human rights?

Key people

Thomas Aquinas (1225–1274) was born in Italy, completed his student studies in Naples and joined the Dominican Order in 1244. He was greatly influenced by the philosophy of Aristotle as can be seen in his greatest work, *Summa Theologica*. His ideas continue to exert great influence on the Catholic Church.

Key quote

'Although it be evil in itself to kill a man so long as he preserve his dignity, yet it may be good to kill a man who has sinned, even as it is to kill a beast.'

THOMAS AQUINAS, *SUMMA THEOLOGICA*, 2.2, QUESTION 64, ARTICLE 30

pay back the injustice caused. It is a view supported in the natural law tradition and by Kant.

Thomas Aquinas, for example, argued that people who carry out terrible crimes that break the fundamentals of natural law (such as the deliberate killing of an innocent person) can no longer be protected by the same rights which protect the innocent. The criminal has abrogated his right to be protected.

The retributivist argument today is expressed through either of these two positions:

- **Rights retributivism** supports the notion that where a person has brutally removed the basic rights of others (life and dignity, for example) it follows that he has forfeited his own right to live and deserves to die. Those who support the 'fair play' argument add that even though the criminal ought by rights to die, there may be other reasons why this may not be carried out (for example, the victim's relatives may not want it).
- **Contract retributivism** argues that where a citizen has blatantly broken his side of the social contract at a fundamental level, for example through an act of treason, by smuggling drugs (as in Malaysia), by blasphemy or through murder, then society is right to regard his action with severity. The threat of the death penalty is a sign of the seriousness in which the social contract is held. A citizen knows what the law is and if he chooses to break it, he can expect to receive his just deserts.

But even those who support capital punishment in theory argue that, although the state has a *right* to kill those who have murdered, it does not have a *duty* to do so.

But many not only find cold-blooded execution of a criminal repellent because of its unnecessary cruelty, but an infringement of all rights conventions. Amnesty International argues against the death penalty for many of the same reasons that it finds torture to be degrading to the society which permits it.

> *The Universal Declaration recognizes each person's right to life and categorically states, 'No one shall be subjected to torture or to cruel, inhuman or degrading treatment or punishment.' In Amnesty International's view the death penalty violates these rights …*

> *The death penalty may also encompass other human rights violations. When a state jails people solely because of their beliefs, it violates the right to freedom of belief and expression. The death penalty is sometimes used to silence forever political opponents or to eliminate 'troublesome' individuals. Whenever and wherever used, it finally and unalterably severs a person's right to hold opinions and to speak freely because it takes that person's life.*

(Amnesty International, *When the State Kills*, pages 1–2)

4 Rejecting rights

Despite the significance of rights and rights language, there are those who caution against rights as the basis of morality and society. Some, such as Marxists, argue that rights create a false set of ideas which have alienated humans from their true humanity. Critics, such as Mary Warnock, argue that rights have corrupted our sense of duty to society and being a good citizen. Some Christian scholars consider that rights have confused our relationships with one another, the natural world and God, whilst philosophers such as Alisdair MacIntyre argue that rights are no more than subjective feelings and fanciful intuitions.

a) Marxism

Marxists share something of Bentham's scepticism of natural rights when he described them as dangerous and nonsensical. But Marxists go further. Rights are the product of a conservative and socially limited culture. It is true that they might challenge the power of the state but their aim is to develop individual egoism at the expense of the collective. Rights increase human sentimentality for life and liberty when what is really needed is to harness the deeper human creative powers towards change. The one basic value that Marxists maintain is that all humans should be involved in the means of production – all other values are relative to this. Rights especially are the product of society that invents goals which reduce the creative spirit and channel it into false ideas, such as the ownership of property, belief in God and obedience to the state.

b) Duty not rights

> It is my contention that a civil society could not function if it subsisted only on indignation where rights have been infringed, without the occasion for admiration as well for those who, like the Good Samaritan, go out of their way to display altruism.

> (Mary Warnock, *An Intelligent Person's Guide to Ethics*, page 74)

Mary Warnock's comment above summarises the feeling of many that rights language has failed society in two ways:

- **Needs and wants**. People often talk of their rights when what they mean are needs and wants. When these are denied they feel that some injustice has been done to them; they speak of this as a 'denial of their rights'. If rights are to exist in any meaningful way they are to uphold the human dignity of those living in community – using rights in this way emphasises the individual at the cost of the community.

- **Rights are not the basis of morality.** Whilst it is sometimes helpful to use rights language, these rights are derived from preceding moral values. For example, if I have promised to pay back the £10 I borrowed from you, then you have a right to be paid back £10. So the moral duty of promise keeping is logically prior to the right of being paid back.

Warnock fears that so much emphasis on rights today leads people to expect society to fulfil their demands, even though in our day-to-day lives with others, personal morality is to do with relationship and a sense of duty born out of obligations. However, we continue to rely on those who *do* have a sense of public duty, for the greater good. This much older idea of morality is derived from the Aristotelian based idea of the virtues such as generosity, moderation and respect for others. It does not need rights language to develop a flourishing society, but rather a revival of duty language.

For example, a teacher teaches her children to the best of her ability because she feels it is her duty as a teacher to do so; she does not teach them well because they have a right to education which she then feels she has a duty to obey.

Finally, although Locke and others have argued that natural rights are part of the divinely ordered creation, many argue that the absolute nature of rights can appear to make obedience to rights more important than obedience to God and the rest of the created order.

Summary diagram

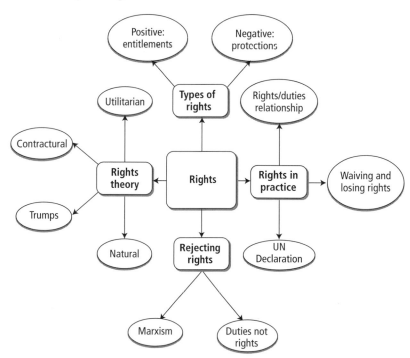

Study guide

By the end of this chapter you should have considered what is meant by rights, and whether these are derived naturally, by considering what is basic to human welfare or agreed on as part of a social contract. You should be able to discuss the problems that rights pose when balancing one set of rights against another. Finally, you should be able to argue why rights may not be in the best interest of society and whether they have made people less morally responsible to each other.

Essay questions

1 a Explain what are meant by natural rights.

1 b 'Only a right which is universal and absolute is a right.' Discuss.

The essay might begin by explaining what rights are for and why (if they are to do with human flourishing) they are intrinsic and universal to humans. The views of Locke and Finnis should be outlined and explained with appropriate quotations.

The natural law position is assumed in the evaluative part of the question. This might be defended on the grounds that unless a right is absolute and universal it cannot protect a person against the state or the immoral behaviour of others. However, the essay may then go on to argue that it is very hard to demonstrate what these natural rights are without falling into the naturalistic fallacy. An utilitarian or contractual position might then be defended.

Further essay questions

2 To what extent have human rights undermined society?

3 'Sometimes the needs of society are more important than the rights of individuals.' Discuss.

4 Assess the view that rights are incompatible with religious belief.

Revision checklist

Can you give brief definitions of:

■ positive and negative rights
■ human rights and legal rights
■ social contract
■ the facts–values distinction
■ mitigation.

Can you give examples of:

■ Locke's basic rights
■ Finnis' basic goods
■ three basic articles from *The Universal Declaration of Human Rights.*

Can you explain:

■ why Bentham rejected natural rights
■ what Dworkin means by rights as trumps
■ Hofeld's four types of rights and duties
■ why Aquinas considered that certain crimes forfeit basic rights
■ why Marxism is suspicious of rights.

Can you give arguments for and against:

■ the use of torture for the good of the many
■ the right to die through assisted suicide
■ rights as the basis of a just society.

Chapter checklist

This chapter considers how women see and understand themselves and how they are seen and treated by society. Three types of feminisms are outlined and discussed: liberal/equality, reconstructionist and radical. Within these, feminism issues such as work, motherhood, reproduction and education are considered. The final section looks at various Christian responses to feminism and the way in which the Bible can be interpreted by some to support feminism and by others to question it.

1 Body and society

Key question

Do men really treat women as equals?

Case study
Lap dancing: where are the boundaries?

Milly took up lap dancing after she was fired from her job and as an easy way, so she thought, to fund her drug and alcohol addiction. She had been led to believe that there were well-defined boundaries which would protect her from becoming part of the sex industry. But she quickly found out that this was not the case.

> *It always crosses the line. So-called boundaries are ludicrous. No one sticks to that. And if you do, you quickly lose out.*

But for Milly the real eye opener was what she learned about men.

> *The worst thing was what I learned about men: that the way to make money from them is to be submissive and pretend to be stupid. What these men wanted was to exert power in the way they felt they could not in normal situations.*

In order to earn money girls were expected to rub their faces in men's groins or let them fondle their breasts.

Milly's disgust wasn't just that lap dancing revealed the continuing sexist attitudes of men but society's toleration of something which treats women as objects.

> *Whether individual women feel degraded by them or not lap dancing degrades all of us because it is providing a socially acceptable place for women to be treated as sex objects.*

Milly is sceptical about whether legislation or regulation will make much difference. For, as along as men hold deep-seated views of women as sexual objects, then they will continue to be exploited. She concluded:

> *The only way to really change things, if there is such a thing as an equal society, is if men learn to understand that paying for sexual stimulation is degrading and does have a negative impact. It's not just a bit of fun. But as long as men are men, there will always be a market.*

(QUOTATIONS FROM *THE TIMES*, 13 FEBRUARY 2010)

Although it is fashionable to argue that feminism is dead, this case study suggests that sexist and patriarchal views of society are still deeply ingrained. Milly's conclusion is interesting. Does she think there is a distinctive male view that cannot be changed? Or does she think that society's consciousness needs to undergo a far more radical change if true equality is to be achieved? Some might argue that it is up to women how they use their bodies, but is this really the case if it means pretending to be something she is not?

Key quote

'The worst thing was what I learned about men: that the way to make money from them is to be submissive and pretend to be stupid.'

THE TIMES, 13 FEBRUARY 2010

a) Women's experience

Milly's case illustrates the complexity of a whole variety of ways in which women have challenged society, which has been termed feminism. The term itself is controversial and provokes negative and positive reactions as much from men as from women. In essence, though, feminism is about how women see and understand themselves in relation to society. Feminism is not just about women. Milly's experience illustrates that for society to function well there is a challenge to men and their **sexist** attitudes and institutions.

It is for these reasons that there is no one single coherent system called 'feminism'. The different experiences of women have inevitably led to a wide range of different perceptions of what it means to be a woman. But if there is one theme running through all forms of feminist thought it is the common desire to value women and liberate them from sexism.

b) Women's voices

Milly's experience of sexism illustrates one of the most controversial debates between feminists and non-feminists alike: the significance of body difference and identity. Some take an essentialist line that there are distinctive feminine and masculine characteristics which are not the product of society but that of biology or nature. Others take an existentialist approach and argue that the body is of little significance and that gender difference is the product of nurture through culture and upbringing. However, in her influential study, **Carol Gilligan** offers an alternative position by considering the power of the voice in creating a view of oneself. Her analysis compares the way in which men and women use their voices to create their identities. Gilligan's unusual approach does not treat voice as a metaphor, but literally. A person's voice, loud or soft, high or low, strident or calm, is a powerful psychological and social means of forming relationships.

Voices change historically and personally over time. Gilligan is interested in the way women's voices in particular have been shaped in Western Europe and especially in the USA. This is because, more so for women than men, women have experienced 'disconnection' between their public voice and their inner voice. For centuries of custom and tradition women have been conditioned not to give voice to their actual thoughts but to view acting selflessly as a virtue. But as her interviews with women of all ages reveals, to act selflessly means to deny oneself an authentic identity. This has not been helped by a society which, when it speaks of 'us', actually defaults to a particularly male view of existence. Most of the time we are unaware that this is so, and it is only in extreme circumstances that the male 'market', which Milly experienced, reveals itself so explicitly.

Key word

Sexism is the discrimination of women by men (and sometimes the other way round) based on cultural or stereotypical prejudices.

Key question

Is there a disconnection between women's private voices and their public voice?

Key people

Carol Gilligan (b. 1936) is professor at the New York University School of Law. Her book, *In a Different Voice* (1982), developed an idea how the voice rather than the body is the source of psychological development. Her revolutionary approach changed many aspects of law, education, psychology and philosophy.

Key quote

'Without voice, there is not possibility for resistance, for creativity, or for a change whose wellsprings are psychological.'

CAROL GILLIGAN, *IN A DIFFERENT VOICE*, XIX

Women's discovery that to be selfless means not to be in relationship is revolutionary because it challenges the disconnection from women and the disassociation within women that maintain and are maintained by patriarchy or civilization.

(Carol Gilligan, *In a Different Voice*, page xiii)

As Gilligan concludes, 'lies make you sick'. The lie she has in mind could apply equally to men as well as to women, but it is particularly women who have suffered by speaking in one voice whilst pretending that the other inner voice does not exist.

2 Liberal or equality feminism

In the rapidly changing societies during the time of the French Revolution, women writers of this period, notably **Mary Wollstonecraft** in Britain and **Olympe de Gouges** in France, argued that if civil rights were being extended to *all* men (regardless of class or belief) then they should also include rights for women. Anything less would be to treat women as means and not as ends in themselves (that is as a form of slavery) and would fail to apply moral duties to *all* people (men *and* women).

The liberal feminism of Wollstonecraft does not argue that the roles of men and women should be the same, but that women should have the same opportunities (to work, to vote, to be educated) and the same rights *as men*. After two hundred years many of these aims have been fulfilled in the West and the number of jobs which are barred to women – even in the armed forces – are shrinking all the time.

a) Equality of opportunity

Another characteristic of the **Enlightenment** philosophers was that reason offered the opportunity to reject anything which could not adequately be explained in rational terms. Traditions, superstitions and religion cannot in themselves be sufficient reason to justify legislation. One of the most influential statements of what we might call the liberal principle is enshrined by John Stuart Mill in *On Liberty* (1859), in the utilitarian principle of the greatest happiness of the greatest number (men and women). The principle is essentially non-judgemental and states that whatever people believe on a personal and private basis is no concern of the state. The function of the state is to maximise personal freedom and only to limit certain behaviour when it interferes with the freedom of others and reduces the overall happiness of society.

The classical liberal feminist position is expressed in John Stuart Mill's *The Subjection of Women* (1869) and his partner (and later wife) **Harriet Taylor's** *Enfranchisement of Women* (1851). Their essays are significant for their disagreement about the nature of women's liberation. Mill held that even though women *are* less capable than men, they should be given the freedom to exercise their talents to the best of their ability. Mill rejected the naturalistic claim that the woman, as wife, has a duty to minister to the needs of the family. Giving women the ability to vote is symbolic of the role of women in a liberal society.

Taylor went further. The inequalities between men and women come from tradition and custom: once women are given equal education, placed in the workforce and share in the running of the state, then it will be apparent that women are equal to men in all these aspects. Taylor argued that if women are to be true *partners* with men they must have the opportunity to earn their own income independently from their husbands.

b) Welfare

Since the 1960s feminists have had to resolve the tension between the woman as mother and career woman. At first the new liberated woman was encouraged to be both – as Taylor had suggested a century before. But the have-it-all 'superwoman' model of the 1960s and 1970s was an impossible aspiration and despite countless magazine articles claiming that women could do both, for many it was simply another form of slavery. The latest phase of the liberal feminist movement is to return to the liberal principle of social reform and ensure that the state provides adequate childcare, flexible working hours and maternity leave for women, and to focus on the particular welfare needs and preferences of women because equality of opportunity is not enough.

Betty Friedan, in her influential book *The Feminine Mystique*, argues that the preference of liberal feminism is only a stage in the historical development of women in society. The next stage will be an androgynous one of 'true' equality between men and women, where gender differences will simply have melted away and women and men can have truly equal roles in society.

c) Criticisms of liberal feminisms

Even though liberal feminism has a number of forms, its aims are sufficiently similar for the following criticisms to apply generally:

- **Androcentric.** The earlier phase of liberal feminism looked for equality for women and men in a man's world. Wollstonecraft wanted girls to be educated in the same way that boys are educated. In other words, the desire to give women rights and opportunities are male centred or 'androcentric' and seen in terms of male values and virtues. True liberation has to acknowledge that in some important areas men and women are different.

- **Reason and rights are masculine**. The enlightenment emphasis on the universal place of reason has been developed entirely in masculine terms. The contention here is that women's logic is more intuitive and co-operative, whereas the kind of rationality that liberalism has accepted to be self-evident is male gender-specific: legalistic and hierarchical. In other words, liberal feminism does not have a coherent idea of women's *identity* and adopts the male tendency to promote mental activity above emotion as superior.

- **False duty**. Some have argued that many women simply do not want to be 'like men'. They do not want to work and feel that their role as wife and mother is undermined by the implicit criticism that if they do not work they have devalued themselves. Women do not have to be members of the public world to be good citizens.

- **Superficial**. Many argue that liberalism only scratches the surface. True feminism needs to be far more revolutionary if *real* social justice is to be achieved. Feminism requires a much more radical reconstruction of society's consciousness. It is true that liberalism may have changed many important laws, but its founding principle has prohibited it from intruding into the private thoughts and values of individuals. Whilst liberalism continues in this form, society will continue to be at heart sexist and prejudiced against women.

3 Reconstructionist feminism

Key word

Patriarchal refers to the values and structures of society which are derived from the male point of view.

The second form of feminism considers that liberal feminism will ultimately fail in its aim to liberate women, because society is, deep down, male and **patriarchal**, and designed to fulfil the needs of men not women. There are two important philosophical influences here: Marxism and existentialism which both offer a radical reconstruction of society and take into account the particular experiences of women.

a) Marxist feminism

Key question

What kind of changes in mindset and the deeper structures of society will enable women to be truly liberated?

Karl Marx (1818–1883) considered that history was divided between those who owned the means of production (the bourgeoisie) and those who were dependent on them (the proletariat). Without the ability to determine their own lives (especially as the result of industrialisation) the proletariat became slaves, exploited economically and mentally. Situations like this are so often considered to be an unchangeable objective reality. But this is **false consciousness**. For feminists it is a false consciousness that women are necessarily economically and mentally dependent on men. To change this situation requires revolutionary reconstruction of society.

Friedrich Engels (1820–1895) was Marx's friend and supporter and argued in *The Origin of the Family, Private Property, and the State* (1884) that whereas in the past men and women enjoyed some degree of partnership, women in industrial society have become increasingly the object of men's power as the means of production (not just in child rearing but in all tasks associated with creating the family). Just as the bourgeoisie exploits the proletariat, so men consider themselves as the owners of women – and this is true in *every* social class. Marxist feminists frequently describe the woman's role in terms of **prostitution** because the metaphor expresses how she is treated sexually and economically by men.

i) Production

A major contribution of Marxist feminism has been to elevate the role of the woman in rearing and sustaining of the family. **Capitalism** has tended to belittle the 'work' of the woman as less valuable than the real work of men (or even women) for wages outside the home. In the past, in pre-industrial Europe, women and men worked with the common aim of sustaining the family. With industrialisation, the means of production moved outside the family into factories; whereas men were able to work *outside* the home, women were left with the primary job of child rearing. The effect has been to devalue the woman's role, because she is not a wage earner and does not contribute publicly to society.

Modern Marxist feminists have argued that liberation for women should not confine a woman to a particular role – wage earner and child rearing are *equally* important and significant. The problem is caused by the capitalist environment, which has set ideas about what constitutes useful work, and liberal reforms which, though designed to protect women and children from exploitation, have in fact, made it harder for women to work as co-equals with men. When women have worked publicly as teachers, nurses, cleaners and secretaries their work has often been regarded as an extension of their family role and consequently paid less than men.

ii) Socialisation of domestic work

One solution is for society to recognise the essential role a woman plays in the home and in the rearing of the family *in society*. In other words, work of this kind is not a private activity but should be recognised as an essential public contribution along with any other paid employment. The socialisation of the woman's role enables her to be placed as an equal with all other workers and gain the respect she deserves. Advocates urged the state to provide an allowance or welfare payment in recognition of the woman's roles. Although this view was controversial among Marxist feminists, it nevertheless inspired the 'wages for housework' campaign in the USA in the late 1960s.

iii) Sexuality and pornography

The Marxist feminist shares a similar view with the liberal feminist in that she does not have a particular view of what a woman ought to be like or whether she has a distinctive gender identity. Relationships are considered almost entirely in terms of whether the economic conditions have exploited or enslaved the woman. Marxist feminists today have concentrated on making radical inroads into the workplace and for equal treatment such as pay and conditions. Engel's views on marriage and sexuality consider that all relationships under capitalism are bound to be unhappy and exploitative. We can see this in the way in which many aspects of the media portray women as commodities to be acquired, adorned and used as sexual objects by men. **Pornography** is viewed as one of the worst aspects of a patriarchal and sexist society. Marxist feminists regard all these social aspects as forms of slavery and typical of capitalist societies where relationships have been reduced to buying and selling. However, Engel's view illustrates the hope that once economic freedom has been achieved, then there will be equal respect between men and women; marriage will not be a form of institutionalised prostitution (that is, slavery) but love between equals.

b) Existential feminism

Existentialism shares with Marxism the idea that humans can only really be fulfilled and happy when they act freely and in accordance with their true nature. But where it differs from Marxism is in its view that humans are by nature productive beings – this limits both women and men. Existentialism is far more radical and argues that there is *no intrinsic human nature*. Jean-Paul Sartre (1905–1980) argued that humans are born with no predetermined nature – their physical existence (*en soi*) precedes their self-conscious essence (*pour soi*). Essence or nature is developed by conscious free action. In Sartre's terms an inauthentic life is when a person is unable to act freely or where they let themselves slip into a stereotypical role. He calls this **bad faith**.

However, it is Sartre's lifelong partner **Simone de Beauvoir** who, whilst sharing many of Sartre's philosophical ideals, reveals a major flaw in his way of thinking. Her influential book *The Second Sex* acknowledges that women have allowed themselves for centuries to become the second sex and to act the role of the wife, the lover, the sex object according to the needs of men. Whilst they continue this form of bad faith they cannot live fully authentic and fulfilled lives.

Women's essence is defined by men for men; women have unwittingly allowed themselves to be defined by men.

> *One is not born, but rather one becomes a woman. No biological, psychological, or economic fate determines the figure that the human female presents in society; it is civilization as a whole that produces this creature, intermediate between male and eunuch, which is described as the feminine.*

(Simone de Beauvoir, *The Second Sex*, page 295)

Key quote

'Now, what peculiarly signalizes the situation of woman is that she – a free and autonomous being like all human creatures – nevertheless finds herself living in a world where men compel her to assume the status of the Other.'

SIMONE DE BEAUVOIR, *THE SECOND SEX*, 29

But whilst this is arguably true, de Beauvoir also senses that women have become trapped by the deeper structures of society, to become objects (like the rest of nature). Far from being equal with men in the existential quest, women are in an impossible position.

Women are not subjects, as men are, able to exercise freedom, but objects fixed by the weight of tradition. De Beauvoir argued that for too long women have accepted and encouraged themselves to believe in 'the eternal feminine', a notion that as the second sex their job is to become what men expect of them. Women have allowed themselves to become the passive bystanders in society. It has been very different for men who have constantly struggled with each other competitively in a **master–slave** relationship but at least have recognised each other's existence.

Key words

Master–slave relationship is an analogy which Hegel used to describe the way in which history and human consciousness have developed through a process of conflict and struggle.

Absolute Other describes how, according to de Beauvoir, women as conscious subjects have been completed ignored by society.

But women have not been part of this power struggle. They have accepted the roles of mothers and homemakers, and believed that that their bodies and minds are essentially passive and feminine. As human subjects they have made themselves invisible to men and become the **Absolute Other** – alienated and disregarded. This false consciousness or *mauvaise fois* now needs to be exposed and reconstructed; the aim of *The Second Sex* is to do this. Women must reject their feminine roles, challenge male consciousness and be recognised as genuine rivals. By defining themselves through their conflict with men, women will also become their own authentic human subjects. Change can only come from a *collaborative* effort of both men and women by altering the consciousness of society so that women can become their own genuine subjects.

c) Criticisms of reconstruction feminisms

- **Work as freedom**. Many have suggested that giving women economic freedom and valuing their work in the family only tackles one aspect of the feminist agenda – it does not go far enough considering the particular sexual needs and interests of women independent of their economic status.
- **Private diversity**. Some have argued that the Marxist feminist emphasis on the social and public value of women and the family belittles diversity of opinion and the private role of the family.

- **Body**. With their concern with authentic existence and emphasis on *pour soi* consciousness the existential feminists have downgraded the body and its significant place when defining the whole person.

4 Naturalist and radical feminism

Key question

What are the moral implications for women if they are fundamentally different from men?

Whereas other forms of feminism have sought either to ignore the body by emphasising reason (liberal feminism) or to consider the public social roles of men and women in a liberated society (reconstructionist feminism), naturalist/radical feminism argues that neither of these two forms of feminism have really considered what it means to be a woman. Naturalist/radical feminism tackles the immensely complex relationship between gender and biology. It is an area fraught with difficulties.

There is no one kind of naturalist feminism. However, what they all have in common is a radical view that because a woman's body is distinct from the male, her existence can only be ultimately complete when she lives as a woman and not in man's image of a woman. But how does one define what is 'natural' and how can one know what characteristics are uniquely female?

Philosophically, the naturalist feminist is quite different from the liberal feminist. Whereas the liberal wishes to be quite clear that moral values *cannot* be derived from biology or nature, the naturalist feminist feels that it is from her biologically unique status that women's values can and must be derived.

a) Reproduction and motherhood

Key question

Does being a mother define a woman?

Is being a mother ultimately the *telos* or purpose of being a woman or is this simply a social idea imposed by men? Radical feminists assert both. One group considers modern reproductive technologies to be the great liberator from biological processes; the other group argues that the ability of women to reproduce and rear a child is a unique experience that gives them the power to distinguish themselves from men. Both groups agree that the basis for women's oppression has been the male's power and control over the process of reproduction. The argument follows on from the Marxist model, but whereas for Marx and Engels social history is determined by class struggle between the property owning classes and the workers, radical feminists argue that the process of history should be understood as the sexual oppression of men over women and the struggle for women to be liberated from sexual slavery.

Key people

Mary O'Brien was born in Glasgow and trained as a nurse before emigrating to Canada. There she taught feminist theory and sociology. She was a founding member of The Feminist Party of Canada (which now no longer exists). She wrote two influential books: *The Politics of Reproduction* (1981) and *Reproducing the World* (1989).

Shulamith Firestone (b. 1945) is a Canadian-born Jewish feminist and co-founded the New York Radical Women in 1969. Her book *The Dialectic of Sex* (1970) synthesises the ideas of Marx, de Beauvoir, Freud and Engels. She argued that in a post-feminist age the nuclear family would cease, as people would live in communes and children would be reared by the state.

Key word

Androgynous means having neither conventional masculine or feminine characteristics or blending both characteristics together.

Key people

Ann Oakley (b. 1944) is a British writer and influential sociologist. She is the founder-director of the Science Research Unit, Institute of Education, University of London. Amongst her publications are: *Sex, Gender and Society* (1972), *Woman's Work* (1976) and the novel *The Men's Room* (1989).

i) Reproduction as liberation

Reproduction and motherhood for writers such as **Mary O'Brien** give women their unique ability to assert their own identity. Using the Marxist model of insiders and outsiders, men are essential outside the reproductive process; only a women is fully able to own the means of reproduction from conception to birth. However, what has happened in the past is that alienated men have tried to reassert their role in the process and determine when and how women should give birth. For many feminists, whereas contraception allows a woman to choose when to reproduce, other forms of artificial reproduction such as surrogacy and artificial insemination by donor are treated with great caution. All aided forms of reproduction allow men to control a woman's means of reproduction and reduce her to the level of a breeder or prostitute.

ii) Reproduction as oppression

However, for many feminists the opportunity offered by reproductive technologies provides the means by which to liberate themselves from the constraints of being a reproducer. **Shulamith Firestone** is perhaps one of the more outspoken representatives of this line of thought. In her utopia, by eliminating reproduction, women will no longer be defined by their biology, and can enter into the public realm as co-equals with men in an **androgynous** society. In the first phase of this revolution women must ensure that they own all the processes of reproduction – abortion, contraception, artificial insemination by donor and so on – as each represent a means by which liberation from reproduction will be possible. Ultimately, technology will make it possible for a woman to be completely free from the 'barbaric' biological aspects of childbirth (which she famously compared to 'shitting a pumpkin') and able to choose when and if she wants a child in her own time.

iii) Motherhood as a cultural phenomenon

Is a woman unfulfilled if she does not want to have and rear children? This strikes at the heart of the radical feminist view that 'motherhood' is the ultimate patriarchal gender construction by men in order to control women. A woman who does not have maternal feelings is considered to be unfeminine.

Ann Oakley presents the view that motherhood is a socially contrived phenomenon and quite separate from being a biological mother. There are three myths or fallacies of motherhood:

all women need to be a mother
all mothers need their children
all children need their mothers

(Ann Oakley, *Woman's Work: The Housewife, Past and Present*, page 186)

Each of these claims can be countered by observation from other cultures and scientific research. Girls are brought up from an early age to play the role of mother – protecting, nurturing and feeding in play with dolls or in the roles assigned for them in the household. 'Maternal instinct' simply does not exist. Many new mothers have no idea how to feed or dress a baby. The most oppressive fallacy is that children need their biological mother more than their father. Oakley argues that children who have been adopted are no less successful than children who have been reared by their biological parents, and that one-to-one parenting has no particular advantage over those children who have been brought up in communes (such as a kibbutz, for example). Other feminists suggest a psychological interpretation of 'motherhood' is a means of compensating for a woman's lack of usefulness in the workplace and justifying her role at home. All these attitudes are created by living in a patriarchal society.

However, not all radical feminists take such a hard line as this. Instead, they suggest that oppression lies in fulfilling the *male* expectation of motherhood – 'real men' do not feed, wash, nurture and 'mother' their children. Liberation comes when children are reared not to associate 'motherhood' just with the woman but with both partners. There is even a sense that, because feminist values are broader than male ones, a child brought up with these will have a greater and richer range of human experiences, without the false gender stereotypes inherent in traditional patriarchal families.

b) Mary Daly

The most radical form of feminism considers that because women's nature is so different from men's nature, then the only whole and ultimately worthwhile life is to be separate from men.

One of the most outspoken and influential writers of this kind of feminism is **Mary Daly**. Her books mark a progression of thought from the acceptance of androgyny to its complete rejection. Her influence, though, is not only important because of her critique of the Roman Catholic church but also her adaptation of the philosophical visionary, Friedrich Nietzsche (1844–1900).

Daly adopts Nietzsche's notion that if society is really to reject God then it needs to undergo a transformation or 'transvaluation'. Through what he calls the **will to power** – what used to be thought of as the negative values of pride, competition, lust and greed replace the old 'slave' mentality of love, forgiveness and tolerance. But Daly goes further. She argues that it is only women who have the strength of character to make this possible because Nietzsche's vision was still strongly patriarchal.

Key people

Mary Daly (1928–2010)
American radical feminist philosopher and theologian. She taught at Boston College for 33 years until 1999. Originally a Roman Catholic she rejected Catholicism and Christianity in her early books, notably *Beyond God the Father* (1973), and then developed her own distinctive feminism and language in works such as *Gyn/Ecology: The Metaethics of Radical Feminism* (1978) and *Pure Lust* (1984). She was dismissed from Boston because she refused to teach men in her classes.

Key word

Will to power
according to Nietzsche is the instinctive basic drive which is the source of all human activities and understanding of the world.

Nietzsche, the prophet whose prophecy was short circuited by his own misogynism wanted to transvaluate Judeo-Christian morality, but in fact it is women who will confront patriarchal morality as patriarchal. It is radical feminism that can unveil the 'feminine' ethic, revealing it to be a phallic ethic.

(Mary Daly, *Beyond God the Father*, page 102)

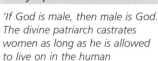

Key quotes

'If God is male, then male is God. The divine patriarch castrates women as long as he is allowed to live on in the human imagination.'

MARY DALY, *BEYOND GOD THE FATHER*, 19

'The liberation of language is rooted in the liberation of ourselves.'

MARY DALY, *BEYOND GOD THE FATHER*, 6

The will to power for Daly is the inner and outer liberation of women as women. As an illustration of what this means, Daly constantly redefines language in its radically non-patriarchal meaning. For instance 'lust' – the title of one of her books, *Pure Lust* – in its male usage refers to manipulative, self-gratifying and exploitative sex, whereas in its female liberated sense it refers to the vigorous, lusty and powerful woman.

It does not follow that all lesbians are necessarily feminists, although, the view of Daly naturally leads her to the position where in order to realise the new feminist vision, free from patriarchal influence, the only satisfactory non-exploitative sexual relationship has to be with other women.

Lesbianism is also a public political gesture. It suggests a public rejection of traditional values and a radically new model of human sexuality that does not involve reproduction, motherhood or submission. It is not just symbolic that there is no penetration by the male of the female in sexual intercourse, for all male sex is about domination (feminists often point out how rape, child molesting and sexual abuse is usually performed by men and rarely by women), whilst lesbianism offers women a wholly different kind of sexual relationship as a meeting of sexual equals.

The Most Unholy Trinity of Rape, Genocide and War is a logical expression of phallocentric power. These are the structures of alienation that are self-perpetuating, eternally breeding further estrangement. The circle of destruction generated by the Most Unholy Trinity and reflected in the Unwhole Trinitarian symbol of Christianity will be broken when women, who are by patriarchal definition objects of rape, externalize and internalize a new self-definition whose compelling power is rooted in the power of being. The casting out of the demonic Trinities is be-coming.

(Mary Daly, *Beyond God the Father*, page 122)

c) Critique of naturalist/radical feminism

● **Feminine values fallacy.** Radical feminists talk as if it is possible to discern unique, fixed feminist values independent of male patriarchal ones. This supposes first, that it is possible to be sufficiently removed from the male view, and their 'false consciousness', and to see beyond. Second, that these values are in themselves only derived from women. Third, that they are necessarily better or preferable or 'good'. Finally, if these values are in opposition to prevailing social (male) values, then as society changes so will women's values.

- **Essentialism**. If women's gender role has been shaped by society then it is equally true that men's gender has been socialised. So, if women seek to be liberated from their perceived gender type then the same is true for men. It does not follow that all men are naturally or essentially potential rapists. Radical feminists have therefore to be consistent and allow that men, just as much as women, can alter their 'false consciousness' and gender perception.

- **Fragmentation and introversion**. The formation of women's groups may give women welcome support and encouragement, but their radical stance often alienates other women and the sympathy of men. Furthermore, by rejecting men, some radical feminists behave in just the same way as the men who treat women as inferior. It is difficult to see how this form of feminism is morally superior to the sexist system it has castigated.

5 Christian responses to feminism

Christianity has always assimilated and adjusted to its cultural and philosophical environment and the various feminisms outlined above have all been instrumental in the formation of Christian feminist theology. The insights of secular feminism have enabled Christian theology and ethics to explore new areas and rediscover ideas which, over the centuries, have become obscured or forgotten.

Key question

To what extent is Christianity compatible with feminism?

a) Feminist theology

There is sometimes a tendency to treat the Bible as if it had all been written by the same person and to treat contradictory passages as evidence of muddled thinking. Biblical theologians today encourage readers to see the text as a *narrative* responding not only to the events they relate, but to the wider story of God's involvement with people. There are indeed passages which might be considered sexist, patriarchal and anti-feminist, but as Wollstonecraft commented, they must be seen as poetical products of the times and circumstances in which they were composed.

i) New social order

In the New Testament it is the four gospels that refer most explicitly to the words and teachings of Jesus. It is often pointed out that Jesus' portrayal in these texts presents a far more radical view of men and women than those in the rest of the New Testament. We should be careful here not to make too sharp a contrast. The gospels themselves

Key word

The Kingdom of God is the term used by Jesus in the gospel to describe a new social order based on an intimate, personal relationship with God now or in the future.

Key quotes

'The women who had come with him from Galilee followed, and saw the tomb, and how his body was laid: then they returned, and prepared spices and ointments.'

LUKE 23:55–56

'And she had a sister called Mary, who sat at the Lord's feet and listened to his teaching.'

LUKE 10:39

Key question

How radical was Jesus' teaching about challenging patriarchal attitudes to women's bodies?

Key people

William Countryman is emeritus professor in biblical studies at Church Divinity School of the Pacific and author of many books including *Dirt, Greed and Sex* (1988). As a liberal theologian he challenges the traditional/conservative teaching on gender and sexuality.

Key quote

'When a woman has a discharge of blood which is her regular discharge from her body, she shall be in her impurity for seven days and whoever touches her shall be unclean until evening.'

LEVITICUS 15:19

were written to present Jesus to different communities, and although there is a higher historical content than in Paul's letters, they are nevertheless theological documents. Jesus was not a feminist; there is no evidence that he had either the philosophical or psychological aims that characterise any of the feminist movements today. But the gospels consistently suggest that his view of women and men challenged many of the deeply ingrained traditions of the time.

Jesus' central idea of the **Kingdom of God** radically challenges the distinction between rich and poor, outcast and conformist, men and women. The following are only a few examples:

- It is the faith of John the Baptist's mother Elizabeth and obedience of Jesus' mother Mary (Luke 1:5–7, 26–38) which permits them to become instruments of God's incarnation in Jesus. It is women who accompany Jesus to the cross, when almost all his male followers have deserted him (Luke 23:27–31), and who are the very first to experience the resurrection (Luke 24:1–11).
- Whereas traditionally in Judaism a woman could not become a disciple of a rabbi, Jesus had many women followers – even when these women were considered social outcasts (Luke 7:36–50, 8:1–3). For this reason Luke uses the story of Mary and Martha (Luke 10:38–42) as a challenge to those who considered a woman's duty to be only domestic chores.

ii) Purity and women's bodies

Many modern feminist theories account for male aggression towards women as fear of women's bodies. Fear of a woman's sexuality as the seducer is illustrated in the wisdom literature (Proverbs 6:24), or her power of reproduction depicted as a punishment (Genesis 3:16). The Book of Leviticus (15:19–24) refers to a woman's monthly period as a time when she became ritually outcast from the community. Judaism's religious, moral and national identity was defined through purity laws. **William Countryman** argues that the early Christian challenge to so many of these taboos, including a radical reappraisal of men and women, was a way in which it eventually defined its own separate identity from Judaism.

A highly significant passage occurs in Mark 5:25–34, when Jesus touches a woman who has had internal bleeding for twelve years. His deliberate action dismisses the taboo of touching a woman in public, and at the same time rejects the Levitical law which made her an outcast because of her prolonged bleeding. Jesus' own empathy for the woman as a person is described as 'power going out of him'; she is cured not because she is a woman but because of her faith and desire to seek a whole life.

Key quote

'God shows no partiality, but in every nation anyone who fears him and does what is right is acceptable to him.'

ST PETER IN *ACTS OF THE APOSTLES*, 10:35–35

Key word

Baptism is the moment when a person becomes a Christian through repentance and accepting salvation through Jesus Christ.

The question of purity rules caused considerable controversy amongst the early Christians. The Council at Jerusalem (Acts 15) debated the question of Gentile admission and whether circumcision was a prerequisite for entry. In these early days, Peter learnt that, just as the ancient food laws (Acts 10:9–16) were no longer applicable, so also 'God shows no partiality, but in every nation anyone who fears him and does what is right is acceptable to him' (Acts 10:35–35). The utterly consistent view held by the very early church was that **baptism** marked a new moment in the life of the convert. Paul, who understood this as the essence of the Christian gospel, concluded in his letter to the Galatians (having justified his rejection of purity rules of circumcision and table fellowship):

For as many of you as were baptised into Christ have put on Christ. There is neither Jew nor Greek, there is neither slave nor free, there is neither male nor female; for you are all one in Christ Jesus.

(Galatians 3:27–28)

There are many implications for Christian feminists today. Purity might imply any circumstance where a women is debarred from a job or employment for no other reason than her sexuality. But overcoming purity taboos also suggests that at a fundamental level, deepseated prejudices about women's sexual inferiority will need a change in male consciousness.

iii) Women's roles

The biggest challenge for the feminist biblical theologian is the interpretation of passages which do not fit into the emerging pattern that 'in Christ there is neither male nor female'. It is often considered that Paul appears to be at the very least inconsistent. In 1 Corinthians 14:34–36 Paul forbids women to speak in Church and stipulates that they should seek to be educated by their husbands at home, a view also reiterated by the author of 1 Timothy (probably a follower of Paul):

Let a woman learn silence with all submissiveness. I permit no woman to teach or have authority over men; she is to keep silent. For Adam was formed first, then Eve; and Adam was not deceived, but the woman was deceived and became a transgressor. Yet woman will be saved through bearing children, if she continues in faith and love and holiness, with modesty.

(1 Timothy 2:11–15)

Key quote

'For as many of you as were baptised into Christ have put on Christ. There is neither Jew nor Greek, there is neither slave nor free, there is neither male nor female; for you are all one in Christ Jesus.'

ST PAUL, *LETTER TO THE GALATIANS*, 3:27–28

To these can be added the 'household rules' – lists of duties for men, women and children, found in 1 Timothy 3:1–13 and 1 Peter 2:11–3:12.

Likewise you wives, be submissive to your husbands, so that some, though they do not obey the word, may be won without a word by the behaviour of their wives, when they see your chaste and reverent behaviour.

(1 Peter 3:1–2)

But for the reconstructionist feminist theologian the passage illustrates just how difficult it was for some early Christian communities to implement the radical social demands of the gospel. For why reprimand the women in the community unless women were *already practising* their new found freedom and causing some embarrassment to Jews and Gentiles. The author of 1 Peter says as much:

Maintain good conduct among the Gentiles, so that in case they speak against you as wrongdoers, they may see your good deeds.

(1 Peter 2:12)

Finally, Paul explicitly mentions the assistance of women amongst his co-workers, Priscilla (Acts 18:1, 18, 26), Apphia (Philemon 2) and Phoebe (Romans 16:1–2). Uncovering the very early history of Christianity therefore reveals a radical challenge to existing society. Knowing this, argues **Elisabeth Schüssler Fiorenza**, enables Christian women today to act in sisterly solidarity with those of the earliest communities which included pioneering women. As she says (quoting Judy Chicago), 'our heritage is our power'.

I argue that on the contrary, that women were not marginal in the earliest beginnings of Christianity; rather, biblical texts and historical sources produce marginality of women. Hence texts must be interrogated not only as to what they say about women but also how they construct what they say or do not say.

(Elisabeth Schüssler Fiorenza, *In Memory of Her*, page xx)

b) Conservative Christian critique of feminism

The Right believes that the only way to have a relationship with God is through gender; in doing so, it dismisses concerns about material oppression and reinterprets women's role as mother and housewife as natural, fulfilling, even liberating … many forms of feminism – both secular and Christian – valorize only those women who go to work.

(Kathy Rudy, *Sex and the Church*, page 43)

The view expressed here by **Kathy Rudy** could well summarise the arguments of the radical feminists who have campaigned for wages for housework and the acknowledgement that a woman's role in the house is *as* valid as a man's external role in the workplace. Although they may share this superficial aim, the 'Right', which Rudy refers

Key question

Has feminism undermined the spiritual and social foundation of the family?

to here, are the powerful Christian conservatives whose influence in the USA has had a profound effect on middle class morality and politics.

A key driving force of the Right is a mistrust of all liberal ideologies and, in particular, feminism. Liberalism and feminism, in both secular and Christian forms, are, they argue, the principal reason for increased divorce, dysfunctional families and sexual immorality (in particular homosexuality), corrupting the morals of the young and ultimately undermining the American social dream of a happy prosperous nation.

Conservative theology believes that men and women were created differently by God, not to be unequal but to have quite different roles contingent on their gender. This notion is grounded in the creation itself:

> *So God created man in his own image, in the image of God he created him; male and female he created them.*

> (Genesis 1:27)

But for the conservative, the image of God is only accomplished when men and women complete the roles assigned to them. In Genesis this is stated after the fall as being:

> *To the woman he said, 'I will greatly multiply your pain in childbearing; in pain you shall bring forth children, yet your desire shall be for your husband, and he shall rule over you.'*

> (Genesis 3:16)

A woman's role is to be wife and mother and create the 'domestic haven' where her husband can escape from the external world. But submissiveness is not equated with weakness, after all, Eve is depicted as the 'mother of the living' and a mother's role is one who brings life into the world, nurtures it and brings it into the knowledge and love of God. Conservative theology is especially critical of those who confuse these roles. A woman who works outside the home not only removes a job from a man, but diminishes a man's role and his *responsibilities* to his wife. Those who are persuaded by feminism are not liberated but exploited.

Summary diagram

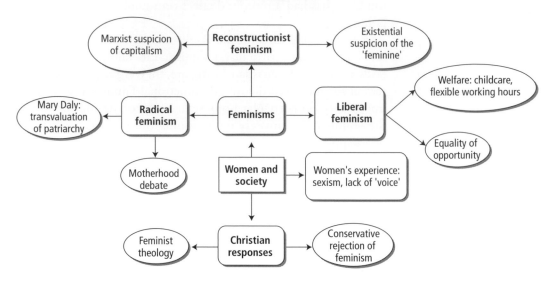

Study guide

By the end of this chapter you should have considered what is meant
by sexism and patriarchy and how this has affected women's sense of
identity, their place in society and their relationship with men. You
will have considered different kinds of feminist response to these issues
and different interpretations of the conditions which will offer women
equality and freedom. You will also have considered how Christianity
has responded spiritually to feminism and whether feminism is or is
not compatible with Christian theology of gender and society.

Essay questions

1 'Feminism and Christianity are incompatible.' Discuss.

The argument might agree that many feminists attribute sexism and
patriarchy to religious, and notably Christian, teaching about men
and women. Examples from the Bible could illustrate Paul's view
that women should be obedient to their husbands or that in the
Old Testament women had fewer rights than men. Furthermore,
many feminists consider that any notion of God automatically
establishes women as the 'other', which, as Mary Daly argued,
reinforces the view that 'if God is male, then male is God'.

On the other hand, many theologians argue that the true
liberation of women must include the spiritual liberation offered by
Christianity and that in Christ 'there is neither male nor female'.
Examples of Jesus' treatment of taboos against women might be
discussed and Fiorenza's argument explored. However, the essay
might conclude by agreeing with conservatives that Christianity and
feminism are incompatible.

Further essay questions

2a Explain the aims of liberal or equality feminism.

2b 'Liberal feminism fails to address the real causes of sexism.' Discuss.

3a Explain why Christianity is divided over the place of women in society.

3b Assess Mary Daly's criticisms of religion.

4 'There can be no equality between men and women because men and women are not the same.' Discuss.

Revision checklist

Can you give definitions of:

- sexism
- patriarchy
- androgyny
- androcentric
- gender.

Can you explain:

- Marxist feminist teaching on work
- Simone de Beauvoir's rejection of the 'eternal feminine'
- Mary Daly's radical feminism of transvaluation
- Conservative Christian criticisms of feminism.

Can you give feminist arguments for and against:

- women as mothers
- marriage and the family
- belief in God
- pornography.

Chapter checklist

This chapter considers the various definitions of human sexuality and gender, what is normal and what is deviant. Religious and non-religious attitudes to marriage and divorce (including annulment) are discussed as well as various types of cohabitation relationships. The ethics of contraception are reviewed. The second part of the chapter discusses the ethics and politics of homosexual and non-heterosexual relationships. The chapter concludes by looking at various normative ethical responses to sexual ethics.

1 Sexuality

Key question

What is sexual integrity?

Case study
Sex and personal integrity

Joseph Fletcher, a moral philosopher, describes a time when discussing a moral dilemma with a young woman:

> Her problem? 'OK. This is it. One of our intelligence agencies wants me to be a kind of counterespionage agent, to lure an enemy spy into blackmail by using my sex.' To test her Christian sophistication, I asked if she believed Paul's teaching about how our sex faculties are to be used, as in First Corinthians. Quickly she said, 'Yes, if you mean that bit in the sixth chapter – your body is the temple of the Holy Spirit – but…', she added, '…the trouble is that Paul also says, "The powers that be are ordained of God".'
>
> The defense agency wanted her to take a secretary's job in a Western European city, and under that cover 'involve' a married man who was working for a rival power. Married men are as vulnerable to blackmail as homosexuals. They did not put strong pressure on her. When she protested that she couldn't put her

personal integrity on the block, as sex for hire, they would only say: 'We understand. It's like your brother risking his life or limb in Korea. We are sure this job can't be done any other way. It's bad if we have to turn to somebody less competent and discreet than you are.'

So. We discussed it as a question of patriotic prostitution and personal integrity. In this case, how was she to balance loyalty and gratitude as an American citizen against her ideal of sexual integrity?

(Joseph Fletcher, *Situation Ethics*, pages 163–164)

Fletcher's case study illustrates the power and contradictions of human sexuality. On the one hand preserving sexual purity is essential to one's sense of personal integrity, but on the other hand for others using one's body sexually as a means to an end is no great deal. The power of the sex drive can be exploited; it can lead to betrayal; it can be directed to others of the same sex or the opposite sex; but it is unclear where this is appropriate and where the boundaries lie. Sex is clearly more than procreation; it is an essential aspect of personal identity and social life.

a) Sex and gender

It has become almost commonplace among many that sex and gender are entirely separate. Whereas sex refers to what one is biologically, gender is determined by one's environment. For example, the feminist writer **Ann Oakley** writes:

Key question

Are sex and gender the same?

Cross-reference

See pages 30–31 on Ann Oakley.

Key words

Intersexual describes those who have an extra sex chromosome (for example, XXY) and whose sex is therefore neither fully male or female. About two per cent of the population are intersexual.

Essentialists believe that there are intrinsic masculine and feminine characteristics. They reject the view that gender is entirely the product of environment.

Sexuality refers to sexual identity.

Key people

Michel Foucault (1926–1984) was a French philosopher, historian and sociologist. Through his multi-disciplinary analysis of prison, madness and medicine he developed his distinctive view of power and knowledge (deeply influenced by Nietzsche). This approach was developed in his seminal three volumes: *The History of Sexuality* (1976–1984).

Key question

Should we reject the idea of there being a normal sexual identity?

Key word

Discourse is any written or spoken communication but Foucault understands discourse to be the way in which language symbols and practices are put together in a particular way.

Much of the confusion in the debate about sex roles comes from the fact that we tend to speak of 'sex differences' when we are really talking about differences of gender. Because of this the rationale of a society based on liberation from conventional gender roles is written off as an impossibility.

(Ann Oakely, *Sex, Gender and Society*, page 189)

But the matter is not easily resolved. Customs associated with gender may well be cultural, such as clothes, hairstyle and social roles, but writers, ancient and modern, have long suggested that the way in which societies are constructed in terms of morality, law and religion is based on an *objective* understanding of the individual sexual body.

Biologically, the process of sex is determined by the relationship of chromosomes, hormones (notably testosterone and Müllerian inhibiting factor) and environment in the womb. Normally, a person is female if their sex chromosomes are typically XX and male if their chromosomes are typically XY. There are some minority of **intersexual** cases, such as Klinefelter's syndrome, where a person's sex is indeterminate or ambiguous.

Some have argued that gender is indeed partly determined by environment but cannot be entirely separate from biology. **Essentialists** such as Freud, argue that gender is largely a result of a person's biological/psychological development.

More recently there are those who have questioned whether it is even possible to talk about sex and gender, and have preferred to think in terms of **sexuality**, which covers a wide spectrum of sexual identities – heterosexual, bisexual, homosexual, lesbian and so on.

b) What is normal?

The French philosopher and historian **Michel Foucault** has been particularly influential in developing a view which challenges whether it is even possible to talk of gender. His analysis of history and human institutions illustrates the constant tension between the open-ended way in which people naturally think of themselves sexually and the tendency of society's institutions to control how people behave. Foucault is interested in the 'production of ideas'. Every age develops its own **discourse** – a mixture of language and practices which organise the social ordering of the body. But, Foucault argues, history demonstrates that humans flourish when social ideologies are questioned and the power of the dominate discourses dismantled.

i) 'Normality'

Foucault argues that normal/abnormal are not meaningful terms; ethics are to be thought of as practices relative to time and place. For example, in ancient Greece sexuality was not defined in natural/unnatural terms but as healthy/unhealthy virtuous living. Erotic love was considered in the same terms as eating and sleeping well, but, like virtuous living, it also required self-mastery, a regard for beauty and balance.

There was a marked difference on the one hand between a heterosexual relationship between husband and wife, where sex was to be seen in the context of running an efficient household (having and rearing children) and erotic love on the other. Homosexuality was acceptable as part of what Foucault terms the **ars erotica** – the experience of sexual relationship based on pleasure and independent from the production of children. It was not uncommon for men to take on a younger boy as a lover, although it was considered bad manners, even immoral to continue with this relationship once the boy reached puberty. So, even in Greek society, sexual relationships were not entirely without control, but the point Foucault is making is that Greek society illustrates how Western society since that time has increasingly developed controls over sex by arbitrarily defining what is normal.

ii) Sexuality as historical construct

The distortion has arisen due to first, an obsession with wanting to classify everything into categories or 'species' (as he calls them), and second, the desire to get people to conform to these categories. By inventing a category called 'human sexuality' society has developed an enormously powerful and *repressive* tool to order people into conformity. The **scientia sexualis**, as he terms it, has in Western society been controlled first by the Christian Church, then especially in the eighteenth and nineteenth centuries by psychologists, sociologists, lawyers and educationists.

> *Sexuality must not be thought of as a kind of natural given ... It is the name that can be given to a historical construct: not a furtive reality that is difficult to grasp, but a great surface network.*
>
> (Michel Foucault, *The History of Sexuality: The Will to Knowledge*, page 105)

However, because for so long homosexuality has been considered a deviant practice it has played a significant role in modern society in liberating sexuality from sex. Its 'reverse discourse' which once served as means of giving gay men and women a sense of their own identity, has now become the tool for querying or **queering** all of society's attitudes to sexuality.

Key word

Ars erotica or 'erotic art' is Foucault's term to describe societies who view sexuality in terms of pleasure.

Key words

Scientia sexualis or 'science of sexuality' is Foucault's term to describe the way in which sexual practices have been controlled and formalised by various institutions in Western societies.

Queering means to challenge all beliefs and structures that seek to fix sexuality as if it is something objective.

Key quote

'The problem is not to discover in oneself the truth of one's sex, but, rather to pursue one's sexuality henceforth to arrive at a multiplicity of relationships.'

MICHEL FOUCAULT, *ETHICS*, 135

2 Marriage and divorce

Even though cohabitation has become more prevalent in the last few decades, the majority of the adult population is married, and marriage is associated with a number of factors, such as educational outcome and health.

(Ben Wilson and Steve Smallwood, in *Population Trends 131* (2008), page 28)

Marriage is a human institution which can be found in every society from antiquity to the present day. Its significance, though, is far more than the union of two people because through it society expresses a range of moral, religious and social attitudes.

At its simplest level, marriage is a man and a woman living together in a sexual relationship at the same residence. So, how is this different from cohabitation, which has increasingly become the modern alternative? There are two key non-religious factors:

- **Marriage as a public event**. In other words, because society formally acknowledges a couple's intentions to live together it formally grants them certain rights and the protection of the law. In many cultures the drawing up of a marriage contract sets out various conditions not dissimilar to the **prenuptial agreements** which have become so popular in the USA today (but are generally not acknowledged in English law). Marriage is a practical affair and its very formality is intended to make day-to-day living as effective as possible.
- **Marriage as long-term commitment**. Cohabitation, it could be argued, is by nature more open-ended, short term, casual and informal. Marriage, by contrast, is about long term, committed relationships. This should not be confused with love. Marriage *may* be about love, but love in many traditions is not a condition of marriage but something which develops later.

a) Traditional natural law view of marriage

The dominant notion for marriage in the West rests on the natural law arguments developed from Augustine and Aquinas. Both theologians begin with the observation that humans, the world-over, pair off for the primary purpose of procreation. From this primary end or 'good' other secondary purposes or '**goods**' can then be deduced:

- Marriage is for the procreation of children.
- Children need to be nurtured, so marriage is about companionship and love.
- As sex outside marriage would result in children being brought into non-stable relationships, marriage is also for the

'containment' of the sex drive into a monogamous, lifelong committed relationship.

The order and way these goods are expressed from writer to writer may vary but the essential ideas remain the same.

It is important also to note that there is nothing especially religious about this argument. This is interesting as many people today associate marriage with those who are religious, perhaps because for two hundred years or so marriage has been almost exclusively run and regulated by the churches.

b) Marriage as religious sacrament

The notion of sacrament is probably the most important factor which distinguishes the religious from the non-religious understanding of marriage. In Christian theology a sacrament is a holy or religious moment, quite often described as an outward and visible sign of an inward state of grace. However, there are several views as to what this means.

- **Essential change.** For Roman Catholics and some Anglicans a sacrament is composed of two parts: the external symbols and its internal essence. The externals in marriage might include the spoken words by the couple (promises to be faithful, the intention to have children), the exchange of tokens (rings for instance) and the blessing by the priest. All these signify that an internal and ontological change has taken place and the couple have become 'one flesh' (Mark 10:8). This view of marriage is **indissoluble** and excludes divorce.
- **Covenant.** For many Protestants sacrament signifies the establishment of a binding two-way promise or covenant. There is no essential change but a significant change in attitude. This suggests that marriage is intended to be a union of minds and bodies in the creation of a loving and stable environment in which children may flourish. In a covenantal marriage divorce is a possibility but usually only on the grounds of adultery.
- **Holy mystery.** For many Anglicans marriage is a holy mystery. In the 1662 *Prayer Book* marriage is defined as a holy mystery, a powerful and effective symbol of the change established through the promises made by the couple in the presence of God. The Church of England's attitude to divorce has always been ambivalent, accepting that where there has been an 'irretrievable breakdown' in relationships then divorce is a necessary evil.

c) Divorce and annulment

Until recently divorce was difficult to obtain and was socially stigmatised, but it is now a common aspect of the Western world. There are many reasons for this, including the decline of the influence of traditional religious teaching, greater independence for women and shifting attitudes to sex. But one view is linked to the understanding of marriage itself. This is a significant, if not obvious, point that divorce merely re-expresses marriage but in negative terms. In other words, as marriage has increasingly been seen in **companionate** terms and less as the means of establishing property rights or legitimacy of children, the grounds for divorce have shifted away from legal fault to relationship breakdown. Even so, the two categories are not necessarily that distinct. A husband or wife who commits **adultery** is equally at fault, having broken their promise to commit themselves to one person, and compromised the trust and fidelity promised to their partner.

Although **annulment** and divorce appear superficially dissimilar, both are concerned with the legal and relational dimension of marriage, although the approaches and emphases are different.

i) Annulment

Annulment is not restricted to Catholicism and is also a possibility within secular British law. But it is within the Catholic tradition that annulment has its fullest expression. Coming from natural law, annulment focuses on the intentions of the couple at the time of the marriage ceremony. Inevitably it is retrospective and those who defend it quite often point to the positive pastoral usefulness of going back over a relationship to see how and when a marriage may have failed. The process may reveal that there are in fact no grounds for separation; on the other hand it may find that from the start the marriage was never fully established.

The first stage is to declare that the marriage is void. The second stage, 'divorce', effects the actual change of status of the couple, which allows them to separate. The nullity of the marriage can be established on two grounds (see *Canon Law*, pages 1083–1095):

- The first grounds are for various **diriment impediments**, such as the failure to satisfy the sexual 'goods' of marriage (for example, impotency), or a vow to remain sexually celibate, or that the person is still married to another.
- The second ground is linked to the sacramental dimension of marriage, which requires the full consent of both parties to marriage. The grounds here may include lack of reason, lack of sound judgement or an inability to understand and carry out the obligations and duties of marriage.

Objections to annulment often fall into two kinds:

- Those who do not share the essential sacramental view of marriage find its retrospective judgement demeaning and wasteful of a relationship which for years may have functioned creatively and fruitfully. Furthermore, if children are born it appears to suggest that they were not conceived into a proper marriage, especially if it has been shown that the original intentions of marriage were defective.

- Others argue that this is the kind of muddle that natural law leads to. The desire to maintain the sacramental status of marriage results in an over legalistic and pastorally weak process. Furthermore, it fails to acknowledge that people can change and intentions may also alter in time.

The second objection may not appear to be as watertight as is commonly thought. It does not necessarily follow that if my intentions appear to change I may not have harboured these desires deep-down long before I became aware of them. Annulment, at least, has the virtue of allowing both parties the psychological freedom to marry afresh (although this is not technically remarriage).

ii) Divorce

In Western societies the attitude to divorce has largely been dictated by Christian teaching. Jesus taught that marriage was lifelong and that divorce had only been allowed in the Old Testament because couples were weak willed. However, two passages suggest that this apparent absolute ruling could be understood as an ideal and that there are exceptions.

The so-called **Matthean exception** appears to allow for divorce on the grounds of adultery, and the Pauline privilege allows divorce (or annulment) in a mixed marriage of a Christian and non-Christian. However, theologians are divided over exactly what these passages mean. Today, though most Protestant traditions do allow divorce, Catholicism permits 'divorce' as legal separation but otherwise maintains Jesus' absolute position.

However, over the past century, for religious and non-religious reasons, the stigma of divorce has become considerably less, as the reasons for marriage have shifted away from contract and sacrament to relationship. The logic is simple: if the marriage relationship has broken down then divorce recognises the situation and is a means of bringing this about legally.

The **Divorce Reform Act 1969** importantly introduced the notion of '**irretrievable breakdown**' as a means of defining the underlying purpose of divorce. The Family Law Act 1996 extended this further by removing the idea of fault altogether. Many ask whether it is by chance that since that time divorce rates in the UK are one of the highest in Europe. An important analysis of divorce in the UK in 2008 states that:

- Forty-five per cent of marriages will end in divorce.
- Providing marriage/death rates remain the same, ten per cent of marriages will celebrate their 60th wedding anniversaries.

Key question

Would a less lenient view of divorce necessarily make people work harder at their marriages?

Cross-reference

See page 63 for a more detailed account of the Matthean exception.

Key word

Irretrievable breakdown defines the underlying causes of marital relationship breakdown.

Key thought

The **Divorce Reform Act 1969** came into effect in 1971 and permitted divorce on grounds of: 1) Adultery; 2) Unreasonable behaviour; 3) Desertion; 4) The parties to the marriage have lived apart for at least two years and both consent to the divorce; and 5) The parties have lived apart for at least five years on the grounds that a relationship had irretrievably broken down. The 1984 legislation allows couples to petition for divorce after one year of marriage.

- For couples who have been married for ten years, fewer than 31 per cent will divorce.
- For couples who have been married for twenty years, fewer than fifteen per cent will divorce.

(*Population Trends*, 131 (Spring 2008), pages 28–36)

iv) Remarriage

Remarriage is particularly problematic for many in the Protestant tradition. There are two reasons for this: theological and pastoral/social.

The theological reasons are those we have already noted when we looked at the Matthean exception. In Matthew's gospel, Jesus says that even if divorce takes place it does not free a Christian to remarry for if a man does remarry he 'commits adultery' (Matthew 19:9)

Those who permit divorce but refuse remarriage have the problematic task of explaining just what they mean by divorce. If they are implying that the person is still in some way married (having made vows of lifelong fidelity), then their view of divorce really goes back to the older idea that divorce is the releasing from the *duties* of marriage but not from the bond itself. This is a possibility in law today when a couple can seek judicial **separation**, which releases each other from any financial obligations for instance.

The pastoral issues related to remarriage mostly focus on the issue of the good *intentions* of those who wish to be remarried. For many there is a *prima facie* case for allowing the innocent party a remarriage. But even this can be problematic. Is it always the case that marriage fails entirely because of one of the parties? The problem is that it can never fully be ascertained just how two people have lived their lives. The same kind of impossibility arises when the person who is asking for remarriage is *not* the innocent party but expresses remorse for their wrongdoings and fully intends to fulfil the marriage promises.

For many years the Church of England has debated how it should deal with marriages which fail. Some treat a failed marriage as a form of death. As Christian marriage permits remarriage after the death of a spouse so does remarriage after the death of a relationship. The conclusion of the Church and its publication of *Marriage After Divorce* (2003) states that although marriage is lifelong:

> *there are exceptional circumstances in which a divorced person may be married in church during the lifetime of a former spouse.*

(www.cofe.anglican.org/info/papers/mcad/index.html)

Cross-reference

See page 47.

Key word

Separation may take two forms. Divorce, when the marriage is dissolved (*a vincula*); or judicial separation (*a mensa et thoro*) when each are released from their duties as husband and wife.

Even so, there is no automatic right for a couple to remarry in church and they will be expected to answer a number of important questions. Each minister has the right to refuse a couple or to refer the case to his or her bishop.

3 Cohabitation

Cohabitation or 'living together' has increasingly become the norm in contemporary Western societies. Whereas in the past, marriage offered emotional and financial stability, women in particular today have considerably more autonomy, sexually (through contraception) and financially (through equality in the workplace), and therefore the need for marriage is far less obvious. Cohabitation also reflects the more informal nature of modern living which does not see the need to formalise relationships, and, with the taboo on **premarital sex** largely removed, living together for a short period of time or for a lifetime has now become a common part of modern living.

At the same time there is an unprecedented rise in the number of people living by themselves through chosen or enforced singleness.

a) Types of cohabitation
i) Casual cohabitation

The least formal cohabitation relationship is characterised by a lack of long-term commitment. It might begin with a casual sexual relationship and develop so that by living together both partners share a common sexual and social life. Often symbolically and for practical reasons one partner may keep his or her home as a sign of independence. Casual cohabitation, unlike marriage, is private, informal and, by its very nature, transitory. Seventy per cent of first partnerships in Britain are casual cohabitation relationships, lasting on average about two years.

ii) Trial marriage cohabitation

Many couples today regard living together before marriage to be important, if not essential. They argue that before taking such a serious step as marriage both partners should be sure that they are compatible to ensure that the marriage will last. This form of cohabitation suggests that it is, at best, conditional, private and short term in preparation for the next stage, marriage. The average age at which men marry is 30.5 and women 28.3. Quite often, if children are born, the additional responsibility may act as a catalyst for marriage so as to give them the benefits of a more stable and long-term environment.

iii) Substitute marriage and ideological cohabitation

Increasingly there are those who *never* marry but who opt for long–term relationships without marriage. There are two broad categories: those who are excluded from marriage and those who chose for ideological reasons not to marry.

Those who are excluded from marriage might include:

- a couple whose families refuse to let them marry outside their religion or class
- a husband or wife who refuses the other a divorce for religious reasons. The separating person is legally unable to remarry and so chooses to cohabit
- one partner who is reluctant to marry.

From the perspective of each of these couples – their intentions are considered to be equivalent to marriage promises. This does not make their relationship licit (lawful) from the point of view of society or a religion – indeed depending on the definition of marriage, a homosexual couple could never fulfil the duties of marriage (that is, through lack of procreation), or a person who cohabits whilst technically married to another commits adultery and may place him or herself outside the communion of their church tradition. But what all these cases have in common is the lack of *public* recognition, which prohibits them from becoming formally married.

Ideological cohabitation refers to those who consciously reject marriage on ideological grounds. For example, some argue that marriage:

- as an institution has failed, as can be seen in the very high divorce rates (almost 50 per cent in the USA and UK)
- is more to do with pleasing others and not oneself
- sets unrealistic expectations about human relationships
- is often perceived to be unnecessarily expensive and bureaucratic
- is a religious commitment which is irrelevant for the non-believer.

Cross-reference

Read pages 25–29 on reconstruction feminism.

Social reconstruction feminists argue that marriage is essentially a patriarchal institution that is more interested in ownership and control of women by men, and an insistence on the role of man as bread winner, than a liberated and genuine human relationship. A woman might feel that she no longer needs to marry for economic survival nor does she have to be a homemaker or even a mother. The traditional purposes of marriage are therefore unnecessary and possibly detrimental for a relationship of equals.

Significantly, many couples feel that a relationship is essentially a private affair. It does not need God or the Church or the witness of other people, or society as a whole, to acknowledge formally the

Cross-reference

See pages 59–60 below on the Civil Partnerships Act.

Key words

Civil partnerships give legal rights and protections to same-sex couples in similar ways as marriage does for heterosexual couples.

Key question

Does genuine commitment in a sexual relationship necessarily mean having the intention to be with that person for life?

Key words

Deontological moral systems are those based on duties and rules.

A cohabitation contract (or agreement) might, for example, set out who is responsible for childcare, who owns what and how assets will be divided if a couple separate.

Key words

A reconstituted family (or step family) is where children from a previous relationship are brought up by at least one non-biological parent.

Cohabitation effect is used to describe the negative psychological effects that cohabitation has on partners and the fact that cohabitation does not lead to long term, stable marriages.

status of a couple. With the changes in the law the rights of both parties are increasingly recognised. For homosexual couples many countries have evolved systems of civil partnerships which offer them similar rights and protection of the law as marriage.

b) Critique of cohabitation
i) Commitment and fidelity

The primary deontological criticism of all forms of cohabitation and especially casual cohabitation is lack of commitment. From a Kantian perspective the danger is that couples are using each other as a means to an end, and in the natural law tradition, if the primary end of sexual relationships is children, then a stable committed environment is a necessary condition for children's welfare. Most Christian deontological traditions share these criticisms, especially where marriage is considered in strong sacramental terms.

However, there is a stronger case to be made for 'substitute marriage' cohabitation. If the intention in this kind of relationship is to be faithful and committed then it is difficult to see what additional moral benefits marriage offers. However, as this kind of cohabitation lacks the same kind of legal protection as marriage, many couples draw up cohabitation contracts setting out the terms and obligations of their relationship to each other. The question then is how, in the end, is this so different from marriage?

ii) Long- and short-term consequences

From a consequential point of view the only relevant consideration is whether cohabitation produces happier people. As in any relationship a break-up causes pain but it is seen as an inevitable part of the process of change. This is not especially problematic for casual cohabitation relationships, except where children are concerned. Some argue that children are robust and can cope with having multiple sets of non-biological parents as in reconstituted families, but others argue that stability and care are the necessary components for happy and balanced children.

Another significant statistical piece of evidence for the utilitarian is the so-called cohabitation effect. This evidence applies particularly to trial marriage cohabitation and is thought to demonstrate that those who cohabit before marriage are far more likely to divorce once they do marry than those who do not live together before marriage.

It is not clear what the reasons for this are. Perhaps for psychological reasons cohabitation gives a couple a sense of freedom which may not translate well into a conventional marriage, whilst other research indicates that the frequency of marriage breakdown is about the same between those who cohabited and then married and those who did not.

Key words

Common law marriage or marriage by repute where a couple have lived together as husband and wife but without going through a marriage ceremony or obtaining a marriage contract.

Finally, many who cohabit believe they have the same rights as married people through **common law marriage**. But common law marriage was abolished in 1753, so unlike marriage there is no automatic entitlement to benefit from a partner's private pension scheme or to inherit property should one partner die.

4 Contraception and the purpose of sex

The use of contraception, whether artificial or natural, means that a couple can have sexual intercourse without the woman becoming pregnant. The contraceptive pill has not only revolutionised the way in which women have been able to govern their own fertility, but has also given them the sexual freedom to conduct their relationships and their working habits on a par with men.

a) Natural law and contraception

God has wisely disposed natural laws and rhythms of fecundity which, of themselves, cause a separation in the succession of births. Nonetheless the Church, calling men back to the observance of the norms of the natural law, as interpreted by their constant doctrine, teaches that each and every marriage act must remain open to the transmission of life.

(*Humanae Vitae*, paragraph 11)

The natural law argument against the use of artificial contraception is most clearly stated in the Pope's encyclical *Humanae Vitae* (1968). It argues that the use of all forms of artificial contraception is morally illicit because every **unitive** sexual act must also *intend* to be 'be open to the transmission of life', that is to be procreative and result in children. More significantly, to allow the separation of the unitive and the procreative undermines the sacramental dimension of marriage and degrades a husband's and wife's relationship.

The only exception to this in Roman Catholic teaching is the **rhythm method**. As this is the use of a natural moment in a woman's reproductive cycle, it is not technically contraception as there is still a possibility that the sex act is 'open to the transmission of life'. *Humanae Vitae* argues:

Key words

Unitive sex means for loving purposes.

The **rhythm method** is the use of the moment just before a woman ovulates where nature provides a moment (or 'rhythm' in nature) when a couple can have sexual intercourse without the probability of having a child.

The Church is coherent with herself when she considers recourse to the infecund periods to be licit, while at the same time condemning, as being always illicit, the use of means directly contrary to fecundation, even if such use is inspired by reasons which may appear honest and serious. In reality, there are essential differences between the two cases; in the former, the married couple make legitimate use of a natural disposition; in the latter, they impede the development of natural processes.

(*Humanae Vitae*, paragraph 16)

Many accuse the natural law argument of unnecessary **casuistry**. They argue that if the rhythm method is permitted as an exception, where nature provides its own 'safe' moment when a couple may have sex for unitive rather than procreative purposes, then artificial contraception is not intrinsically wrong and Church teaching should be revised.

For example, the liberal Catholic psychologist **Jack Dominian** argues that sex has many purposes – all of which serve to enhance the husband–wife relationship. He names four – love, procreation, pleasure and relief of tension – of which 'the single most important is the presence of love, which represents the highest unity of body and person' (*God, Sex and Love*, page 30). By broadening the notion of procreative sex to mean life-giving in its psychological sense, Dominion reinterprets *Humanae Vitae* to include what he considers to be an equally valid non-procreative sexual relationship, where both husband and wife are still *creative* as they grow and sustain each other.

> *The full potential of sexual intercourse is to be seen as a source of life for two people who are relating over time. It is powerless to operate when it is experienced in transient, unreliable and unpredictable circumstances.*
>
> (Jack Dominian and Hugh Montefiore, *God, Sex and Love*, page 32)

b) Arguments for the use of contraception

Until fairly recently Protestant churches held a view not dissimilar to the Roman Catholic Church. The primary concern was that contraception would encourage irresponsible behaviour and separate sex from its proper place in marriage. However, most Protestant churches today hold that there is a distinction between sex for unitive purposes and sex for procreation, and these are reflected in the way in which marriage is considered first to be for companionship and second for the creation and raising of children.

There are, in addition, good pragmatic and utilitarian reasons for the use of contraception:

- Couples need to be able to provide for families financially and humans are called to be good stewards of the world's resources.
- A responsible control of family size contributes to the well-being of society.
- Condoms reduce the spread of sexually transmitted infections (STIs) including the Aids virus.

Contraception, therefore, is not necessarily contrary to marriage, but used responsibly is an aid to a loving, intimate relationship between husband and wife.

c) Moral objections to contraception

Besides the natural law objections to artificial contraception other objections include:

- **Respect for people**. Many feminists have argued that contraception has reinforced male control over women. Most forms of contraception have relied on women regulating their fertility, a practice reinforced by men. How many men would choose sterilisation (vasectomy) or would take an equivalent of 'the pill'? Contraception reduces the companionship element in a relationship by making sex an end in itself without consequences. It can diminish male respect for women by thinking that sexual intercourse is all that a relationship is about.

- **Means of power**. Some see the opportunities that contraception gives to institutions to interfere with a basic right of every human being to reproduce. For example, in 1983 the Chinese government issued a directive which stated that women with one child must have **IUD**s inserted and one spouse in a couple with two or more children must be sterilised. In that year 21 million sterilisations, 18 million IUD insertions and 14 million abortions took place. In the West there have been a number of cases where the local health services have enforced contraception or sterilisation on very young or mentally ill women when they have considered it to be in her 'best interests'.

- **Exploitation**. Many have criticised natural law objections to artificial contraception for causing poorer countries hardship through over population. A response to this is often that the size of family is part of more complex structures. In some cases a small family is simply unable to have the working power to survive. Smaller families destroy the networking that large and extended families enjoy. Poverty is to do with other resources apart from the size of family.

- **Promiscuity**. Contraception can encourage **promiscuity** and adultery. The lack of serious consequences (that is, through the birth of a child) has legitimised sexual permissiveness and harmed the institution of marriage and the family.

Cross-reference

Read pages 29–31 on feminism and motherhood.

Key word

IUD or intrauterine device is a small piece of plastic or copper inserted into the womb that acts as a contraceptive.

Key word

Promiscuity means casual and indiscriminate sexual intercourse with many partners.

5 Homosexual and non-heterosexual relationships

Key word

Difference in its general sense means accepting a wide range of sexualities. In its philosophical usage *différence* is the endless play of existence that seeks to disrupt any dominant ideology (such as heterosexuality).

a) Difference

For lesbians and gays **difference** describes the fundamental psychological or even spiritual dimension of a wide spectrum of sexualities. For some, these sexualities are analogous to visiting a different country with a very different culture from one's own, which viewed from the outside might seem to be exotic,

Key word

LGBT is the acronym for lesbian (women attracted to women), gay (men attracted to men), bisexual (attracted to men and women or being both heterosexual and homosexual) and transgendered (where a person's biological sex does not match their perceived gender identity).

Key quote

'Pseudo-radicals have no interest in non-monogamous, flamboyant, lesbian, gay and bisexual people.'
ELIZABETH STUART, 'SEX IN HEAVEN' IN SEX THESE DAYS, 187

Key question

Are there legitimate grounds for limiting homosexual behaviour?

Key people

Jeremy Bentham (1748–1832) was a philosopher, social and legal reformer. He was a founder of utilitarianism, and as an atheist believed that the law should be revised according to a simple objective human standard: does the law produce the greatest happiness for the greatest number?

frightening and even bizarre, but once encountered become acceptable on their own terms. The preferred collective term today for non-heterosexual difference is **LGBT** – lesbian, gay, bisexual and transgendered people.

As for some feminists, homosexual difference often entails rejecting many heterosexual values, traditions and social structures. For instance, in some countries where homosexual marriage or 'registered partnership' are possible, radical queer theorists, influenced by Foucault's analysis, consider this 'normalising' of homosexual relationships to be entirely false as it is based on heterosexual values that are alien to LGBT identity. For some lesbian feminists, inclusion into patriarchal institutions, such as marriage, is a double enslavement to male patriarchy as well as heterosexuality.

For radical queerists difference means developing lifestyles which are authentic in themselves and avoiding, as Foucault argued, the normalising influence of the dominant social institutions. Elizabeth Stuart, for instance, criticises liberal 'pseudo-radical' Christians who argue for the inclusion of lesbians and gays but on their heterosexual terms and values.

If Stuart and others are correct, homosexual difference and especially lesbianism, when driven by radical feminism, does indeed 'queer' or pose fundamental challenges to ethicists, legislators and theologians alike.

b) Homosexual consent and harm

Fundamental to all liberal societies is whether a human activity should be prohibited because it is harmful and lacks consent. One of the founders of modern liberal thinking, **Jeremy Bentham** gave some considerable thought to the issue of same-sex relationships. His aim was to consider whether anal sex or 'unnatural' acts between men and men, including children, should be considered criminal acts. Bentham argues in *Offences Against One's Self: Paederasty* (c. 1785) that if there is mutual consent for pleasure, then sex between an older man and younger male cannot be wrong:

> *As to any primary mischief, it is evident that it produces no pain in any-one. On the contrary it produces pleasure, and that a pleasure which, by their perverted taste, is by this supposition preferred to that pleasure which is in general reputed the greatest. The partners are both willing. If either of them be unwilling, the act is not that which we have here in view; it is an offence totally different in its nature of effects; it is person-al injury; it is a kind of rape.*

> (Jeremy Bentham, *Offences Against One's Self: Paederasty* quoted in Blasius and Phelan *We are Everywhere*, page 16)

But Bentham's argument begs the question: is a younger person sufficiently rational to know whether he really is giving his full consent and even allowing that there may be no physical harm, how is one to judge what kind of mental harms are caused and to whom?

i) Consent as contract

Bentham argues that those who oppose 'unnatural' sexual acts do so on irrational prejudice or superstition (or religion) and not on rational utilitarian principles. Bentham's principle probably strikes many people as being self-evident; providing both parties are in agreement, then that is sufficient reason to justify *any* sexual relationship (including under age sex, prostitution, adultery and LGBT). However, there are difficulties determining whether this notion of consent as contract is entirely coherent. For example, consent:

- May fail to take into account long-term harmful psychological side effects.
- Is contingent on determining whether a person is *capable* of making a reasoned decision.
- May be 'apparent consent'. I may consent to lend you my car because you have asked me as a favour. Nevertheless, it is not something I do willingly because I know you are a bad driver.
- Is only possible when all things really are equal. Marxism claims that until economic and class distinctions are overcome, there will always be one party who stands to gain more than the other.

ii) Moral harm

John Stewart Mill's liberty principle, which was adopted by the **Wolfenden report** in its proposal for the decriminalising of homosexuality, is whether lifestyle choices or 'experiments in living' should be limited because they cause harm. It is easy to see from a utilitarian point of view that if harm is caused to society then overall happiness will be reduced and the law has a legitimate purpose in intervening. But happiness, just as much as harm, is an ambiguous notion and hard to define and judge.

Mill argues that harming oneself is no reason for the state to intervene, but harm to others is sufficient reason to interfere with someone's autonomy:

> *The only purpose for which power can be rightfully exercised over any member of a civilised community, against his own will, is to prevent harm to others.*

(J.S. Mill, *On Liberty*, page 68)

The question is whether self-harm *alone* is a sufficient reason for the law to intervene. Mill states that self-harm might be a necessary condition for intervention; the sufficient condition is when there is lack of rationality (that is, a child or someone who is mentally ill). So, for example, if a person engages consentingly in a strange form of sadomasochistic sexual activity, however harmful this might be, this is

Key question

Why is consensual sex not sufficiently good reason to permit any kind of sexual activity?

Key question

What reasons does the state have to give to prohibit someone's sexual activities?

Key thought

The Wolfenden report was produced by Lord Wolfenden in 1960 and was the basis for the 1967 Sexual Offences Act which decriminalised homosexuality.

not a good reason for anyone to interfere. On the other hand, if I could show that self-harm of this kind is irrational, then and only then would I have reason to intervene *even if it did no harm to others.*

iii) Public and social harm

Harm might also occur because it offends other people's moral values and sense of decency. This is far more elusive, and judging when this actually threatens public stability is notoriously hard to define.

- Mill argued that causing moral *offence* to others is not a sufficient reason for outlawing it. However, this begs the question: if many people are offended then might not this be a necessary condition of harm? If it could be shown that homosexuality causes widespread offence, then there is good reason for the law to make it illegal.
- Can one really claim that private consenting acts have no effects on public morality? Some argue that *all* our actions and attitudes affect society. So, for instance, if I enjoy watching hardcore pornographic videos at home, many argue that this will inevitably alter the way I think and treat others. This view challenges Mill's notion of private morality.

There has been a long-standing view that some same-sex relationships cause harm to public decency. In ancient Greece, same-sex relationships between older men were considered to be corrupt. St Paul cites homosexuality as a reason why Roman society had degenerated morally and in the eighteenth century the 'Societies for the Reformation of Manners' was instrumental in the raids and closure of many 'molly houses' or gay clubs because it considered such places as undermining public decency.

iv) Physical harm

The discussion above has so far considered the cultural and moral challenges to a heterosexual society. But there are many who argue that leaving out any specifically moral evaluations, homosexuality (and male homosexuality in particular) is dangerous, as empirical evidence suggests, its sexual practices and lifestyle pose great health risks to its participants and to society. Thomas Schmidt is representative of many conservative Christian thinkers who take this line. In his book, *Straight and Narrow?* (1995), Schmidt concludes:

> *But no honest look at current scientific research allows us to view homo-sexual practice as peaceable and harmless. For the vast majority of homosexual men, and for a significant number of homosexual women – even apart from the deadly plague of AIDS – sexual behavior is obses-sive, psychopathological and destructive to the body. If there were no specific biblical principles to guide sexual behavior, these considerations alone would constitute a compelling argument against homosexual practice.*

(Thomas Schmidt, *Straight and Narrow?*, page 130)

Key question

Are homosexual practices necessarily physically harmful?

Whilst it might be the case that a greater use of higher risk practices such as anal and oral sex have posed a much higher threat to society from Aids and STIs it does not follow necessarily, as Schmidt implies, that society has reason to restrict homosexual practice. To respond consistently with Schmidt's criticisms, society would be compelled to outlaw *all* 'dangerous' practices whether heterosexual or homosexual, however, not only might that be considered impractical but also a gross intrusion into personal sexual liberty.

c) Sexual liberty and law

Key question

Should homosexuals have exactly the same rights as heterosexuals?

It is recognised that, for whatever reasons, four to five per cent of the population consider themselves to be gay men or lesbian women. Since 1967, the Sexual Offences Act has permitted homosexual relationships in private for consenting adults over 21; in 1994 the law was amended to reduce this to 18, and reduced again to 16 in 2000. The basis for the 1967 law was the liberal principle that the state should not interfere in an individual's freedom in a private relationship. Many people today argue that although they may personally dislike homosexuality, there is no reason why, as a matter of basic human rights, LGBT people should not be able to express their sexuality. But there is still dispute about whether LGBT relationships should have exactly the same rights and privileges as heterosexual ones, such as the right to marry, have children and so on. Besides general changes in the law, the most decisive change has been the introduction of **civil partnerships** in 2004.

Key words

Civil partnerships give legal rights and protections to same-sex couples in similar ways as marriage does for heterosexual couples.

The question of homosexuality poses an important challenge to the liberal principle of law. Should the law permit all types of sexual practice on the grounds that what consenting adults do in private should be left to their own moral discretion even if many are morally offended? Bentham argued on utilitarian grounds that prohibition could only increase suspicion and fear, but there is also the question of equality and rights to consider.

i) Liberty

Mill states the liberal principle in this way:

> *The only freedom which deserves the name is that of pursuing our own good in our own way, so long as we do not attempt to deprive others of theirs or impede their efforts to obtain it. Each is proper guardian of his own health, whether bodily or mental and spiritual. Mankind are greater gainers by suffering each other to live as seems good to themselves than by compelling each to live as seems good to the rest.*

(J.S. Mill, *On Liberty*, page 72)

Key word

Positive and negative liberty. Negative liberty is freedom from interference from others. Positive liberty is the active involvement of citizens in the control of state.

Liberty may be defined in two ways: **negative liberty** is the least interference of the state or anyone else to restrict individual behaviour, and **positive liberty** is the freedom to fulfil one's potential by being actively involved in government. Mill's position, expressed in the quotation on the previous page, is largely a defence based on negative liberty. Mill supports negative liberty especially when it comes to 'experiments in living' because, in utilitarian terms:

- variety of lifestyles enhances the richness and enjoyment of society
- liberty allows individuals to 'flourish and breathe' according to their own wishes and rational choices
- no one can have a monopoly on morality; people should be allowed to make their own moral choices (even wrong ones)
- tolerance makes for a happier society.

There are many responses to Mill's notion of liberty and in particular to 'experiments in living', which would today include LGBT practices:

- Variety does not necessarily make for a happier society. A community working within common values and aims and sense of purpose might feel freer.
- A profusion of sexual LGBT lifestyles may simply lead to confusion, distrust, anxiety and unhappiness.
- It does not follow that freedom of all forms of sexual expression makes society a richer and more imaginative place.
- Mill's negative liberty presumes that people are their own best judges. But even he acknowledges that this is not always the case and we need 'competent judges' who have better and more expert knowledge to decide what is best for society as a whole. Some forms of queer behaviour are deliberately subversive and should not be recognised by law.

ii) Civil Partnerships Act

The major change in the UK has been the introduction of the Civil Partnerships Act (2004) which became law in 2005. A civil partnership means giving legal recognition to a same-sex relationship. A couple may register their partnership at a registry office or other approved place.

- Anyone between the ages 16–17 must give written consent.
- The documentation enables the couple legally to adopt a common surname.

A civil partnership may be ended by:

- a 'dissolution order' which dissolves a civil partnership on the ground that it has broken down irretrievably
- a 'nullity order' which annuls a civil partnership that is void
- a 'presumption of death order' which dissolves a civil partnership on the ground that one of the civil partners is presumed to be dead

- a 'separation order' which provides for the separation of the civil partners.

(*Civil Partnership Act* (2004), Chapters 1, 2, 37)

Civil partners have equal treatment to married couples in a wide range of legal matters, including:

- tax, including inheritance tax
- employment benefits
- most state and occupational pension benefits.

(www.direct.gov.uk/en/RightsAndResponsibilities)

A civil partnership is different from marriage because in a marriage registration takes place when the couple exchange spoken words, whereas a civil partnership is registered when the second civil partner signs the relevant document.

6 Normative ethical responses to sexual ethics

a) Natural law

i) Heterosexuality

In traditional natural law, marriage, as Augustine argued, is a sacrament ordained as 'containment' for sin and to control the sexual urge. He also took seriously God's command in Genesis that humans are to 'be fruitful, multiply, and fill the earth' (Genesis 1:28). Humans are therefore 'naturally disposed to pairing'; marriage allows the proper ordering of sex, and is the right environment in which to raise children. Aquinas believed the primary purpose of sex was reproduction, and so by extension (as a secondary precept) the purpose of marriage is to provide a stable environment for raising children. It is also the basis for a relationship based on trust, mutual obligation and stability. More controversially, he believed marriage completes woman as, 'the male is both more perfect in reasoning and stronger in his powers'.

Roman Catholicism today continues the natural law teaching. The *Catechism* states that 'the vocation to marriage is written in the very nature of Man and Woman as they come from the hand of the creator'. Marriage is the basis of a healthy life and family, and the building block of human relationships and strong society. It provides the moral basis for the development of children by providing fellowship, love and grace. Roman Catholics highlight the fact that sex within marriage fulfils both a unitive and procreative function. For this reason the use of artificial contraception is intrinsically wrong. In addition to natural law, Roman Catholic doctrine also holds that marriage is a sacrament. The couple administer the

Cross-reference

Read pages 52–54 on the strengths and weaknesses of natural law teaching on contraception and in particular Jack Dominian's views.

sacrament of marriage to each other when they consent to live together in faithful union for the rest of their lives. A new and indissoluble bond is formed.

The Catholic Church does not recognise the possibility of divorce – except as a form of separation where marital reconciliation appears impossible, or the relationship appears to have broken down irredeemably. If a marriage has taken place then no one is capable of dissolving it by decree. The implication of this is that remarriage after separation constitutes adultery.

However, the most common response in a range of situations is to say that the marriage never actually took place ontologically, and there are a number of diriment impediments in which an annulment is granted by the Church. These include non-consummation, underage unions, forced marriage, consanguinity (blood relationship) or affinity (related to each other through law). It can also be granted on the basis that one of the partners failed to consent to the marriage vows through a lack of reason, judgement or psychological ability.

ii) Homosexual and non-heterosexual relationships

The Roman Catholic Church regards homosexuality as contrary to both Scripture and natural law. Homosexual sex is regarded as an improper and misdirected use of the sexual organs given the impossibility of conception. Homosexuals are called to **chastity**, disinterested friendship and self-mastery. The Church has declared homosexuality 'intrinsically disordered':

> The number of men and women who have deep-seated homosexual tendencies is not negligible. They do not choose their homosexual condition; for most of them it is a trial. They must be accepted with respect, compassion and sensitivity …
>
> (*The Catechism of the Catholic Church*, page 505)

The Church's more developed theology of the single life (in the priesthood for instance) enables it to distinguish a fulfilled (though homosexual) life from a physical sexual relationship. The latter is confined through marriage exclusively to heterosexual couples.

Therefore, homosexuality is never a possibility in traditional natural law teaching because the purpose of sex, as Aquinas established using the principle of the 'emission of semen' (or the purpose of sperm), must always intend to be procreative:

> It is evident from this that every emission of semen, in such a way that generation cannot follow, is contrary to the good of man. And if this be done deliberately, it must be a sin. Now, I am speaking of a way from which, in itself, generation could not result; such would be any emission of semen apart from the natural union of male and female … Moreover, these views which have just been given have a solid basis in divine authority. That the emission of semen under conditions in which

Cross-reference

Read pages 45–48 on divorce and annulment.

Cross-reference

Read Michael Wilcockson's *Sex and Relationships* pages 83–84 for more detail on annulment.

Key words

Chastity means to refrain from sex.

Key quote

'*Homosexual persons are called to chastity. By virtues of self-mastery that teach them inner freedom, at times by the support of disinterested friendship, by prayer and sacramental grace, they can and should gradually and resolutely approach Christian perfection.*'

THE CATECHISM OF THE CATHOLIC CHURCH, 505

offspring cannot follow is illicit is quite clear. There is the text of Leviticus (18:22–23) 'thou shalt not lie with mankind as with womankind …'

(Aquinas, *Summa Contra Gentiles*, 3.2. 122, quoted in Robin Gill,
A Textbook of Christian Ethics, pages 484, 466)

Many find the natural law teaching on homosexuality to be unsatisfactory. For instance:

- The notion of a *telos* is ambiguous. Sex may equally be regarded purposeful for recreational and loving ends. If the lack of intent to reproduce does not condemn a heterosexual relationship, it could equally be applied to a homosexual one.
- Aquinas' argument is a judgement on *all* sexual genital acts that are conducted without the intention to reproduce. This is not a judgement on homosexual orientation as such but all (including heterosexual) anal/oral sex and use of artificial contraception.
- Aquinas' argument does not explicitly condemn lesbian sex.
- Modern scientific consensus does not regard homosexuality to be a deviant pathology. Being in a minority is not in itself contrary to any natural law, any more than being left-handed.

At the heart of the homosexuality debate is the central issue of what constitutes normal sexual behaviour. At the start of this chapter we considered Foucault's analysis that 'normal' is usually an idea established by those who have a vested interest in controlling society by supporting a *scientia sexualis*. According to Foucault there is no homosexual nature, just sexuality. For these reasons Foucault is suspicious of the very limited procreative purpose of sex suggested by Aquinas.

However, for some theologians natural law can still provide an important moral basis for gay relationships once the purpose of being human is expanded to be more than merely procreation. The process theologian **Norman Pittenger**, for example, argues that:

We do not know the 'origins' of homosexuality: neither do we know those of heterosexuality. Both are present in every culture; both are found, by those who are involved, to be fulfilling and satisfying; lack of opportunity to accept one's primary inclination, and the rejection of the possibility of acting thereupon, can only be recognized as inhuman and inhumane. To deny opportunity and to condemn acting upon it would be tantamount to asking someone to reject something basic to his or her nature and hence to live an inhuman life … I suggest that the 'controls' for homosexual expression of human sexuality are the same as those for its heterosexual expression. They are based upon the centrality and primacy of love — love which is mutuality, sharing, giving and receiving, life together in the most radical sense of the phrase.

(Norman Pittenger in *Towards a Theology of Gay Liberation*,
pages 87–88)

Key quote

'It is evident from this that every emission of semen, in such a way that generation cannot follow, is contrary to the good of man.'

AQUINAS, *SUMMA CONTRA GENTILES*,
3.2:122

Cross-reference

Read pages 42–43 on Foucault and sexuality.

Key people

Norman Pittenger (1905–1997) was an Anglican priest, professor at the General Theological Seminary in New York and later a member of the Divinity Faculty, Cambridge University. He was also Vice-President of the Campaign for Homosexual Equality.

b) Revealed ethics

i) Heterosexuality

Cross-reference

Read Michael Wilcockson's *Sex and Relationships* pages 98–102 for a more detailed analysis of biblical teaching on marriage and divorce.

Key quote

'Go take to yourself a wife of harlotry, for the land commits great harlotry by forsaking the Lord.'

HOSEA 1:2

Key word

Porneia is from the Greek translation of the Hebrew *erwat dabar* from the book of Deuteronomy 24:1. In English it is often translated as 'indecency' or 'improper'.

Key people

Martin Bucer (1491–1551) played a leading role in the reformation. His liberal views on toleration eventually meant he had to flee Strasbourg and he settled in England where he later died.

Key quote

'As the church is subject to Christ, so let wives also be subject in everything to their husbands. Husbands, love your wives, as Christ loved the church.'

EPHESIANS 5:24–25

The Bible teaches very little explicitly on marriage. It says more about divorce and from this we have to infer what this implies about marriage. The Bible often equates marriage to be parallel to the God–human covenant relationship. There are many ways to understand this: trust, obedience and fidelity, but love is paramount. Hosea described Israel's failure to carry out the covenant to be like his failed marriage, where he likened his wife to a prostitute.

New Testament teaching on divorce, however, is complex. Jesus' teaching appears to reinforce the notion that marriage is for life and that there can be no grounds for divorce. But in Matthew's Gospel Jesus allows for an exception. He says, 'And I say to you: whoever divorces his wife, except for unchastity, and marries another, commits adultery' (Matthew 19:9).

The problem here is the interpretation of 'unchastity' or the Greek word '**porneia**' which even in Jesus' day was much debated by rabbis. A strong version is represented by Rabbi Shammai who interpreted it to mean adultery. But Rabbi Hillel's weak version rendered *porneia* to refer to any situation where a wife had failed in her contractual duties to her husband. Jesus appears to have sided with Shammai, although he extended divorce to be the prerogative of both parties not just of the man. But it wasn't until the Reformation that **Martin Bucer** famously championed the weak version. Bucer had argued for a companionate view of marriage well before the church and society had adopted it. He therefore suggested that any relationship which had become unpleasant, hurtful or just 'broken' constituted *porneia*. Luther defined it in terms of desertion, that is the clear failure to keep to the duties of husband and wife to each other.

Protestants today share with Catholics many of the ideas about the nature and purpose of marriage. They do not, as a whole, hold an essentialist view of sacrament, and downplay both natural law teaching and Church tradition in deference to the word of God in scripture. Protestants emphasise the importance of mutual faith and companionship in a relationship, and the duties of husbands, wives and children set out in the various 'household lists' in the New Testament. All duties are based on love as expressed in Christ's relationship to the church. These texts often pose problems today, even for conservative theologians, because the wife appears to be submissive to her husband. Even so, some theologians argue that by first-century standards they offer a radical breakthrough by demanding that husbands should love their wives.

ii) Homosexual and non-heterosexual relationships

Homosexuality presents all the Churches with a considerable moral and spiritual challenge because, as the following extract from the Church of England report *Issues in Human Sexuality* (1991) illustrates, the biblical view is that heterosexual marriage is the normative place for sex:

> *There is, therefore, in Scripture an evolving convergence on the ideal life-long, monogamous, heterosexual union as the setting intended by God for the proper development of men and women as sexual beings. Sexual activity of any kind outside marriage comes to be seen as sinful, and homosexual practice as especially dishonourable.*

> (*Issues in Human Sexuality*, page 18)

However, the report goes on to say that God does not condemn homosexuals because 'God loves us all alike':

> *This leads directly to our second fundamental principle, laid upon us by the truths at the very heart of the faith; homosexual people are in every way as valuable to and as valued by God as heterosexual people. God loves us all alike, and has for each of us a range of possibilities within his design for the universe.*

> (*Issues in Human Sexuality*, page 41)

Conservative Christians argue that the Bible condemns all forms of homosexual practice because it breaks the covenant relationship between God and his people.

- The towns of Sodom and Gomorrah were destroyed by God because of their practice of homosexual rape (Genesis 19:1–8). This story in particular has become synonymous in Christian tradition for the evil of homosexual sex.
- Leviticus 18:22 states that 'If a man lies with a male as with a woman, both of them have committed an abomination; they shall be put to death'.
- In 1 Corinthians 6:9–11 St Paul considers that 'sexual perverts' – that is, homosexuals – cannot enter the Kingdom of God. The two Greek words used here to translate sexual perverts ('malakoi' and 'arsenkoitai') represent the passive (soft) and active partners in the homosexual relationship.
- Paul condemns homosexual and lesbian practices, which he uses to illustrate Gentile depravity in Rome and the reason for God's judgement. He argues that these practices not only go against the natural order but conscience (Romans 1:18–32).

Liberal Christians argue that the God of love includes many forms of sexuality. They argue that when the Bible is interpreted in its historical

Key quote

'Where are the men who came to you tonight? Bring them out to us, that we might know them.'

GENESIS 19:5

Key quote

'And you shall not lie with a male as with a woman; it is an abomination.'

LEVITICUS 18:22

Key quote

'Men committing shameless acts with men and receiving in their own persons the due penalty for their error.'

ST PAUL, *LETTER TO THE ROMANS* 1:27

and sociological context, it is clear that whilst certain homosexual practices are condemned, homosexual *relationships* are not.

- Jesus preached to all kinds of people and did not distinguish between them because of their sexual orientation.
- Sodom and Gomorrah are condemned because of all kinds of social wickedness, including violence against strangers and rape (homosexual and heterosexual). Ezekiel 16:49–50 cites Sodom as a place whose abominations included failure to help the poor and needy, and in the New Testament Jesus chooses Sodom's notorious lack of hospitality as an example of the events which will be particularly judged on the Day of Judgement (Matthew 10:14–15).
- Leviticus 18 condemns all things which upset the natural order of things – a field must contain one kind of seed and a garment one kind of fibre. Homosexuality is included in the same list and probably refers to the homosexual *prostitution* of the Canaanites, not gay *relationships*. Furthermore if homosexuality is condemned so also are children who curse their parents and those who wear clothes of mixed fibres. The purpose of Leviticus 18 is to maintain religious purity and this is not exactly the same as moral purity.

- St Paul is referring to two practices in 1 Corinthians 6 which the translation of the two Greek words ('malakoi' and 'arsenkoitai') as 'sexual perverts' fails to do justice. It in fact refers to masturbation (malakoi) and male prostitution (arsenkoitai) – not the same as having a gay lifestyle. At the end of Romans 1, Paul also includes a list of other sins against the natural social order: covetousness, malice, envy, gossiping, etc.
- In his letter to the Romans, Paul persuades Jews to convert to Christianity by arguing that the 'unclean' Gentile practice of homosexuality is still condemned. However, he then proceeds to show that as cleanliness laws have been superseded by Jesus' death, so homosexuality is no more a sin than failing to keep to the food laws.

c) Kantian ethics

i) Heterosexuality

Kant gave many lectures on sexual ethics and whilst his arguments largely support traditional Christian teaching his particular idea of the rational and universal 'moral law' developed it in several subtle ways.

Marriage is based on promise keeping and duties, the two fundamentals of Kantian ethics. What is important is the nature of the duties of husband and wife to each other. Kant argues that sex either out of a sense of duty or from lust fails to treat either husband or wife with the respect that moral law requires. So, sexual relations must be freely given, absolutely equal and mutually consenting and if any of these are infringed then the couple become no better than animals. Most importantly, as both would be treating each other as a means to an end, neither would truly respect each other as persons. Finally, marriage must be companionate not merely for sex. If it were merely for sex then as soon as people became too old for sex they would cease to have a reason to be married. This is to misunderstand the nature of the promise on which marriage is predicated, which is permanent, unconditional and lifelong.

Kant gives two reasons for divorce: adultery and impotence. Adultery breaks the promise on which marriage is based and indicates that 'one party thereby seeks to withdraw from the primal duty' (Kant, *Lectures*, page 379), and impotence makes it impossible to have a reciprocal sexual relationship. (This doesn't refer to impotency later in marriage but undisclosed impotency before marriage).

Prostitution, one-night stands and promiscuity are therefore unsupportable because the relationship is not between equals and based on mutual respect. A relationship based on lust treats the other person as a means to an end; it demeans both people.

> It follows from this that nobody can make themselves into an object of the other's enjoyment if it is injurious to their personality, and that strictly incumbent obligation to consummate a promise of carnal intercourse cannot be admitted.

(Immanuel Kant, *Lectures on Ethics*, page 378)

Kant does not discuss cohabitation, but we have already considered why a Kantian might argue for substitute marriage cohabitation, whilst rejecting other forms of cohabitation because they are not founded on an unconditional mutual promise.

ii) Homosexual and non-heterosexual relationships

It is because Kant has established that the only place for sexual intercourse is mutually within marriage that he argues that homosexual sex cannot be other than lust and 'demeans man below the beasts' (Kant, *Lectures*, page 381).

But does Kant's own judgement on homosexuality necessarily follow? If we consider that homosexuals are rational, autonomous beings, and gay sex can be expressed in a loving, exclusive, mutually committed manner, then there is no contradiction in accepting the validity of homosexual relationships within the moral law. However, this view doesn't take into account gay and lesbian ideas of difference and might be accused of trying to normalise homosexuality by fitting it into an essentially heterosexual model.

Key quote

'In general, a promiscuous desire with unfettered inclination to choose any object for satisfaction of its lust, cannot be allowed to either party.'

IMMANUEL KANT, *LECTURES ON ETHICS*, 380

Cross-reference

Read page 51 on a Kantian analysis of cohabitation.

d) Virtue ethics

i) Heterosexuality

The value of virtue ethics is that in the discussion of sex, what is emphasised is the internal aspect that determines what kind of people we want to be and what qualities contribute best to human flourishing. The great weakness, it is argued, of utilitarian and natural law approaches to sex is that they concentrate on what effect actions have and whether they achieve their appropriate end, whilst entirely forgetting that actions or sexual practices are the outcome of the kind of people we are and in turn shape what kind of society we wish to live in.

For example, the utilitarian might argue that there is no harm in prostitution, providing sex is consensual and safe. On the other hand, the natural law ethicist might well argue that as prostitution is non-procreative and outside marriage, it disorders society and is therefore intrinsically wrong. But neither argument considers what kind of person practises prostitution and what this says about his or her relationship with people in the wider community. If virtue is about developing good habits and the skills (phronesis) of living well, sex has to be understood within the context of all human interactions.

The virtue that is often overlooked but which virtue ethicists often consider to be fundamental to making ethical decisions is friendship. But how is friendship to be defined and how does it operate? Below are two original ideas of Aristotle (who represents classical thinking) and Jeremy Taylor (who represents Christian thinking).

Key question

How is friendship as a virtue to be defined and applied?

Cross-reference

Read pages 96–97 for a more detailed account of Aristotle on friendship and race.

- **Aristotle and philia.** For Aristotle, friendship (*philia*) is the basis for all the virtues (such as courage, altruism, non-possessiveness): those in authority have a particular responsibility to set an example through the practice of friendship. Friendship requires self-control (*phronesis*) over irrational passions (such as lust) and just treatment, even for those whose status is different from one's own. Friendship begins with self-love. As the virtues govern the kind of character we should become, no one who loves themselves wishes to hurt themselves and so by extension the good person does not aim to harm his neighbour. Complete friendship (*teleia philia*) depends on mutually willing each other's good. There are other forms of friendship (for example, business partners) that depend on what goods are gained or exchanged – for lovers that might include erotic love or pleasure – but whilst these are not bad they lack the unconditional, controlled desire for good of *teleia philia*.

- **Jeremy Taylor and love.** For Taylor, although *philia* in its classical sense of friendship is missing from the New Testament, in fact it exists in a new form of 'charity' or love; as Taylor says, 'Christian charity is friendship'. True friendship is not exclusive to Christians because Christ's life and example was to renew friendship as it was originally intended to be – universal, generous, sacrificial and equal. Friendship is achieved through humility, prayer, doing no harm, desiring and doing good. Unusually for his time Taylor presents marriage as the paradigm or 'queen of friendships', because it is the expression of the whole human – physically, emotionally, spiritually and morally. Married partners should share their friends and enjoy their company including friendship between men and women as equals. All friendships are in a sense 'marriages', however imperfect they might be, because only heaven is the perfect place of the 'religion of friendship'.

ii) Homosexual and non-heterosexual relationships

If virtue ethics considers that human relationships have to be viewed holistically, that is physically, mentally and spiritually and in relation to others, what does this imply for same-sex relationships?

First, virtue ethics questions the narrow way in which same-sex relationships have been defined. For centuries, men and women have enjoyed same-sex relationships without thinking of them in specific sexually orientated terms. As an ancient way of thinking, virtue ethicists can show that, historically, intense same-sex friendships have often displayed more fully the virtues of love and mutual respect than, for example, heterosexual friendships. Many examples from before the eighteenth century (the time when same-sex relationships begun to be regarded as perversions) were intensely physical and emotional without being regarded as odd or dangerous. A paradigm that was often referred to was Jonathan and David's intense friendship in the Old Testament.

Virtue ethics, therefore, ensure that in the spectrum of relationships, intense same-sex friendships have an important place in human relationships without the necessity of categorising them as being gay, lesbian or bisexual.

Second, and much more problematic for virtue ethicists, is to what extent the notion of gay and lesbian difference or *différence* make it possible to develop the idea of koinonia/community. Some radical queer theorists such as **Queer Nation** deliberately subvert or queer the dominance of heterosexuality by arguing that sexual freedom is not a private experience but should be public through de-heterosexualisation of society. Other queer theorists are separatists and have founded their own queer only communities based on specific virtues such as exuberance and permissiveness. One can see how these virtues might offer a radical reinterpretation of Aristotle's *philia*, beginning with self-love (of one's own sexuality) and recasting mutuality as in a celebration of sexual difference. But for others these are not virtues but vices that subvert values of decency and, above all, threaten the very nature of a civil society.

e) Utilitarianism

i) Heterosexuality

There can be no particular utilitarian notion of marriage. By the analysis of the marriage act, the utilitarian is more likely to judge marriage in terms of the quality of relationship that marriage as an institution might offer. Increasingly people today do not sharply distinguish between cohabitation and marriage and the trend is for couples to live longer together before marriage. As utilitarians do not share the Christian view that marriage is a sacrament or covenant with God, then the onus is on the couple to decide on the scope and commitment of their relationship.

From a preference utilitarian point of view, what matters is the mutual sharing of interests. For some, marriage may be preferable to cohabitation because it offers better protection of rights and duties by the state and its formality offers long-term security. But for others, who have no long-term view of a relationship, their interests are best served by the informality, flexibility and open-endedness of cohabitation.

Finally, there is much controversial sociological evidence as to whether cohabitation or marriage produces happier people. Some argue that in cohabitation relationships there is a higher rate of alcoholism, increased death rate due to cancer, higher abortion rate and greater frequency of sexually transmitted diseases. We have also considered that some believe that cohabiting couples are more likely to divorce if they marry, causing pain for the couple and any children.

In the face of lack of firm evidence, the utilitarian, therefore, does not give priority to cohabitation or to marriage. But how does the utilitarian regard adultery or an affair outside the relationship? The utilitarian does not consider adultery to be intrinsically wrong and it can perhaps only be judged on what the couple establish themselves. Some might have an **open marriage** which is non-exclusive and where the couple agree that the other can have extramarital sexual relationships. Whereas this may work

Cross-reference

Read pages 51–52 on the cohabitation effect.

Key question

Does a utilitarian necessarily consider adultery to be wrong?

Key word

Open marriage is where both partners agree to allow extramarital relationships without being considered unfaithful.

Key word

Monogamy means being married to one person at a time or having a sexual relationship with only one person.

Cross-reference

Read pages 55–56 on Bentham and gay sex.

Cross-reference

Read pages 55–58 on harm and consent.

for some, many find this unsatisfactory as it can cause mistrust and jealousy. For the rule utilitarian, as **monogamy** or exclusive sexual relationships bring about greater satisfaction, then there is sufficient reason that there should be a rule that prohibits adultery or sexual affairs.

ii) Homosexual and non-heterosexual relationships

We have already considered Jeremy Bentham's bold arguments for same-sex relationships. The key requirement for all utilitarians is that both partners consent to the relationship and avoid harm. Utilitarians argue that rejection of homosexuality is frequently based on irrational homophobic prejudice, superstition and religious tradition, none of which take seriously the happiness or interests of same-sex couples.

Moreover, as Foucault argued, satisfying preferences for different types of sexual expression does not cause society to collapse, if anything the reverse might be true. In a liberal society, as John Stuart Mill argued, people have the right to rule their own bodies. A society that encourages a wide range of 'experiments in living' is good because diversity gives individuals greater scope to express themselves according to their sexuality.

However, as in all utilitarian calculations, an assessment has to be made of pain or harm caused. Some argue that if a sufficient number of people are morally outraged by the idea of homosexuality, then based on the greatest number principle, it should be made illegal.

Some, as we have seen, consider that some homosexual sexual behaviour is physically harmful and others argue that children brought up by a gay or lesbian couple are likely to suffer from the prejudices of some heterosexual people or be emotionally confused. But those who reject these criticisms argue that if homosexuality is wrong because of certain sexual practices (such as anal and oral sex) then many heterosexual relationships should also be criticised for using the same acts. Finally, there is no conclusive evidence that children suffer by being brought up by same-sex parents; what matters is the quality of relationship.

Summary diagram

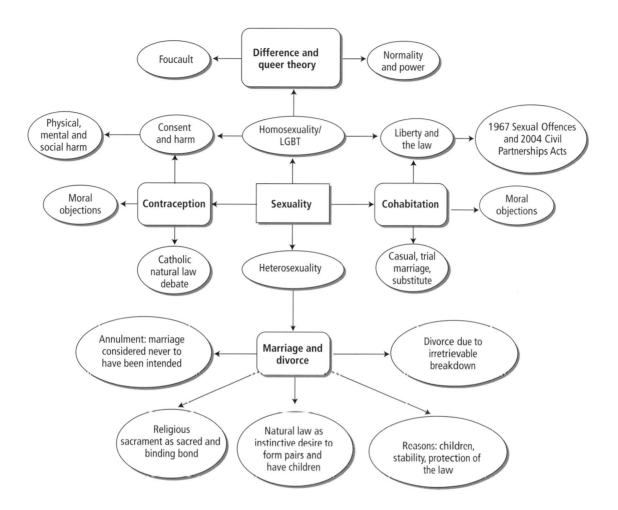

Study guide

By the end of this chapter you should have considered whether 'normal' is an appropriate term to judge different types of sexual behaviour. You should also be able to discuss in what ways marriage might be considered different from cohabitation and which might be considered more desirable. You should also be able to discuss the reasons for and against contraception. Finally, you should be able to explain and evaluate various types of non-heterosexual practices.

Essay questions

1 To what extent are issues of sexuality best evaluated by virtue ethics?

The essay might begin by explaining that many ethical theories fail to acknowledge the complex relationship between human actions and character. The argument might commend virtue ethics because it is about the skill of developing good habits. This might be illustrated with Aristotle's idea of friendship as the basis for love and Taylor's argument that marriage is a form of friendship. The qualities of friendship should be discussed. Friendship might also be discussed as a way of developing same-sex ethics.

However, it might be felt that virtue ethics does not offer a substantial critical means for evaluating sexual behaviour; queer 'virtues', for example, might be felt to undermine the values established through natural law or Kantian ethics.

Further essay questions

2 'From a utilitarian point of view cohabitation is just as good as marriage.' Discuss.

3 a   Explain the moral issues in the use of artificial contraception.
3 b   'It is only natural law which objects to contraception.' Discuss

4 a   Explain why Michel Foucault argued that there is no such thing as 'normal' sexuality.
4 b   'There are some sexual practices which are simply wrong.' Discuss.

Revision checklist

Can you give definitions of:

- discourse
- monogamy
- irretrievable breakdown
- adultery
- LGBT
- chastity.

Can you explain:

- what Foucault means by the *ars erotica*
- what Christians mean when they describe marriage as a sacrament
- the difference between divorce and annulment
- the problems over defining consent and harm in sexual relationships.

Can you give arguments for and against:

- cohabitation
- natural law teaching on contraception
- liberal Christian teaching on homosexuality.

Chapter checklist

This chapter considers the problems of defining race in terms of biology, ethnicity and sociology. It then analyses the causes and reasons for racism and the particular issue of institutionalised racism. The chapter then looks at the problems of identity, the reasons that have prompted anti-racism and a quest for a fairer society (such as affirmative action and race relations policies). The chapter concludes by reviewing various normative ethical responses to race and racism.

Key question

Is Kilroy-Silk a racist?

Case study
'We Owe the Arabs Nothing'

In January 2004, the former Labour MP and television presenter of the chat show *Kilroy*, Robert Kilroy-Silk (b. 1942) published an article in *The Sunday Express*, 'We Owe the Arabs Nothing'. The article caused a storm of protest but it did not stop Kilroy-Silk going on to become a Member of the European Parliament representing the United Kingdom Independence Party (UKIP). The article begins:

We are told by some of the more hysterical critics of the war on terror that 'it is destroying the Arab world'. So? Should we be worried about that? Shouldn't the destruction of the despotic, barbarous and corrupt Arab states and their replacement by democratic governments be a war aim? After all, the Arab countries are not exactly shining examples of civilisation, are they? Few of them make much contribution to the welfare of the rest of the world. Indeed, apart from oil – which was discovered, is produced and is paid for by the West – what do they contribute? Can you think of anything? Anything really useful? Anything really valuable? Something we really need, could not do without? No, nor can I. Indeed, the Arab countries put together export less than Finland.

(*The Sunday Express*, 4 January 2004)

Kilroy-Silk's article illustrates some of the characteristics of racism: it differentiates between 'us' and 'them', the 'other'; it generalises the characteristics of the other race as being culturally and morally inferior; it suggests that the other race is dangerous and barbaric; it warns that allowing these kinds of people into our own society (as asylum seekers or as immigrants) will undermine our own way of life; it accuses liberal minded defenders of multi-racial societies of being weak, treacherous and unpatriotic.

1 What is race?

Key words

Phenotype is the visible characteristic of an organism as the result of its genetic make-up and its relationship with the environment.

Subspecies describes humans (or plant or animal) who have distinctive appearances but who can still interbreed.

Key people

Arthur de Gobineau (1816–1882) was born into a noble French family. He worked as a diplomat and later as foreign minister. His most influential work was *Essay on the Inequality of Human Races* (1853–1855).

Charles Darwin (1809–1882) studied medicine at Edinburgh and theology at Cambridge but dropped both in his pursuit of natural history. His travels round the world provided him with the evidence needed to help to popularise the theory of biological evolution. In his influential book *The Origin of Species* (1859) he argued that all living things have developed naturally from earlier forms which he then applied to humans in *The Descent of Man* (1871).

In very general terms, to be racist is to hold the view that it is morally acceptable to discriminate against another human being because of his or her race. In many cases, as in the Kilroy-Silk example, discrimination is based on the notion that the other race is socially inferior, or as he put it, 'not exactly shining examples of civilisation'.

However, in practice, as biologists and sociologists have shown, 'race' is a very broad term and open to a range of possible interpretations.

a) Biology and genetics

The narrowest view of race is that biologically human beings belong to distinct and separate races. This view of race argues from external appearances or **phenotype**, such as hair, skin colour and eyes, that are used to categorise people either according to type or **subspecies**.

The writings of **Arthur de Gobineau** in particular developed the racial purity view. He argued that a distinctive Aryan race had migrated from the East and brought with it a superior way of life responsible for the great civilisations such as Egypt, China, Greece, Rome and Assyria. Gobineau's ideas greatly influenced the Nazis' policy on cleansing Germany of Jews and others racial groups during the Second World War.

Another influential view in the nineteenth century was developed from **Charles Darwin**'s theory of evolution. Darwin's view is that humans have developed and adapted themselves according to environment. Humans have therefore slowly developed many subspecies. Natural selection meant that those subspecies best suited to their environment have survived whilst others have died off. Furthermore, he suggested that due to sexual selection females have selected males most attractive to them in that environment. In this way particular racial types have developed in different parts of the world.

Whilst Darwin's views are neutral about racial differences, the work of the **social evolutionists** such as **Herbert Spencer** argued that only those races that had developed the most sophisticated and complex societies would survive and flourish. For example, if a native race in a conquered nation was unable to adapt to the new way of life imposed by its invaders, then it clearly showed it was inferior.

However, the dominant view today is that there is no biological justification for separate races; sociologists argue that race is a social invention based on the way in which people develop their own interpretations of phenotype differences. The change in view is based largely on the work of geneticists who have shown that the genetic difference between the so-called races is so minimal as not to justify the term race. For example, the geneticist **Steve Jones** argues that:

- For races to be distinct there has to be a larger variation of genetic distinction than skin colour.
- Genetic diversity is often greater within countries than between countries. The overall differences between 'races' is no greater than between nations of the same 'racial' type.
- Genetic variations in humans are far less than in other species. In his own particular research field of genetic difference among snails, Jones concludes, 'The genetic differences between the snail population of two Pyrenean valleys are much greater than those between Australian Aboriginals and ourselves. If you were a snail, it would make good biological sense to be a racist: but you have to accept that humans are tediously uniform animals'.

b) Ethnicity

Many argue that if race is not determined biologically or genetically then it should be thought of in terms of lifestyle and culture. Difference is therefore **ethnic**, meaning having a shared culture of morality, customs, ancestry, religion and language. Those who argue race as ethnicity consider that what is important is the perception of distinctiveness that one group has from another.

However, it is not always clear what constitutes an ethnic group. Some argue that a group has to have a sense of its own origins to support this idea through stories, myths and ideologies, but:

- Many ethnic groups can be subdivided.
- The criteria for determining ethnicity varies from scholar to scholar and therefore categorising ethnicity is often no clearer than biological views of race.

c) Immigrant-host

Some sociologists explain 'race' in terms of **migration** and the social effects this has on the host nation. Race therefore describes outsiders/foreigners (the migrants) and insiders (the host society). For example, up to 1961 immigration from new Commonwealth countries (such as Pakistan, India and the West Indies) was encouraged by the British government to solve serious labour shortages. More recently, immigrants have been largely from the European Union (EU), as EU laws allow freedom of movement and work between nations. The tensions between immigrant and host are sometimes described in '**race relations**' terms. As in the ethnicity argument, 'race' is being used here to describe the distinct cultural characteristics of a group, but in the more limited terms of the migrant outsider's relationship to the host society.

Those who hold some form of immigrant-host view of 'race' argue that with time, adjustment and through **assimilation**, these differences and competition disappear as the immigrant group adapts to the customs, language and culture of the host nation.

But others are less sure and consider that assimilation is too optimistic; there are many reasons why assimilation will not inevitably follow. For example, external phenotype differences can be much harder to accommodate by the host society because they indicate that the migrant is still essentially an outsider.

Key words

Migration means moving from one country or area to another.

Race relations refer to the tensions between immigrant people and their host nation.

Assimilation is the process by which one group takes on the cultural characteristics of a larger group.

2 What is racism?

Key question

Can there be more than one kind of racism?

Key word

Stereotype is a simplified generalisation about a group which may or may not be based on fact.

a) The problem of definitions

Racism is defined as the combination of two ideas: prejudice and discrimination.

- **Prejudice** refers to a set of beliefs and ideas that are learned and which are biased for or against a certain group. Some definitions suggest that prejudices are based on **stereotypes**, insufficient evidence and irrational arguments. Although this may be true, it merely begs the question how a prejudice is formed. Prejudices do not necessarily lead to actions.
- **Discrimination** is the act of unfavourably treating another group according to one's prejudices.

The word 'racism' first came into usage in the 1930s to refer to the nineteenth-century scientific theories of race, but it also came to describe Hitler's beliefs about the Aryan race.

By the 1950s as views about scientific racism had come to be doubted, racism took on its modern form to be a combination of prejudice (that is, the false idea that different races are superior or inferior) and discrimination. However, as we have seen, 'race' has since been broadened to refer to ethnicity and immigrant–host. Modern definitions of racism will depend not only on how ethnicity is categorised but also on how different ethnic groups react to each other.

Here are two different contemporary definitions of racism:

- Racism is a conscious theory and belief that there are differences between 'ethnic groups' some of which are inferior or have undesirable qualities.
- **'New racism'** considers that racism is a form of discrimination based on ethnic difference, not necessarily because an ethnic group is considered to be inferior or because people hold particular beliefs or theories about race.

These two definitions question to what extent racism has to be intentional or unintentional, rational or irrational, personal or institutional.

Key word

New racism is a term used by sociologists to describe the way racism is practised by ordinary people as opposed to those who self-consciously develop a theory of race.

b) Exclusion

The obvious manifestation of racism is the experience of exclusion of ethnic minorities from everyday life. Where racism exists, it is not uncommon for ethnic groups to find themselves experiencing discrimination in one or more of the following ways:

- **Violence and harassment** – for example, murder, assaults, attacks on property and abusive language.
- **Employment and earnings** – for example, unequal pay, lack of interviews for employment, restrictions on positions of responsibility.
- **Housing and living conditions** – for example, being offered inferior accommodation, living in overcrowded homes and deprived areas in cities or towns.
- **Education** – for example, low expectations by schools for certain ethnic groups, or assumed stereotypical jobs.

c) Eugenics and ethnic cleansing

Eugenics literally means 'well born' and refers to the process of producing the healthiest offspring. The term was first used in 1883 by Francis Galton, when discussing the conditions that could improve (or hinder) the quality of future generations. Eugenics can be applied through selective breeding, by ensuring that couples with genetic defects do not reproduce or by genetic screening or genetic engineering.

Eugenics, though, took on a more sinister meaning after the Nazis carried out their experiments on Jews to perfect their understanding of reproduction, with the ultimate aim of producing a superior race. The programme also built on the social evolutionary notion of the

Cross-reference

Read page 76 on social evolutionism.

'survival of the fittest', which, combined with the belief in the superior and purer Aryan racial type, linked eugenics and racism.

However, is the practice of eugenics necessarily racist? In the way that Galton and others understood the categorisation of races by higher and lower intelligence, then a ban on breeding across races is both discriminatory and prejudicial, yet people may still choose to marry members of their own class and background and dissuade others from marrying out.

Finally, eugenics need not be part of a systematic process of discrimination based on higher qualities. The 'new racist' model of discrimination shows how irrational and sudden a eugenic position can erupt as ethnic cleansing. Groups who have lived side by side for many years can be provoked into extraordinary acts of violence, in which ethnic identity, however it is defined, becomes a factor for cleansing society of the other group. The war and genocide of the Tutsis by the Hutus in Rwanda (1994) is one such example.

d) Xenophobia

Racism need not be based on any scientific sense of racial superiority but simply a dislike or even fear of foreigners, that is **xenophobia**. The immigrant-host model of racism helps to explain why a host society might resent having their way of life disrupted by an influx of 'others' who bring different traditions and values to their own. Whilst it could be argued that these new customs are enriching and expand the range of cultural experience, for some people any change that destabilises the community is construed in negative and racist terms.

It is therefore not unusual for xenophobic type racism to be linked with **scapegoating**, that is passing the blame for loss of moral values, degeneration of family and lack of employment for the foreigner.

However, xenophobia need not necessarily be racist. Dislike or even fear of strangers does not have to be based on ethnic difference, just fear of any outsider or any different culture. The problem that xenophobia poses is just how far can 'new racism' extend? Nowadays, it is not uncommon to link religion and racism. For example, Muslims are often discriminated against and blamed for many social evils in the West. Yet, Islam is not in itself a racial designation but a belief system. However, as Islam is frequently associated with foreigners and terrorism, as Kilroy-Silk's article illustrates, it has become stereotyped as dangerous, inferior, undemocratic and un-Western.

e) Culture, nationalism and reversal

Scientific racism in the nineteenth century was closely related to nationalism and the sense that Western nations were clearly more sophisticated, cultured and developed than the other nations of the world.

Key word

Xenophobia is the fear of foreigners.

Key word

Scapegoating is when a person or people are made to take the blame for others.

Cross-reference

Read page 74 for Kilroy-Silk's argument.

However, in its modern guise the argument has attempted to avoid the inaccuracies of these claims (such as the weaknesses of biological racism and the evidence of ancient civilisations established by races now regarded as being backward). The new nationalism that has developed argues that anti-racist discourse has advantaged the ethnic minorities to such an extent that it has excluded the nationals who had established the society before these ethnic groups arrived. Furthermore, they argue, the real racists are the ethnic minorities who not only fail to assimilate but force society to discriminate against the host population, turning them into second-class citizens.

Using the 'new racist' model, groups such as the French *Le Club de L'Horlogie* (made up of businessmen, civil servants and intellectuals) have developed their own version of 'new racism', using the notion of difference which has been characteristic of those seeking to develop 'new racism' race relations. They argue that 'difference' should now recognise the excluded white members of society by reversing the privileges given to ethnic minorities. This view formed the intellectual basis on which **Jean-Marie Le Pen** established his ultra right-wing party. Its attraction, in 'new racist' terms, is that Le Pen argues that what he says is common sense, it is not racist to argue for ordinary French people to enjoy their own culture, not to be discriminated against and exercise the 'right to be different'. He adds that if ethnic groups do not like French culture then they do not have to stay. Finally, and as a challenge to liberals and socialists, his arguments employ many of their ideas and language. For example, he:

- shares with liberals the desire to live in a harmonious and homogenous society
- rejects utopian views of society in favour of what will work in practical terms
- argues for the 'right to be different' (the left-wing slogan of the 1970s)
- defends liberty, capitalism and self-governing local communities
- calls on the state to provide security for people and property
- supports republicanism (the view held by socialists and liberals).

But Le Pen's argument (like many other contemporary neo-nationalists) is disingenuous. His 'reverse discourse' argument and 'differentialism' hides the fact that deep down he believes in scientific biological racism. If he were genuinely anti-racist he would universalise human dignity first and difference second. He does not think that being born in a country is enough; national identity requires a shift in cultural values and Le Pen does not think that is possible if one is not ethnically French.

Key people

Jean-Marie Le Pen (b. 1928) born in Brittany, France. He fought for the Foreign Legion and began his political career in 1956 as deputy in the shopkeepers' party. In 1972 he established the Front National (FN), an ultra right-wing movement. In 2002 he shocked the French establishment when he made it to the final round of the presidential election.

Key quote

'People cannot be summarily qualified as superior or inferior, they are different, and one must keep in mind these physical and cultural differences.'

JEAN-MARIE LE PEN (QUOTED IN *SOLOMOS*, *RACISM*, 209)

Key quote

'I love North Africans, but their place is in the Maghreb … I am not racist but a national … For a nation to be harmonious, it must have a certain ethnic and spiritual homogeneity.'

JEAN-MARIE LE PEN (QUOTED IN SOLOMOS, *RACISM*, 210)

f) Institutional racism

The term 'institutional racism' was first used in the black power movement in the USA by Stokely Carmichael and Charles Hamilton in 1967 to refer to the deep, ingrained culture of injustice and inequalities suffered by the black population and the advances automatically experienced by whites.

> *When white terrorists bomb a black church and kill five black children, that is an act of individual racism, widely deplored by most segments of the society. But when in that same city – Birmingham, Alabama – five hundred black babies die each year because of the lack of proper food, shelter and medical facilities, and thousands more are destroyed and maimed physically, emotionally and intellectually because of conditions of poverty and discrimination in the black community, that is a function of institutional racism.*
>
> (Stokely Carmichael and Charles Hamilton)

Institutional racism suggests that the structures of society make it impossible for there to be true equality between races. Areas such as housing, health care, education, employment and wealth, racial and ethnic minorities find themselves disadvantaged not because any one person or group is being consciously racist but because laws and traditions fail to take into account the needs of these minorities.

i) Intention

An important feature of institutional racism is that no one is consciously intending to be racist, but ideas and actions are affected by racist structures and policies. This notion provides a very important starting point for legal reform and the review of the way institutions work. With sensitivity and reflection all these areas can be reformed.

However, as Ali Rattansi has argued, in practice the unintentional/intentional distinction has often been blurred and instead of looking at the complex underlying relationship of class, gender and ethnicity, more recent statements about institutional racism have focused on intentional and conscious racism within specific institutions. For example, in Rattansi's analysis of the **Macpherson Report** he says that Macpherson's investigations focused in particular on the police and accused them of institutional racism by their failure to treat Stephen Lawrence's murder as racially motivated and by their lack of urgency and commitment to finding the culprits. In his paper *The Stephen Lawrence Inquiry* Macpherson defined institutional racism as:

> *The collective failure of an organisation to provide an appropriate and professional service to people because of their colour, culture, or ethnic origin. It can be seen or detected in processes, attitudes and behaviour which*

Key question

Can an institution be unintentionally racist?

Cross-reference

Read Ali Rattansi's *Racism,* pages 133–136.

Key thought

The **Macpherson Report** (1999) was the result of the murder of the black teenager Stephen Lawrence in 1993. The report has been seen as a defining moment in race relations in the UK.

amount to discrimination through unwitting prejudice, ignorance, thoughtlessness and racist stereotyping which disadvantage minority ethnic people.

(*The Stephen Lawrence Inquiry*, Chapter 6.34)

Yet, Rattansi finds in this definition a blurring of distinctions which have led to considerable confusion between the impersonal processes of an organisation, the personal intentional attitudes of individuals (such as stereotyping) but also the unintentional or 'unwitting' prejudice.

ii) Beyond institutional racism

Rattansi goes on to argue that although the term institutional racism has served a useful purpose in the past, a more subtle view of racism illustrates that often it is a blunt means of dealing with a complex issue. For example, institutional racism has been used in recent years to focus too much on *one* organisation when that institution is part of a wider society. It fails to consider why racism persists when the structures of society have changed; it also fails to consider other important factors such as class and gender attitudes, which, although not explicitly racist, can lead to discrimination. Finally, it does not take into sufficient consideration attitudes of the ethnic minorities themselves whose historical conditions of oppression may persist well beyond changes in society as a whole.

3 The causes of racism

Theories about the causes of racism cannot exist separately from the ideas of race and ethnicity that we have already considered. Each of the three theories of racism set out below suggests how an idea of race has led to the wrongful exploitation of human beings. This presupposes a philosophical or moral position that all humans deserve equality of treatment.

a) Essentialism

Cross-reference

Read pages 75–76 on scientific racism.

Essentialism is the belief that there are some races that are naturally inferior to others. We have already seen how, in the nineteenth century, scientific racism attempted to find biological evidence to support the view that certain races had smaller brain sizes than others and would necessarily be less intelligent and sophisticated than other races.

Since then, various factors have led scientists to consider that this position is scientifically wrong. Therefore, those who persist in thinking that there are biological or genetic hierarchies between races, which determine how sophisticated they are, are considered to be racists.

Another form of essentialism is based on an ideology of 'otherness'. Otherness developed as an ideology before scientific racism, and has therefore been termed 'ethnocentrism'. Otherness is a means of defining oneself in terms of power over others; it assumes a superior position that understands other human beings better than they understand themselves. Racial essentialism of this kind is not necessarily exploitative but it may and indeed has viewed others in a **paternalistic** way, regarding others as interesting and intriguing but lacking some important qualities that require 'our' help. For example, in 1910 Lord Balfour argued that the Egyptians needed British occupation and rule because they were incapable of doing it effectively themselves.

b) Class and capitalism

Followers of Marxism reject the essentialist claims that humans are intrinsically superior or inferior because they adopt the existential notion that there is no predetermined human nature; every human is free to develop his or her own destiny. Racism is the result of those who own the means of production and power falsely creating ideas about the existence of ethnic groups. It suits those who have power to designate ethnic groups into inferior and superior types often based on physical (phenotype) characteristics, but the real cause of racism is competition and economic power, that is **capitalism**.

For example, the black Marxist sociologist, Oliver Cromwell Cox (1901–1974) argued that racism is really the competition between classes that has developed in modern industrial societies. In the ancient world racism did not exist at least not in the sense that people were essentially superior/inferior because of their race. However, the rise of capitalism and colonialism has conveniently been supported by scientific racism to justify the superiority of the whites and their exploitation of blacks. For example, the black underclass or 'proletariat' in America is alienated from ownership of the means of production by the white 'bourgeoisie' in whose interests it is to maintain the black ghettos.

However, many criticise this kind of Marxism because it fails to deal with capitalist societies that do not fall neatly into proletariat and bourgeoisie. Recent Marxist theories about racism note how many oppressed ethnic groups even accepted racist beliefs and perpetuated them. Contemporary Marxists, looking at Europe since the 1970s, have taken a more subtle and wide-ranging view of the environment which has given rise to racism. Developing the 'new racism' view, they argue that, in addition to capitalism, deeply entrenched views such as nationalism, xenophobia, family values, unemployment and working-class values have led to racism. In this view, racism is not necessarily developed by the upper classes but has also resulted from an identity crisis of the working classes.

Key word

Paternalism means literally to 'act in a fatherly way' and justifies overriding a person's or people's autonomy if it is for their own good.

Key question

To what extent is racism the result of class and human competitiveness?

Key word

Capitalism see page 26 for a definition.

Key word

Modernity describes the present trend in culture which values reason, democracy, science, capitalism and so on.

Cross-reference

Read page 75 on Arthur de Gobineau.

Key word

Holocaust is the general term used to refer to the systematic isolation and subsequent extermination of Jews and others by the Nazis in the Second World War (1939–1945). From 1942 onwards the Nazis chose wholesale extermination rather than deportation.

c) Modernity and reason

The liberal position developed famously by John Stewart Mill in his book *On Liberty* (1859) would at first appear to be an argument condemning racism. Mill's key idea is that:

> *Over himself, over his own body and mind, the individual is sovereign.*
>
> (John Stewart Mill, *On Liberty*, page 69)

Liberalism sets out to resist any undue interference from the state especially the 'tyranny' of the majority over the minority so as to maximise personal freedoms as much as possible. Yet Mill, like many others, only intended the liberal principle to apply to those with sufficient reason to exercise it without interference. Mill, like the eighteenth-century philosophers Hume and Kant before him, considered that many races were incapable of living by reason, and there was good evidence to show how undeveloped and barbaric other races were in comparison.

Liberalism is an example of the modernist thinking that developed during the period of the Enlightenment, which placed reason as the sole source of human authority. Yet, it is modernity that gave rise to scientific racism, and eventually to the theories of pure Aryan races developed by Arthur de Gobineau and subsequently the systematic extermination of the Jews by the Nazis.

The **holocaust**, taken as an example of racism, was not an irrational act. It was planned, it had an ideological basis (the efficient running of the country) and those who were instrumental in the transportation and eventual execution of the Jews knew what they were doing. If those involved felt any emotional disturbance from what they were doing, reason was able to justify their obedience to the state, and that the ends justified the means.

4 Law and race

The Race Relations Act (1976) replaced the two earlier race relations acts of 1965 and 1968. It banned discrimination on grounds of 'race, colour, or ethnic or national origin' in the workplace, housing, education, provision of goods, facilities and services.

The Act begins with the following definition:

> *(1) A person discriminates against another in any circumstances relevant for the purposes of any provision of this Act if – (a) on racial grounds he treats that other less favourably than he treats or would treat other persons; or (b) he applies to that other a requirement or condition which he applies or would apply equally to persons not of the same racial group as that other …*
>
> (www.statutelaw.gov.uk)

The Act considers that discrimination can be direct and indirect. **Direct race discrimination** occurs when a person treats another person less favourably on the grounds of colour, race, nationality, ethnic or national origin.

Examples include:

- refusing to serve ethnic minority clients
- ignoring racial harassment of employees.

Indirect race discrimination occurs when a condition or requirement which:

- *a smaller proportion from the victim's racial group can comply with,*
- *is detrimental to the victim because s/he cannot comply with it*
- *cannot be shown to be justifiable irrespective of the colour, race, nationality or national and ethnic origins of the person to whom it is applied. For example, requirement of a certain height.*

The Act safeguards people who exercise their rights, including people who help others in pursuing complaints regarding race discrimination.

The Race Relations Amendment Act (2000) came into being due, in part, to the Macpherson Report on the murder of Stephen Lawrence. The report noted a level of institutional racism in the Metropolitan Police and criminal justice system. The Act extended the 1976 regulations to ban discrimination in the police, the National Health Service and agencies providing public sector services. It also made it an active duty for public bodies to enable procedures to prevent racism, unlawful discrimination and promote equality of opportunity. A further amendment (2003) made it illegal to discriminate on grounds of religious belief.

Cross-reference

See pages 81–82 above for an analysis of the Macpherson Report.

Key quote

'All human beings are born free and equal in dignity and rights They are endowed with reason and conscience and should act towards one another in a spirit of brotherhood.'

THE UNIVERSAL DECLARATION OF HUMAN RIGHTS, ARTICLE 1

5 Anti-racism

Key question

Is it fair to give minority ethnic and racial groups preferential treatment in society?

a) Affirmative action

A year after US Congress passed far-reaching rights legislation forbidding public segregation, President Lyndon B. Johnson made the following statement which implicitly justifies the use of affirmative action in the process of combating racism and making society a fairer place:

> *But freedom is not enough. You do not wipe away the scars of centuries by saying: Now you are free to go where you want, and do as you desire, and choose the leaders you please.*

> *You do not take a person who, for years, has been hobbled by chains and liberate him, bring him up to the starting line of a race and then say,*

'you are free to compete with all the others', and still justly believe that you have been completely fair.

(Lyndon B. Johnson, 'To Fulfil These Rights', Commencement Address at Howard University, 4 June 1965)

Those who advocate affirmative action or preferential treatment for racial and ethnic minority groups justify its use because, as President Johnson's comment above argues, giving these members of society freedom and rights are not enough. It is not enough because in order to combat continuing prejudice and years of exclusion the passing of race discrimination laws do not suddenly create a level playing field.

There are two versions of affirmation action (or preferential treatment):

- **Backward looking affirmative action** argues that it is right to favour racial/ethnic minorities as a means of compensating them for the many years they were excluded from education or jobs to which they are entitled. In other words, compensation enables there to be fair competition in order to make the principle of 'equality of opportunity' truly equal.
- **Forward looking affirmative action** justifies preferential treatment in terms of what produces the best consequences for society. By giving preference to those who are racially disadvantaged (by recognising their potential) not only do they benefit but so does society as a whole. Therefore, society in the long term increases its skilled workforce and in addition becomes a more just and happy place to live in.

Although backward looking affirmative action as a form of compensation initially appears quite reasonable, there are those who criticise it for the following reasons:

- **Lack of consistency.** There are many members of society other than racial/ethnic minorities who are just as disadvantaged in terms of lack of opportunity. If affirmative action were to be widely practised then these members of society should also be favoured.
- **'Colour blind'.** A truly democratic society should be aiming to treat all citizens in the same way regardless of colour. This is the proper meaning of 'equality of opportunity'.
- **Lack of discernment.** Compensation for *all* racial/ethnic minorities fails to take into account that within these groups some are more disadvantaged than others. For example, poor black people are more in need of preferential treatment than middle-class black people. This illustrates the overall weakness of

the compensation as a way of justifying preferential treatment, which is the difficulty of calculating just what is and what is not appropriate compensation and who deserves it.

Cross-reference

Read pages 91–92 for Peter Singer's utilitarian discussion of affirmative action.

The consequential nature of forward looking affirmative action is criticised for the following reasons:

- **Resentment and racism.** A common criticism is that affirmative action can stir up racial hatred and resentment. It might be that favouring those who are less well qualified but happen to belong to an ethnic minority is manifestly unfair and is itself a form of racial discrimination.
- **Rights violation.** Affirmative action appears to violate the rights of those who have a legitimate claim to exercise them. This does not respect the 'colour blind' nature of rights and the principle that all human beings should be 'equal in dignity and rights'.
- **Equality of interests.** Where the interests of people are the same, then they should be given the same moral value, not to do so is arbitrary and irrational (that is, the very reasons why racism is wrong).

However, there is a case that justifies forward looking affirmative action which does not infringe rights, and that is to regard race as a necessary qualification for preferential treatment. For example, it is reasonable to prefer a black applicant to the police force over a white applicant where a black community would be better served by having more black police officers because their race offers them the unique skills necessary for building up trust and reducing crime.

b) Race relations

Key question

Is Britain a racist nation?

As we have observed earlier in this chapter, tensions between immigrant and host communities are sometimes described in 'race relations' terms. Tensions are caused for all the many reasons we have considered so far. These are not necessarily to do with race as such, but ethnic differences and the host group's sense of threat from the 'other' as well as gender, ethnicity and class. Since 1945, when Britain welcomed ex-Empire nationals to settle in the UK, through to the 1976 Race Relations Act, Britain's race relations policies have often been considered to be a model for other nations to emulate. But have they worked in reality?

Cross-reference

Read Rattansi's *Racism*, Chapter 8.

Rattansi's analysis in *Racism* presents an ambiguous picture. Some have warned that despite legislation Britain is sleepwalking into racial segregation of 'US-type nightmare' proportions. The reality of the situation post 1945, Rattansi argues, is very different from the happy acceptance of Jamaicans and South Asians in the post-war years. Behind the scenes the government were far from happy about the influx of non-white colonials and were worried by inter-race marriages.

Famously in 1968 the Conservative MP Enoch Powell gave what became known as his 'rivers of blood' speech in which he likened Britain in the future to be a blood bath of racial friction, just as in ancient times a Roman predicted that the Tiber would be 'foaming with much blood' caused by foreigners. But his predictions have not occurred and to that extent race relations have worked. There are now many ethnic minority MPs in all the major political parties, there have been no sustained races riots (as Powell predicted), black and South Asian culture is popular and even cool, inter-racial marriage is the highest in Europe and ethnic groups (especially Indians and African Asians) are increasingly represented in the professions – law, medicine, teaching and so on.

However, the following suggest that below the surface, race relations have much to resolve:

- **Unemployment**. African-Carribean groups are twice as likely to be unemployed than other ethnic groups.
- **Ethnic penalty**. Even well-qualified ethnic minority groups find themselves subtly discriminated against through the 'glass ceiling' effect where less qualified white professionals are promoted and they are not. Others find themselves unable to get a job interview based on prejudices associated with an ethnic sounding surname.
- **Education**. Educational achievement is particularly poor among African-Caribbean boys, which is further exasperated by lower teacher expectation.
- **Housing**. Ethnic minorities are often housed in poorer residential areas, causing separation of friendship groups, schooling and language. For example, Bradford, Burnley and Oldham have almost totally separate non-white/white communities.
- **Riots and gangs**. Among poor black boys a macho knife subculture of gangs has developed, clashing with white youths. There have been periodic riots, most recently in 2001 in Oldham between the black community and the police.
- **Right-wing nationalists**. There has been a rise in support for right-wing groups such as the British Nationalist Party (BNP), who, like Powell, play on popular fears of the lack of immigration control, the influx of asylum seekers as well as Islamophobia.

Some have questioned the suitability of race relation policies themselves. 'Diversity training', for example, which aims to celebrate ethnic difference can also have the unintended consequence of promoting separation. Confusions over race and religion have often meant suppression of Christian customs for fear of upsetting other religious traditions, with the effect that so-called political correctness has caused resentment from 'white' communities and annoyed non-Christian religious groups who regard such actions as part of a liberal secularising agenda.

6 Normative ethical responses to race and racism

a) Natural law

The starting point for natural law is to ask what is the nature of humans and what ought they to become in order to live full and worthwhile lives. Following Cicero's maxim that natural law is right reason in agreement with nature, Aquinas argued that there are five primary or basic principles from which all other moral laws may be derived, including the ability to learn and live by reason and to establish an ordered society. But these two principles beg the racist questions: are there some people who are unable to live by reason?; and, if society is to be ordered, are there some whose place is to be subservient to others?

i) Natural law and scientific racism

As we have seen, two scientific groups support a natural law position for racism. The eugenics movement and social biologists of the nineteenth century both presented the empirical evidence that there are some races which are intrinsically more rational, cultured and sophisticated than others. Racism, in this sense, is not considered to be irrational but rather a considered view that if societies are to flourish then they should be organised according to the order of nature.

In its more benign version this form of racism simply acknowledges, as the medieval world termed it, that there is a **great chain of being** from God to the lowliest creature and that the hierarchy of being extends itself through human society. Just as people are born to rule or to be ruled in every society, so there are races which are naturally superior and inferior to others. The history of humankind bears witness to this: various empires have brought their 'superior' culture to 'barbaric' peoples.

But scientific racism has a darker side. In extreme cases it has led to ethnic cleansing, genocides and persecution. But today modern biology has clearly demonstrated that the notion of racial purity is predicated on an entirely erroneous view of race. The genetic variations between races is marginal and phenotype differences make no difference to intelligence and the powers of reason. As Steve Jones argued, there is greater genetic variation between snails and 'humans are tediously uniform animals'. The essential racist position finds few supporters today.

ii) Natural law and natural rights

It might be argued that as natural law does not begin with racial difference but with shared humanity then an ordered society is one which gives rights to all regardless of race and ethnicity. Once the error of scientific racism is removed, then other forms of racism have no foundation. This was the basis of Martin Luther King's argument.

King pointed out that even though the American Declaration of Independence (1776) had stated 'that all men are created equal, that they are endowed by their Creator with certain unalienable Rights', it did not include black Americans. The emancipation of black slaves, declared by Abraham Lincoln in 1863, went some way to remove legal restrictions, but King's civil rights campaign finally achieved the potential (a 'promissory note' as King puts it) implied by the Declaration. As King famously stated in Washington, DC:

> So, we've come here today to dramatize a shameful condition. In a sense we've come to our nation's capital to cash a check. When the architects of our republic wrote the magnificent words of the Constitution and the Declaration of Independence, they were signing a promissory note to which every American was to fall heir. This note was the promise that all men, yes, black men as well as white men, would be guaranteed the unalienable rights of life, liberty, and the pursuit of happiness.
>
> It is obvious today that America has defaulted on this promissory note in so far as her citizens of color are concerned.

(Martin Luther King, *I Have a Dream*, 28 August 1963)

But do natural law and natural rights go far enough? Scholars argue that reason alone is not able to explain or make sense of racism. People feel strongly about their ethnicity, they feel threatened by outsiders (as the immigrant–host analysis suggests), the liberal argument that different peoples will gradually assimilate and develop a new culture belittles the cultural identity which defines a group.

Finally, natural law has also to consider the rightness or wrongness of affirmative action. It seems reasonable for natural law to support a backward looking version of affirmation action that compensates racial/ethnic minorities for past injustices. In the natural law tradition of the Catholic Church, compensation is defined in moral terms due to the maligning of character and physical harm. But it is far from clear in what form and to what extent reparation or compensation should be made.

However, it is difficult to see how, having established the 'colour blind' nature of rights, forward looking affirmative action can give preferential treatment to racial/ethnic minorities without contradicting itself.

b) Utilitarianism

It would appear from Bentham's maxim, 'everybody is to count for one; nobody for more than one', that discrimination on the grounds of race has no justification in the utilitarian world. If the ethically correct choice is always to create the greatest happiness of the greatest number of human beings then it is very difficult to see why

Key quote

'Every offence committed against justice and truth entails the duty of reparation, even if its author has been forgiven … This reparation, moral and sometimes material, must be evaluated in terms of the extent of the damage inflicted. It obliges conscience.'
CATECHISM OF THE CATHOLIC CHURCH, PARAGRAPH 2487, 530

Cross-reference

Read pages 85–87 on affirmative action.

anyone would choose to give up their freedom to become a slave or allow a situation where they were refused education, employment or housing because of their racial or ethnic identity.

However, critics of utilitarianism argue that utilitarianism does not offer a sound argument against racism because:

- It has no adequate justification for the protection of minorities against majorities if the happiness of the majority outweighs the pain of the minority. For example, if the economy flourishes because of the use of black slaves (as it did in the nineteenth century), then as the ends justify the means there can be no other external moral objections.
- Conversely it does not adequately deal with the situation where a few extra happy people's pleasure outweighs the pain of the majority (as in the case of apartheid in South Africa where the minority white rulers discriminated against the black majority to support their lifestyle). Both objections challenge utilitarianism to formulate a view of equality which takes into account current objections to racism.

i) Equal consideration

Singer's argument for the protection of the minority over the majority is part of his version of utilitarianism, which, rather than focus entirely on the pleasure/pain aspect of the maxim, emphasises Bentham's satisfaction of interests. If utilitarianism is to count each person as one, then what matters, regardless of race, intelligence, talents and so on, is whether people's hopes and aspirations receive equal consideration. For example, a child's interests are different from an adult's as his intellectual and emotional needs are less sophisticated, but clearly he still has them. And if that is so, a racist would have to argue that a child of his own race should therefore have less consideration given to him than an adult of a race he regards to be inferior. Furthermore, if the racist thinks the other race is less intelligent than his own (using the 'genetic hypothesis'), this can only be a statement about average intelligence and therefore he would be forced at times to discriminate against lower intelligence adults of his own race if he is to hold consistently to his belief in the genetic hypothesis.

Race, therefore, for the utilitarian, is factually irrelevant; racial discrimination is intrinsically wrong if it precludes the consideration of interests of all.

Finally, Singer argues that even if the genetic hypothesis were true then there is all the more reason for the utilitarian to support the disadvantaged minority group as they are less likely to be able to fulfil their plans, hopes and aspirations. It is to this group that greater effort should be given to distribute goods such as housing and education to balance their intellectual disadvantage.

Key quote

'My view is that the preferences we should satisfy, other things being equal, are those that people would hold if they were fully informed, reflective, and vividly aware of the consequences of satisfying their preferences.'

PETER SINGER, *REPLY TO MARTHA NUSSBAUM*, THE TANNER LECTURES ON HUMAN VALUES, 2002, WWW.UTILITARIAN.NET/SINGER

Cross-reference

See Peter Singer's *Practical Ethics*, Chapter 2.

Key question

Is utilitarianism really concerned about the interests of minorities?

ii) Distribution of goods

How, therefore, is the distribution of goods to occur equally and fairly? This question presupposes that, due to existing racist attitudes, society has not acted according to the equal consideration of interests up to this point, but must now rectify the situation according to utilitarian principles. Singer considers two positions to implement practical justice:

- **Equality of opportunity**. This is the level playing field position that thinks society should give everyone an equal start in life – housing, education, income, etc. But, even if this could be achieved, it cannot alter a person's upbringing and the aspirations which are instilled by parents and other environmental factors (such as inherited skills and talents). As Singer concludes, 'So equality of opportunity is not an attractive ideal. It rewards the lucky, who inherit those abilities that allow them to pursue interesting and lucrative careers' (*Practical Ethics*, page 39).
- **Affirmative action**. Affirmative action cannot defend a quota system whereby an institution (university, the police force, political party, etc.) must fill a certain number of places with a racial minority group. This fails the equal consideration of interest principle through reverse discrimination/racism. However, a system of compensation which takes into account the disadvantages of a person's background (race, class, gender, etc.) and then offsets these disadvantages to make some equivalence with those who have not been disadvantaged cannot be accused of reverse racism. Finally, affirmative action might justify itself on the grounds of **diminishing marginal utility**, that is by reducing the frustration experienced by a racially discriminated group, the long-term good consequences benefit everyone as hostility is reduced and greater trust is built up as racial minority groups have their own professionals in the workplace.

c) Revealed ethics

Key question

Which aspect of Christian theology most challenges racism?

The Christian view is that as all people are created in the image of God and are therefore intrinsically valuable, any form of discrimination that devalues or alienates one person from another, or one group from another, is morally wrong and sinful. Racism is one of the great social evils.

However, as we have seen, the issue of race and ethnicity is complex and Christianity offers no simple solution on how to value ethnic difference and yet maintain social harmony. Furthermore, despite the position just outlined, Christians have supported and justified slavery and racism. This has led to a basic reappraisal of theology and the assumptions it has made about God and his relationship with the world.

i) Incarnation and image of God

There are no gradations in the image of God. Every man from treble white to bass black is significant on God's keyboard, precisely because every man is made in the image of God.

(Martin Luther King Jr, *The American Dream*,
in *A Knock At Midnight*, page 88)

The basic position as stated in Genesis 1:26–27 is that if all humans are created in the image and likeness of God then all humans should be treated with equal dignity. As all life is sacred, and has intrinsic worth, then any form of behaviour that degrades, dehumanises and objectifies a human being as an 'other' must be considered morally wrong and evil (as in the cases of genocides and ethnic cleansing).

Furthermore, the Christian belief in the **incarnation** illustrates how God reaffirms his relationship with humans by becoming fully part of their history. In a striking image Paul describes the incarnation, in terms of Jesus Christ, as God 'emptying himself' of all arrogance by becoming a slave or servant. The image is particularly striking because Paul knows how the Jews themselves have suffered racially as slaves in Egypt and so for God to become a slave means that he sides with those who are oppressed.

It is for these reasons that some black theologians have described Jesus as the black messiah. One of the leading black theologians, **James Cone**, argues that in order for Christians to understand that the incarnation is not a neutral event in history but a decisive affirmation of justice against injustice, the incarnation has to be understood as a 'black event'. Jesus had a racial identity, he was not white (as he is often depicted), he was not middle class (as the Churches often appear to present him) and like so many American black slaves he died by being 'lynched' at the hands of the mob.

Christ's blackness is both literal and symbolic. His blackness is literal in the sense that he truly becomes One with the oppressed blacks, taking their suffering as his suffering and revealing that he is found in the history of our struggle, the story of our pain, and the rhythm of our bodies …

To say that Christ is black means that God, in his infinite wisdom and mercy, not only takes color seriously, he also takes it upon himself and discloses his will to make us whole – new creatures born in the spirit of divine blackness and redeemed through the blood of the Black Christ.

(James Cone, *God of the Oppressed*, page 125)

Finally, Jesus' own treatment of the marginalised and racially oppressed challenged many of the existing taboos of the time. In response to the question 'who is my neighbour' he deliberately chose to illustrate his answer by the example of a Samaritan (Luke 10:25–37). The

Key people

Martin Luther King (1929–1968) was a Baptist minister who became a leader of the successful boycott of the Montgomery City Line buses. His central message was 'the end is reconciliation … the creation of the beloved community'. He influenced President Kennedy 'to banish segregation and racism from this land'. He led the march on Washington in 1968 where he gave his famous 'I have a dream' speech and was assassinated shortly afterwards.

Key word

The **incarnation** in Christian theology is the belief that God took on human form in the person of Jesus.

Key quote

Jesus Christ 'who though he was in the form of God … emptied himself, taking the form of a servant, being born in the likeness of men.'

ST PAUL, *LETTER TO THE PHILIPPIANS*, 2:5–7

Key people

James Cone (b. 1938) is the Charles A. Briggs Distinguished Professor of Systematic Theology at Union Theological Seminary, New York City. His book *Black Theology and Black Power* (1969) was one of the first to inspire the black theology movement.

Key quote

'Then God said, 'Let us create man in our image, after our likeness.'

GENESIS 1:26

Key question

Does Cone's black theology suggest that Christianity should not be colour blind?

Key quote

'The stranger who sojourns with you shall be to you as the native among you, and you shall love him as yourself; for you were strangers in the land of Egypt.'

LEVITICUS 19:34

Samaritans were regarded by Jews at the time as 'others' because racially, religiously and socially they had intermarried with the Assyrians in the eighth century BC. Yet, it is the Samaritan in Jesus' parable who attends a man attacked by robbers, who overcomes taboos against blood contamination and who keeps the Jewish laws concerning treatment of strangers (Leviticus 19:33–34) far better than the Jewish officials (the priest and Levite).

ii) Equality and the Kingdom of God

The vision of a world redeemed and harmony restored is summarised by the term 'the Kingdom of God'. Martin Luther King often described the Kingdom as the 'beloved community' in which race differences are overcome through love. As he says in the sermon *The American Dream* (1965) – which echoes his famous 'I have a dream' speech given in Washington DC (1963) – the dream or vision of the future is one also expressed in Isaiah 40:4–5, a world of racial equality (expressed using the imagery of filled up valleys and flattened mountains) where all humanity shall experience God's glory equally. King's vision considers the common ancestry of all people because they are all created in the image of God. His notion of the Kingdom is therefore essentially political, because it is not merely a state after death, nor an inner experience but the transforming power of God's love through human agency.

> *I have a dream this morning that one day all men everywhere will recognize that out of one blood God made all men to dwell upon the face of the earth.*
>
> *I have a dream this morning that one day every valley shall be exalted, and every mountain and hill will be made low; the rough places will be made plain and the crooked places straight; and the glory of the Lord shall be revealed, and all flesh shall see it together.*
>
> *I still have a dream this morning that the truth will reign supreme and all of God's children will respect the dignity and worth of human personality.*
>
> (Martin Luther King Jr, *The American Dream*, in *A Knock At Midnight*, page 100)

Martin Luther King (centre foreground) leads his 'Mississippi Freedom Marchers'.

Key quote

'For as many of you as were baptized into Christ have put on Christ. There is neither Jew nor Greek, there is neither slave nor free, there is neither male nor female; for you are all one in Christ Jesus.'

PAUL, *LETTER TO THE GALATIANS*, 3:27–28

Key question

How might Christianity have been used to support racism?

Cross-reference

Read pages 82–83 on the notion of the other.

The Kingdom of God is also a time when God's spirit is at work in the hearts and minds of those who are inspired by love and justice. In his letter to the Galatians, Paul concluded that through baptism the Christian now lives by the spirit of God and therefore enters a radically new set of relationships in which race, sex and class difference are irrelevant in God's Kingdom on earth.

James Cone went further. Eschatological discussion of the final completion of the Kingdom of God, which dwells on reward in the afterlife is a convenient myth for racists. Heaven, though, is the 'white man's lie' and developed during the time of slavery, becoming a common theme in the black churches, but the time has now come to focus instead on justice for the oppressed in society.

iii) Racist theology

I assert most unhesitatingly, that the religion of the south is a mere covering for the most horrid crimes – a sanctifier of the most hateful frauds, – and a dark shelter under which the darkest, foulest, grossest, and most infernal deeds of slaveholders find strongest protection.

(Frederick Douglass, *Narrative of the Life of Frederick Douglass, an American Slave*, page 117)

Frederick Douglass, a freed slave writing in 1845, often commented on the paradox that the Christianity he read about in the Bible and the racist Christianity of the slaveholder appeared to be two different things. If anything, the Christian slaveholder was often more vicious and racist than his non-religious counterpart. Throughout Christian history, Christianity appears to have supported racism, from the persecution of the Jews, to the apartheid system of South Africa. So does this suggest that Christianity is racist?

In the earlier part of this chapter we considered how a 'new racist' approach to racial and ethnic discrimination need not have its roots in any systematic theory of race but justifies itself through many existing ideas. In the case of Christianity, racism has developed for some of the following theological reasons:

- **The other as barbaric.** An influential story in Genesis supports the view that some humans are not only less civilized than others but essentially barbaric and outside God's redemption. In Genesis 9:20–27 Ham sees his father Noah, who is drunk at the time, naked but fails to avert his eyes. When Noah recovers he is disgusted at Ham's barbaric behaviour and curses Ham's son, Canaan, and all his descendents. They will suffer for ever as 'the slave of slaves' (Genesis 9:25). Later tradition even suggests that Ham was a black person.
- **Purity and election.** As we have seen in the ideas of Arthur de Gobineau, Nazi Aryanism, and in versions of the immigrant-host theory, there has been a long history of the idea of racial purity.

The notion can be supported in the biblical idea of election and religious purity. For example, in South Africa the white minority argued that the Bible supported the view that God had called some people to rule and others to be ruled. The idea of election is supported by Jesus' saying that 'many are called, but few are chosen' (Matthew 22:14). Those who are chosen are evidenced by their superior ruling powers and by St Paul's injunction that it is entirely right that 'slaves obey in everything those who are your earthly masters' (Colossians 3:22). As the chosen people, the whites' duty was to prepare for the coming of God's Kingdom by establishing justice and order, just as Israel had also regarded herself as God's elected nation. Moreover, the Dutch Reformed Church in South Africa supported apartheid by arguing against mixed marriages between blacks and whites on the grounds that mixing of blood would reduce the effectiveness of white leadership as part of God's plan. Levitical purity laws are especially severe on the contamination of the pure with the impure.

However, many would argue that it is not Christianity that is racist. Christianity does not lend itself to 'scientific racism' but has become the means by which political power and xenophobia have been legitimised through it.

d) Virtue ethics

For Aristotle, Aquinas and MacIntyre, and many others, the virtues can only be properly exercised and developed within the community. The question, as far as racism is concerned, is what kind of community does one want and what virtues support such a community. The problem for all virtue ethicists, therefore, is whether virtues are derived from pre-existing moral principles, or whether virtues exist independently from moral principles and inform and shape them.

This poses a chicken and egg dilemma. Is the kind of community we wish to live in shaped by the virtues we admire and wish to live by or are the virtues we live by ones derived from the kind of community we admire and wish to create?

This point can be considered via an analysis of Aristotle, whose writing on politics and virtues have been the point of departure for medieval thinkers, such as Aquinas, as well as contemporary philosophers including MacIntyre.

The basis for Aristotle's theory of the virtues – the qualities of character needed to live the good life – is **friendship** or *philia* (Greek). Aristotle argues that as *philia* governs all relationships it must therefore be the foundation of all the virtues, as it expresses the highest aspect of human nature: to love another for his or her own sake and for no other reason. But true friendship is only possible between equals who are mutually conscious of each other,

Key quote

'You shall be holy to me; for I the Lord am holy, and have separated you from the peoples, that you should be mine.'

LEVITICUS 20:26

Cross-reference

Friendship is discussed at length in Aristotle's *The Nicomachean Ethics* books VIII and IX.

Key question

How might friendship be used as a basis of race relations?

Key quote

'After this the next step will be to discuss friendship; for it is a kind of virtue, or implies virtue, and it is also most necessary for living.'

ARISTOTLE, *ETHICS*, 1155A3

as he says, 'equality and likeness are friendship' (*Ethics* 1159b2) and for that to be possible true friendship can only be between those who share the same experience or common ground.

So, even though slaves are owned by citizens, are their property and have no rights or liberty, masters are governed by the principle that the ownership of property is not absolute; property must also be used for the general good. Therefore a master has a duty out of friendliness to act fairly and generously with non-citizens because failure to do so would not lead to a well-balanced society nor enable the slave to work to the best of his ability.

Aristotle shares many of his contemporaries' disdain for foreigners (that is, non-Greeks) but does not feel that they are intrinsically subhuman. Of them he argues that it would be better for them to give up their freedom and make the best of their potential in Greek society, for at least they would be living a more noble life than in their barbaric uncivilized countries.

In summary, Aristotle's teaching on the virtues suggests that even in a hierarchical society:

- Everyone (free citizens and non-citizens) should be motivated by goodness to achieve their full potential.
- Friendship, as the basis for the virtues (such as courage, altruism, non-possessiveness), is an active process at every level of society. It is therefore not an optional practice but requires skill, especially from those in authority.
- Friendship illustrates that citizens have to exercise self-control (phronesis) over irrational passions (such as xenophobia) and just treatment even for those whose status is different from one's own.
- Friendship is based on self-love. As the virtues govern the kind of character we should become, no one who loves themselves wishes to hurt themselves and so by extension the good man does not aim to harm his neighbour.

Key question

Can Aristotle's idea of the virtues be adapted to deal with race relations today?

Cross-reference

See page 80 for Le Pen's nationalist arguments.

Therefore, with some adaptation to the contemporary world, Aristotle offers some important insights into racism and society, especially the thought that the far right-wing nationalist, who wishes to exclude racial and ethnic groups from the community, does so, not because of sound reasoning about the need to preserve community and national identity, but through lack of love for himself and an unconscious promotion of a society which regards hate as its foundational virtue.

Virtue ethical approaches might also provide ways of allowing for difference within unity by reappraising the undervalued place of friendship in community. In conclusion to her study of friendship, Liz Carmichael comments:

The love of friendship in this study is love that sets people free to be and to become in their own individual uniqueness, and which is essentially directed towards, hopes for and invites, reciprocal love and the joy of ful-filment in mutual relationships: but without possessively demanding it. Friendship so understood is a fundamental attitude characterizing our whole approach to others.

(Liz Carmichael, *Friendship*, page 200)

e) Kantian ethics

Key question

Is the Kantian approach to racism too optimistic?

The starting point of Kantian ethics is the autonomy of reason. What is good is derived from the human rational will not God's commands or society's rules. According to this, the categorical imperative of what I will for myself is only truly good if it can be equally willed for all humans. Kant's universalising principle offers a vision of society in which each person is both law maker and law receiver. In other words, the perfect society ('the kingdom of ends') is one which rejects selfish, self-centred nationalistic behaviour in favour of one which respects all human beings regardless of race and ethnicity.

The Kantian view is essentially optimistic. In his *Anthropology from a Pragmatic Point of View* (1798) he writes that national characteristics are 'based on the collected historical experience of all times and among all peoples'. In other words, if there are differences between nations these are not due to the *essential* different properties of people and nations but traditions and experiences. These differences, of course, cause friction, but as all humans desire peace then laws and treaties between peoples and nations can work to achieve harmony. Kant's vision is typical of all those who share in the liberal hope that sees race prejudice slowly becoming a thing of the past.

The character of the species, as evident based on the collected historical experience of all times and among all peoples, is the following: that they, taken collectively (as a human race as a whole), are a mass of persons that exist next to one another and after one another who cannot do without peaceful coexistence and yet cannot avoid constant strife amongst one another.

(Immanuel Kant, *Anthropology from a Pragmatic Point of View* 7.331, in Kleingeld (editor), *Toward Perpetual Peace*, page 174)

Furthermore, the Kantian position should lead to the conclusion that prejudice based on colour and other racial phenotype characteristics, irrational fears of outsiders (xenophobia), scapegoating and exclusion of other human beings for no other reason than their race or ethnicity, ought all to be rejected as being based on emotion not reason.

Key quote

'I am apt to suspect the Negroes in general and all species of men (for there are four or five different kinds) to be naturally inferior to whites. There never was a civilized nation of any other complexion than white.'

DAVID HUME, OF NATIONAL CHARACTERS (1753 EDITION)

Cross-reference

See page 76 for Steve Jones' argument.

Cross-reference

Read page 84 on reason and racism.

However, despite all these apparently anti-racist conclusions, if it could be shown as a *fact* that certain human beings lack reason then it follows from the Kantian *a priori* that these people cannot be included in the moral community as members of the kingdom of ends. This indeed appears to be Kant's own conclusion. He accepted, apparently without question, the conclusion of David Hume (1711–1776) that as black culture is clearly inferior to European civilization then all black people must lack certain powers of reason. Kant gives the example of a Negro slave who was fond of criticising white clergymen for the way they treated their wives. But Kant is entirely dismissive of the reasonableness of the Negro's comments and concludes:

> in short, this fellow was quite black from head to foot, a clear proof that he was stupid.

> (Immanuel Kant, *Observations of the Beautiful and the Sublime* (1764))

So, in Kant's anthropology, even though the black person may possess the good will, what he lacks, due to his colour, is sufficient reason to be a full member of society. Oddly, for a man of Kant's intellectual rigour, he fails to test this scientific racist claim, and as Steve Jones and many others have argued today there is no biological evidence that certain races are more 'stupid' than others.

In conclusion, we might observe why some postmodern commentators on racism, such as Ali Rattansi, have been suspicious of arguments that have relied too heavily on the place of human reason, because to do so is either to fall into the trap of essentialism (that is, scientific racism) or to give an insufficiently subtle account of human identity.

Summary diagram

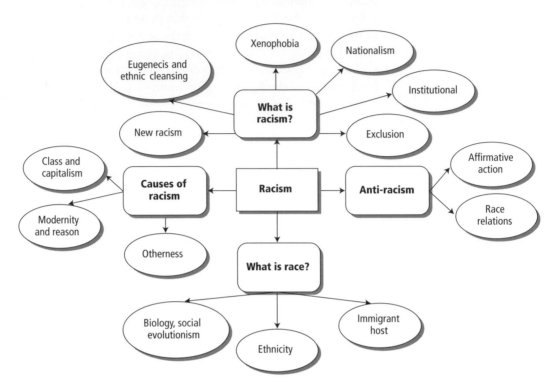

Revision checklist

Can you give definitions of:

- immigrant-host
- assimilation
- eugenics
- xenophobia
- scapegoating
- new racism.

Can you explain:

- why ethnicity is sometimes preferred to race as a means to describe difference
- how class and capitalism may be causes of racism
- the aims of race relations
- how Aristotle's virtue of friendship might be used to overcome racism today
- Martin Luther King's anti-racist theology.

Can you give arguments for and against:

- the use of the term 'institutional racism'
- affirmative action to combat racism
- presenting Jesus as the black messiah.

Study guide

By the end of this chapter you should have considered the problems of defining race and the various causes for racism. In particular you should understand why the term 'institutional racism' is controversial and the distinction between ideological racism and new racism. You should also understand why affirmative action is not always considered the most appropriate way of tackling racism. Finally, you should be able to apply various normative ethics to the issues of race and racism.

Essay questions

1 a Explain how Kantian ethics might be used to approach issues of race and ethnicity.

1 b 'Kantian ethics are too optimistic when dealing with racism.' Discuss.

The essay might begin by explaining that, whereas race refers to biologically determined characteristics, ethnicity is a broader term which describes cultural difference. Kantian ethics should be outlined: the categorical and practical imperatives; and the kingdom of ends as a just and fair society. Kantian ethics therefore regards racial prejudice as irrational and determined by historical not intrinsic factors. Some reference might be made to Kant's own view of ethnicity.

In the evaluation, various areas might be discussed and considered against Kantianism. For example, how might a Kantian reason for or against affirmative action or race relations? Might Kantianism lead to scientific racism? Finally, Kantianism might be a poor basis for race and ethnicity policy in a postmodern age when relationships are more to do with power than the exercise of practical reason.

Further essay questions

2 'Christian ethics cannot support any form of racial discrimination.' Discuss.

3 Assess the view that the principle of the greatest happiness of the greatest number will inevitably lead to the exclusion of racial minorities.

4 'Can one be a nationalist and not a racist?' Discuss.

Chapter checklist

This chapter considers whether there is a need for business ethics, and in particular attitudes to consumerism, materialism and work. It then looks specifically at business practice and the balance between achieving a profit and treatment of people (consumers, employees, managers, stakeholders). The issue of business espionage (insider trading and hostile takeovers) and the impact of globalisation on business and environment form the second part of the chapter. The chapter concludes by looking at various normative ethical responses to business.

1 Do we need business ethics?

Key question

Should Allen Lam be sent to prison for insider trading?

Case study
Insider trading in Hong Kong

Allen Lam, a banker, working for the broker CLSA gave an illicit tip-off to Ryan Fong in 2005, having overheard plans by J.C. Decaux Pearl & Dean, an outdoor advertising company, to buy a 73.38 per cent stake in Hong Kong-listed Media Partners International (MPI) Holdings.

In addition, as a senior banker, Lam also had access to confidential information about the proposed takeover, and passed on the information to Mr Fong, a friend, in three emails in August and September 2005, giving the proposed deal the codename 'the French car'.

Mr Fong, at the time a portfolio manager and asset manager with HSZ Hong Kong, then bought 2.43 million MPI shares for himself and 8.2 million shares for an investment fund managed by HSZ. Mr Lam's wife was an investor in the fund. In September, Mr Fong sold all MPI shares at a profit of

HK$1.03m ($133,000) for himself and HK$3.39m for the fund. Mrs Lam sold her investment in the fund in April 2006 at a profit, of which about HK$69,000 was attributable to MPI. Mrs Lam has not been charged with any offence.

Both men were found guilty by Judge Eddie Yip and sentenced with imprisonment. Mr Lam's defence counsel, Michael Blanchflower, argued for leniency saying, 'He was a passive recipient of information that he overheard' and had gained nothing personally from the information.

Based on *The Financial Times*, 8 July 2009

Business ethics as an area of academic and professional study is a comparatively recent development. Even up until the 1980s most people would have argued that there should be no difference between personal and social values and the ethical values in business. This may well be true, but developments in the social construction of Western societies and changing global relationships between cultures means that it is not always easy to presume a common set of values on which business is to be conducted.

Another significant factor is the development of **multinational corporations** (MNCs) in the late-twentieth century which has meant that national governments have played less significant roles in determining the values of society. As governments have legislated more and more, the rules under which businesses may operate, and real power, in terms of how day-to-day life is lived among the majority of citizens, has increasingly been determined by the values established by MNCs. Business ethics, therefore, is the self-consciousness process by which businesses, especially large corporations, consider and reflect on their influential role in society.

Finally, business ethics are necessary because for almost everyone, work is part of everyday life and the practices and values of the workplace determine how we are treated and how we treat others. As Peter Vardy notes, people often behave quite differently in the work place than at home. For example, an employee might think it morally right to overcharge mileage on a business trip, take home photocopy paper or use the telephone to ring friends as 'perks of the job', when they would not dream of taking petrol at a petrol station without paying for it, or stealing paper from a stationery shop or using a friend's telephone without asking permission first.

Key word

Multinational corporations (MNCs) or transnational corporations are businesses which trade, produce and offer services in more than one country. Often their income or revenue is greater than the gross domestic product (GDP) of some countries.

Cross-reference

Peter Vardy's *Business Morality,* page 68.

2 Consumerism

a) People as consumers

Calling people consumers rather than customers or clients suggests a subtle but significant shift in the way businesses regard people. By regarding people as consumers the role of business (whether it is making goods or providing a service such as education or health) is to satisfy the needs of the consumer at whatever price the market place can bear.

There is nothing morally wrong with this view if that is indeed what it means to be human. At a basic level humans need to consume food to stay alive, find shelter, exchange goods and services and seek entertainment. **Ethical egoists**, such as the economist **Adam Smith**, argue that humans as individuals act only in regard to what satisfies their own interests and desires. If they do things for other people it is essentially because it benefits themselves. Smith suggested that the market place acts as a moderating influence on personal selfishness because if I wish to live the kind of life I want then some consideration of others' needs and wants have to be taken into account. A business person, who thinks as an ethical egoist, knows that if he produces a bad product it may harm the consumer and still make profit, but in the long term other businesses will offer a better, more effective product which more consumers will purchase.

But for others, the consumer model is not only demeaning to human nature but allows us to treat humans as objects and not as persons. For an ethicist, people have special value. Whereas things may be disposed of when they cease to be effective we do not dispose of people when they cease to be productive. As we have seen in Chapter 1, the development of human rights suggests that every human being is to be regarded with equal dignity, to be an integral part of society whatever state of usefulness they might be to it. Many ethical systems, therefore, might resist the tendency to think of humans merely as consumers. In the Jewish and Christian traditions humans are described as being made in the image of God (Genesis 1:27) and Kant rephrased this in non-religious terms, that as all humans are rational creatures then we all have a duty to treat others as we treat ourselves. That means, because I would never wish to be treated as an object or thing, that I must never treat another human being as a means to an end (which would make them an object) but ends in themselves (as a person). Therefore, it is quite wrong to think of people as consumers as it 'instrumentalises' them as objects and a means to achieve profit or material gain.

Key word

Ethical egoism is the belief that morality is entirely based on self-interest.

Key people

Adam Smith (1723–1790) was a philosopher, political and economic theorist. His philosophical theories on human nature and morality are expressed in *The Theory of Moral Sentiments* (1759). His influential work on the commercial society was *An Enquiry into the Nature and Causes of the Wealth of Nations* (1776).

Cross-reference

Attitudes to the material world are discussed at greater length in Chapter 7 on the environment.

b) Materialism

How we regard humans as people or consumers is fundamental to the way in which business ethics views the purpose of business and the material world. The term materialism is ambiguous. For some it has negative connotations because it appears to support the consumerist view of humans and denies other values such as love, honesty, trust, fidelity, and so on. For others, materialism is a positive description of the world, which is there for us to use for our own benefit. In broad terms, as far as business ethics are concerned, there are two views of materialism:

- **Capitalism.** The idea (for example, in the version which Adam Smith put forward) that humans flourish when they seek and fulfil their own desires and interests in a competitive market place. For many religions, notably Christianity, Adam Smith's ethical egoism could be modified so that the young, the old and the sick who cannot work should be cared for because the material world offers us the means to do so as stewards of creation.
- **Marxism.** Marxists regard capitalism as the source of injustice and exploitation, especially of the weak and vulnerable. Marx compared capitalists to vampires sucking the life force out of workers. Marxists argue that we are all equal members of the material world so there is no justification for any one person or group to own it any more than anyone else. All people should have equal access to the 'means of production' according to their various abilities. Marx argued that there is a dialectical relationship between humans and the material world, by this he meant that just as we rely on the material world for our existence so the material world relies on us. Both should be treated with respect.

Key quote

'Capital is dead labour, that, vampire-like, only lives by sucking living labour, and lives the more, the more labour its sucks. The time during which the labourer works, is the time during which the capitalist consumes the labour-power he has purchased off him.'

KARL MARX, *CAPITAL* 1, PART III, CHAPTER 10, SECTION 1

3 Profit and people

The aim of business is profit. If a business does not make a profit then it will eventually fail and cease to exist. However obvious this might seem there are other reasons for businesses to exist which are not necessarily unconnected with the aim of profit. Businesses serve the human need to work, to be a member of a productive society and in turn to contribute to its welfare.

a) Profit

In an influential article **Milton Friedman** argued that business corporations only have a social duty to increase profits because:

- Corporations are not human beings and cannot in themselves have moral responsibilities. Only the individuals in corporations can have true moral responsibilities.

Key question

Does a business only have a duty to make a profit?

Key people

Milton Friedman (1912–2006)
American economist, Nobel Prize winner and leader of the Chicago School of economics. He held a liberal view of economics which advocated monetarism, the view that central government should not micromanage the economy. His essay 'The Social Responsibility of Business is to Increase its Profits' (1970) was one of the major contributions that launched the idea of business ethics in the USA.

Key word

Organisational culture refers to the collective moral and social values which are derived from a business' organisation, system and structure.

Cross-reference

For a fuller account of Kant's argument see pages 114–116.

Key word

Stakeholders are all those affected (harmed or benefitted) by the aims and activities of a business.

- The responsibilities of managers are to its shareholders. Providing that managers act within the law then the only purpose for which a manager may act is to increase profit, any other reason is a form of 'theft' from the shareholders.
- Social issues are not the primary concern of businesses but of the state. Businesses are not designed to, or managers trained to, achieve social goals. Furthermore, as businesses are unelected it would be wrong for them to do so.

But Friedman's analysis of the moral dimension to corporate business has been challenged, primarily because any business that has an organisational structure by which its beliefs, values and operations are determined, must also have what some have termed an **organisational culture.** Therefore, a corporation may have a *collective* responsibility for social issues just as much as it may be blamed for its immoral actions.

b) Corporate social responsibility

Corporate social responsibility (CSR) is the phrase used in business ethics to indicate that businesses have a moral duty to society in addition to the duty to their shareholders to make a profit.

The first line of argument that justifies CSR is largely pragmatic, uses Adam Smith's version of ethical egoism and is often summarised as enlightened self-interest. Put simply, a business that is seen to buy its goods from renewable sources or that refuses to deal with corrupt regimes or supports local charities presents itself as a morally responsible and trustworthy player in society. This in turn encourages people to buy its goods or services.

However, from some moral points of view it is dubious whether this could be called a *moral* act at all. From a deontological point of view the egoist's action is entirely for self promotion and has very little direct concern for society. Kant gives the example of the so-called honest shopkeeper who only gives the right change to his customers because the increase in their trust of him is good for business. But Kant's criticism is that the shopkeeper has not acted with any genuine sense of duty for people.

On the other hand, as there is no direct evidence that CSR does improve profits, then perhaps Kant's argument that duties are necessary because businesses are significant members of society and, therefore, like the individual citizen (but more so) have obligations to society from which they benefit. Businesses have duties to right wrongs when they impact on the local community, and most importantly businesses have to bear in mind that shareholders are not the only ones who depend on the success or failure of a business. Other **stakeholders** might include employees, consumers/customers, suppliers and other businesses in the local community.

There are many versions of CSR but an influential one cited by Crane and Matten is a four-part model where each part responds to an aspect of society at any particular time. Each aspect in the four tiers indicates the appropriate business duties and responsibilities to society:

Cross-reference

Read Andrew Crane and Dirk Matten's *Business Ethic,* pages 43–46.

- **Economic responsibility.** Duties are to shareholders for a reasonable return on their investments, employees who want fair pay and reasonable working conditions, and customers who want good products at competitive prices. This is the basic level on which the three other levels are based.
- **Legal responsibility.** Firms should abide by the law of the land and laws explicitly regulating businesses (such as insider dealing, price fixing, monopolies, etc.). Duties are not optional but required by society.
- **Ethical responsibility.** Businesses may choose to act in an ethically reasonable way by society's wider standards even though they may not be obliged to do so by law. This might be the result of a pressure group or feelings expressed through the letters pages of the local paper. The firm acts because its good standing and reputation is at stake.
- **Philanthropic responsibility.** The highest level is based on the principle of philanthropy or 'the love of one's fellow human being' and is mirrored in Kant's idea of unconditional duty, the golden rule (to do to others as you would have them do to you) and the Christian notion of loving one's neighbour. The duties performed here cannot be demanded by society. But Quaker firms, such as Cadbury and Rowntree in the nineteenth century, built schools, hospitals, decent housing and parks for the local community because they felt that, as influential members of society, it was their Christian duty to do so. A more recent example was in 1998 when the UK firm SmithKline Beecham gave drugs to developing tropical countries to combat Lymphatic Filariasis (known commonly as elephantiasis) which affects 120 million people each year. It cost SmithKline Beecham £100m.

Key quote

'The stakeholder theory of the firm is probably the most popular and influential theory to emerge from business ethics.'

ANDREW CANE AND DIRK MATTEN, *BUSINESS ETHICS*, PAGE 50

Key question

To whom should a manager be most responsible – shareholders, employees, customers, local community?

Key word

Fiduciary relationship is the relationship of trust between the trustee (i.e. managers) and shareholders whom he represents.

c) Duties of managers

In the previous section we noted that business not only has duties to shareholders but to other stakeholders. This most recent development in business ethics extends the duties of managers and directors outside the narrow limits of business to include government, competitors, local community, pressure groups and so on.

i) Responsibility to shareholders

In traditional and legal terms managers have a primary **fiduciary relationship** with their shareholders to act in their best interests, that is to maintain the aims and objectives of the firm, to operate within the law and to make a profit. However, even these aims suggest a wider responsibility other than to shareholders. The aims and objectives of the business might include fair treatment of employees and to give customer satisfaction. Even Friedman acknowledges that there are those who have a stake in the business other than shareholders.

ii) Responsibility to other stakeholders

European law protects many workers' rights such as pay, working conditions, maternity and paternity leave and so on. But other stakeholders may impose *moral* duties on a business. For example, other businesses, shops, schools and local amenities may be directly or indirectly dependent on the existence of a firm. It might be argued that these stakeholders ought to have a greater claim over the running of a business than shareholders whose main interest may only be to speculate in order to make money.

However, how are managers to weigh up the various demands of the stakeholders? Consequentialists, such as utilitarians, will advise, depending on the situation, as to what makes for the greatest happiness or benefit of those involved. Managers will also have to consider long- and short-term consequences and these are often very difficult to determine. But for deontological based ethics, such as Kantian or natural law, the question is whether managers have an equal duty to all stakeholders and whether all duties carry the same weight. W.D. Ross developed a **prima facie** duty system which argued that situations have to be taken into account in order to determine what duty is most appropriate in that circumstance. But this might appear to make principles or duties more important than people.

iii) Management style

More recently, developments in virtue ethical theory offer an important contribution in resolving the problems posed by consequentialists and deontologists, and that is the style or manner in which managers run their businesses. Aristotle's virtue based approach to ethics understood that it is not just what we do that matters but the way in which we do it. Further, he argued that the good person does not operate in isolation but within the community. The virtues are what we need to learn in order to become a good person. Aristotle argued that some virtues have to be taught (the intellectual virtues) and others learnt through observation and upbringing (moral virtues). Therefore, the good manager not only learns to get the best out of others but is himself an example of the good citizen. The key virtue is **phronesis** or practical wisdom. Phronesis is the ability to judge in any situation

Key word

Prima facie duties were developed as an idea by W.D. Ross (1877–1971) to mean that some duties can be overridden by a stronger moral duty. Prima facie means literally 'on first appearance'.

Key word

Phronesis is the Greek word used by Aristotle and others meaning practical wisdom or the ability to make sound moral judgements.

What skills and qualities does a good manager need?

Key word

Total quality management (TQM) is a style of management which encourages co-operative, not authoritarian, management style throughout the whole process of production.

whether a virtue is being pushed to excess or to an extreme or is deficient through lack of exertion. Aristotle added that learning how to avoid the vices of excess or deficiency is not something to be learnt in a day but is a lifetime's project.

There are many models today of what makes a good manager. Increasingly the move has been to merge leadership qualities with management skills. A manager is one who sets targets and objectives and makes the most efficient use of resources to achieve these ends, whereas a leader is one who influences others to achieve aims or objectives. Today it is recognised that a good manager has also to be a leader.

Some people argue that leaders are born to lead (known as 'trait theory'), but modern theorists generally argue that leadership skills can be taught. Although there are many management styles, most fall into one of three types: authoritarian, paternalistic and democratic.

Aristotle's intellectual virtues might be equated with what is referred today as **total quality management** (TQM). TQM is critical of the authoritative style of management and is a practical guide to managers which includes:

- A fundamental requirement of senior management to commitment.
- A genuine commitment generates a vision which must be meaningful and achievable.
- Changes should not be implemented top-down but must involve everyone.
- The vision for the organisation must always be translated into practical actions.
- Integrating TQM into the business includes consideration of the mission statement, strategies and plans, reviewing the management structure, and enabling the workforce to be an active part of the process.
- Senior managers must have long-term commitment to eliminate false departmental pride barriers, avoid setting arbitrary goals and develop experts through training.

(Based on John Oakland and Peter Morris, *Pocket Guide to TQM*, page 41)

d) Duties of employees

In simple terms, an employee enters a contract with his employer which binds him to carry out the role for which he is hired. But no job description can be so comprehensive that it covers every eventuality and the employee is protected by employment laws whether the contract states these or not. Even though an employer cannot ask an employee to break the law there are times when an employee has to balance a number of conflicting considerations.

- **Loyalty to the company.** An employee has a duty to his employer. In return the employer has a duty of care to ensure that he complies with health and safety regulations in the workplace.
- **Conscience**. Even without the legal requirements an employee might feel he or she has a moral and professional duty to their clients or the general public. But to inform them would be to betray their loyalty to the firm and face almost certain dismissal. Those employees who choose to be 'whistleblowers' know that taking action of this kind does not just have consequences for them from this particular firm but from the industry as whole. No one likes or trusts a troublemaker. There are some organisations such as 'The Freedom to Care' who support whistleblowers but this does not make their decisions any easier.
- **Balance of benefits**. In return for their loyalty to their employer, employees should expect to be reasonably treated.

4 Business espionage

A narrowly defined consequentialist view of business ethics might argue that provided a business makes a profit the means by which it achieves that end are justified. Consequentialists are not interested in the value of means in themselves, but that consequences are good and that any negative side effects are outweighed by the desired ends. If this is true, then, does it matter whether a business is acquired in a gentlemanly manner or as a hostile takeover? Or does it matter whether shares for a business are acquired in the open market as an 'act of faith' or through 'insider knowledge'?

a) Insider trading

In a perfect market, buying and selling of stocks and shares is always an act of faith. Those who invest in stocks and shares know that they cannot predict for certain whether these will make or lose them money. The shrewd investor will find out as much as he can about a particular firm and then make his gamble. This assumes that information about a business is all public knowledge.

However, supposing a firm does not reveal their total situation because to do so would unsettle the value of their shares, but certain investors know the real situation, which enables them to buy or sell shares to their advantage. It would be like betting on a horse already knowing the result of the race before it became public knowledge.

This 'insider trading' is considered to be bad business practice because it destabilises the markets and creates doubt and mistrust about financial knowledge. If left unchecked the long-term effect could be to destroy the entire stocks and shares marketplace with colossal damage to business in general. But there are other moral considerations which condemn insider trading:

- **Stealing of property**. Some argue that all information about a firm is in effect part of its property. Divulging information secretly to others, even within the firm, is a form of theft.
- **Harm to innocent people**. Insider trading can cause ordinary investors in the market considerable harm. Those who invest their savings in stocks and shares for their future pension, for example, do so knowing the market can change, but they do so trusting that the market is a level playing field. Insider trading badly distorts the market causing harm to those who have done no wrong. A basic principle of deontological moral systems such as natural law, is that the innocent must be protected and only those who have caused harm must be punished.
- **Trust**. Insider trading not only distorts the market place but it can destroy the fiduciary relationship between shareholders, managers and employees within the business itself. As insider trading is carried out by a few for their own selfish benefit, then the system of trust which is the hallmark of a good business, is severely threatened.

However, there is a fine dividing line between insider trading and legitimate trading and the problem is at what stage does it become immoral for a business to withhold certain information.

b) Hostile takeovers

Whilst some argue that a takeover cannot take place unless some of the shareholders are willing to allow a takeover, others argue that hostile takeovers undermine several important moral considerations:

- **Fairness**. It might be that a few senior executors on the board persuade other board members to accept a takeover encouraged by the prospect of 'golden parachutes'. A golden parachute is the promise made by the takeover firm to the executors that when the merger has taken place they will be paid a large redundancy fee.
- **Dishonesty**. In what has been called 'greenmail' (as opposed to blackmail) the executors agree to buy back shares after the merger at a higher price than the market so as to secure their jobs using money from the firm.
- **Betrayal**. In some cases a hostile takeover occurs when an ailing firm is made such a generous offer that it feels it cannot refuse. However, the new owners have no intention of maintaining the business and then proceed to sell off land and other assets, possibly keeping the rights to brand names and patents. The side effect of this 'asset stripping' process is that employees and other stakeholders lose their jobs.

Key word

Hostile takeover is when 'an investor, or a group of investors, intends to purchase a majority stake in a corporation (often secretly) against the wishes of its board' Crane and Matten *Business Ethics* page 193.

However, it might be argued that in each of these cases business is just being business. With the exception of the golden parachute example, the greenmail tactic might merely be regarded as acting in the best interests of the business by ensuring that the chief executive officers keep their jobs and have some influence on the future of the business, and in the asset stripping case an ailing firm could have decided to sell off various aspects of the business itself and perhaps offered better redundancy terms for its employees than the firm making the takeover.

5 Globalisation

a) What is globalisation?

Globalisation is an ambiguous term and used in a variety of ways both negatively and positively. Economically, it is often used to refer to the ease of cross border transactions and deregulation of trade restrictions between countries. Socially, as Manfred Steger suggests, it describes the way in which human lifestyles, consciousness and fashions have influence each other from one side of the globe to the other. This is reflected in the way in which Western culture (for example, music, media and dress) has been exported to the Far East.

Globalisation has been facilitated by the advancement of technology (communication and internet) and politics (through the liberalisation of laws that makes travel comparatively easy). Crane and Matten have therefore defined globalisation as 'deterritorisation'. The impact of deterritorisation is making it less significant where businesses are geographically located.

However, some consider that globalisation has undermined long-established values and customs. For others, a deregulated market makes it far harder to hold businesses to account. The result is that globalisation has increased poverty, exploitation of resources and destruction of local economies.

b) Accountability to LEDCs

Multinational corporations (MNCs) have considerable power, often owning and controlling media such as television and newspapers and able therefore to determine what we see and what we want. But to whom are they accountable? Unlike a government, who can be re-elected from time to time, MNCs are only responsible to a few shareholders who have very little control over the day-to-day running of the company.

The impact of MNCs is particularly great on less economically developed countries (LEDCs). MNCs have the resources and control to exploit people in poor countries both as workers and as consumers. MNCs are able to use a poor workforce to produce goods for a fraction of the cost in regularised Europe, which is controlled by factors such as a minimum wage and maximum working hours. MNCs are also able to transcend local culture and through the media offer a consumer vision of society which is not only unreachable but at odds with the values of that community.

Perhaps it just has to be accepted that that is the way in which the world is developing. But for many it seems that MNCs are managing to avoid some of the basic human rights and duties, which govern the cultures from which they are operating. Sometimes MNCs learn the hard way that if local customs and values are not respected then they will lose trade because people will vote with their feet and refuse to buy their products or services. But the problem remains of how MNCs can be held accountable unless governments across the world develop agreed trade standards.

c) Sustainability

Since the Rio Earth Summit (1992) the issue of sustainability has become the cornerstone of almost every business ethic. Sustainability is not just about the use of resources and impact of businesses on the environment but also the way in which business can create and destroy communities and cultures.

Globalisation has created particular moral problems for businesses. For example, there is presently considerable debate about the use of bottled water. Bottled water is big business. It is estimated that between $50 and $100 billion is spent globally each year on bottled water, which is good for business but evidence suggests bad for many communities and the environment.

- Bottled water produces up to 1.5 million tons of plastic waste per year. According to some research the plastic requires up to 47 million gallons of oil per year for its production.
- Although the plastic used is of high enough quality to be recycled, over 80 per cent of plastic bottles are simply thrown away.
- Additional costs and effects on the environment are caused by the fuel needed to create and transport bottles.
- Because of changing climate conditions and industrial pollution, fresh water is rapidly becoming the new 'blue gold'. Water supplies are increasingly becoming privatised throughout the world by MNCs for bottled water.
- Local communities (especially in LEDCs) no longer have control over what should be theirs by right, access to a safe and affordable water supply.

Key question

Should the production of bottled water be banned if it has a negative effect on the environment?

Cross-reference

Read pages 106–107 on the problems of CSR.

Key word

Sustainable development is a term coined by the World Commission on Environmental Development in 1987. 'Development' is the aim to improve human living conditions and dignity.

However, the solution is not necessarily to stop selling and buying bottled water. One of the unintended side effects of stopping people drinking too may fizzy drinks, such as Coca Cola, for dietary and dental reasons has been to increase the use of bottled water. There are therefore health benefits to bottled water so the onus is either to improve the taste of tap water or encourage the recycling of the plastic bottles and increase the CSR (corporate social responsibility) of MNCs in countries where water is scarce.

As the bottled water solution suggests, **sustainable development** is not a simple idea. In reality, there have to be a number of trade-offs between what has been termed the 'triple bottom line' of economic, social and environmental values.

6 Normative ethical responses to business ethics

a) Kantian ethics

Early in his analysis of morality in the *Grounding for the Metaphysics of Morals* Kant distinguishes between two types of duty: duty that comes from compulsion and duty that is derived 'from some selfish purpose'. Both are false kinds of duty because they are not driven by a genuine 'good will', which wills our neighbour's good for his or her own sake, but some other selfish motive. He illustrates the selfish 'duty' with the following example of the 'prudent merchant':

> *For example, that a dealer should not overcharge an inexperienced purchaser certainly accords with duty; and where there is much commerce, the prudent merchant does not overcharge but keeps to a fixed price for everyone in general, so that a child may buy from him just as well as everyone else may. Thus customers are honestly served, but this is not nearly enough for making us believe that the merchant has acted this way from duty and from principles of honesty; his own advantage required him to do it. He cannot, however, be assumed to have in addition an immediate inclination toward his buyers, causing him, as it were, out of love to give no one as far as price is concerned any advantage over another. Hence the action was done neither from duty nor from immediate inclination, but merely for a selfish purpose.*

> (Immanuel Kant, *Grounding for the Metaphysics of Morals*, paragraph 397)

Kant's argument seems very strange at first. The dealer has not overcharged his customers, he has earned a reputation for honesty, his customers return to him and so it would appear to be a model of good business ethics. But for Kant the whole set-up lacks genuine moral motivation. In this case the outcome may be good, but the principle on which the merchant acts is expedience or utilitarianism, which might be expressed as follows:

Key quote

'Act in such a way that you treat humanity, whether in your own person or in the person of another, always at the same time as an end never simply as a means.'

IMMANUEL KANT, *GROUNDING FOR THE METAPHYSICS OF MORALS*, PARAGRAPH 429

Cross-reference

Read Immanuel Kant's *Grounding for the Metaphysics of Morals*, paragraph 402 on the lying promise.

If I act honestly with my customers
Then I will build up their trust and they will trade with me
So I can make a profit and continue in business

We can see here that honesty is not being exercised for its own sake because it is contingent or dependent on the situation rather than an act done freely and autonomously. Furthermore, this 'hypothetical imperative' as Kant calls it, is clearly not interested in people for their own sake but uses them as a means to an end, the success of the business. Kant's argument is that genuine duty keeping always treats people as ends in themselves. Duty to people must precede profit.

A genuine duty, or as Kant calls it the categorical imperative, can be tested by reason (not emotions such as love or desire) and judged to be a duty if it can be universalised regardless of situation. Kant's example of promise keeping illustrates the absolute nature of the categorical imperative. A genuine promise is not contingent, so a promise with conditions such as 'I will only keep my promises to keep me out of trouble' is no promise at all because I both want promises to be kept by others but not to be bound by them myself. A contradiction of this kind makes it impossible to live in an ordered and law-abiding society (Kant's 'kingdom of ends'). In business ethical terms Kant's foundational position is a reminder of the phrase used for centuries by merchants and the motto of the London Stock Exchange, 'my word is my bond'.

The attractiveness of Kant's deontological position is that it regards business ethics to be no more than an extension of the morality which governs day-to-day life in society as a whole. There are no special exceptions for businesses; therefore MNCs increasingly have the power and influence to set an example of good citizenship with regards to corporate social responsibility (CSR), equal treatment of stakeholders as people, sustainability, and the avoidance of deceits and lies involved in business espionage.

However, although Kantianism may act as a generally attractive goal it fails to deal with the practical day-to-day life that businesses have to negotiate. Not everyone is rational enough to see the good sense that Kant encourages and in the competitive market place compromises have to be made. In particular, Kant does not offer a method of resolving clashing duties. For example:

- **Duties to stakeholders.** In the Friedman view of business there is only one duty and that is to shareholders. But in order for this to work at a Kantian level all other stakeholders would have to be viewed as impersonal aspects of the market and not as people. As this is not possible, then the Kantian manager has the difficult job of maintaining his duty to all of them equally. But do they all necessarily have equal demands? In order to distinguish between them might entail a consequential assessment of their respective

Cross-reference

See page 114 for the triple bottom line argument.

needs; but that appears to make duties contingent and hypothetical, and to undermine the integrity of the categorical imperative.

● **Profit and people.** A more taxing problem, as illustrated in Kant's example of the prudent merchant, is that if people are placed prior to profit then businesses will almost certainly fail. The Kantian aim of treating all stakeholders with respect is not to be undervalued but as we have seen in business the 'triple bottom line' argument suggests that duties have to be traded off between economic, social and environmental needs, depending on circumstances. This is closer to Ross's *prima facie* argument for duties, where situation determines which duties are more relevant in that circumstance, but once that is acknowledged as a factor then the universal aspect of Kantian ethics is lost.

b) Utilitarianism

As we have seen from many of the discussions above, utilitarianism offers a practical and simple method of calculating good outcomes when a number of considerations have to be taken into account. As a consequential system it begins with Adam Smith's observation that society works best when individuals are left to judge for themselves what is most useful or expedient. Smith argued that the 'invisible hand' of the market generally means that unless I take into account the wishes of others then it is unlikely that my business will succeed.

Adam's enlightened self interest is the principle developed by Bentham and Mill, and the later utilitarians, all of whom argued that *unless* I aim for the greatest good of the greatest number then society will not flourish and I will not be happy. Bentham's hedonic calculus, by which he suggested that happiness or pleasure can be approximately calculated and quantified, lends itself particularly well to the aspect of business ethics which thinks in terms of **cost–benefit analysis**. Put simply, cost–benefit analysis calculates whether a product or service is worthwhile in terms of the labour, materials and time taken to create a product and the short- and long-term predictions of its success and financial returns. Furthermore, utilitarianism is well suited to managers weighing up the various demands of stakeholders and judging therefore what is in the best interests of the business.

However, utilitarianism is not without its problems.

Key word

Cost–benefit analysis calculates whether a product or service is worthwhile in terms of: labour, materials, time taken, short-/long-term success or failure.

i) Depersonalising

If one takes the view of Freidman then the aim of businesses is profit. Businesses are not people but the means by which profit is achieved. This might suit the authoritarian manager who regards his employees as part of the process and customers as consumers to be satisfied, but for many this aspect of utilitarian business ethics is far too calculating and depersonalises everyone involved.

ii) Rights and numbers

Cross-references

For Freidman's view read pages 105–106.

For Bentham on rights read page 6.

Although the utilitarian might take rights into account, Bentham famously dismissed natural rights as nonsense, so there is no essential protection of minorities as far as the act utilitarian is concerned. An employee who is considered inefficient or not a team player may be fired without warning. This often happens in small businesses where despite employment law workers are uneasy about exercising their rights knowing that other businesses will regard them as troublemakers. Often MNCs use cheap labour in LEDCs knowing that an employee has to decide between sweated labour or poverty, or even death.

iii) Quantity not quality

Cross-references

See pages 113–114 on business and sustainability.

See pages 106–107 on CSR (corporate social responsibility).

The example of sustainability and bottled water illustrates how often MNCs justify their product because it is purchased by many regardless of how it has been produced or whether it is good for the customer. In this matter utilitarians are divided. Mill distanced himself from Bentham preferring to pursue 'higher pleasures', whereas Bentham regarded all pleasures are equal if they produce happiness. Mill's distinction indicates a desire to give utilitarianism more noble human ends but in practice the distinction between higher and lower pleasures is hard to distinguish. For example, if, as in the case of cigarettes, products can be shown to have negative effects on the quality of people's health, do businesses have a duty to stop manufacturing them? Despite the factual evidence, the smoking industry has continued to manufacture cigarettes because as there are no intrinsic duties in utilitarianism there is no obligation to observe CSR unless enforced by law to do so.

iv) Lack of integrity

Bernard Williams' analysis of utilitarianism suggests that one of the major weaknesses of utilitarianism's consequential outlook is the unnecessarily sharp distinction between ends and means. Quite often the means are morally significant and cannot be overridden even by an end which may appear to be rationally justified. In an example which Williams gives, an employee who finds out that the product he is making can be used in the production of weapons of mass destruction, one could argue in utilitarian terms that what he is doing has no *direct* effect on others and furthermore if he gives up his job others will fill it and then he and his family will suffer. But such reasoning fails to account for his existing moral commitments (Williams calls them 'basic or lower-order projects'). No amount of reasoning will justify acting in a narrowly utilitarian way without sacrificing these commitments and thereby undermining his sense of personal integrity. The utilitarian demands are, therefore, unrealistic and 'absurdly superficial and shallow' (*Utilitarianism: For and Against*, page 111).

Utilitarianism would do well then to acknowledge the evident fact that among the things that make people happy is not only making other people happy, but being taken up or involved in any of a vast range of projects, or – if we waive the evangelical and moralizing associations of the word – commitments. One can be committed to such things as a person, a cause, an institution, a career, one's own genius, or the pursuit of danger.

(Bernard Williams, *Utilitarianism: For and Against*, page 112)

c) Natural law

i) Natural rights

Natural law offers a deontological basis for business that has the advantage of supporting human rights which allow the individual the freedom to operate and flourish within society. Natural rights, as developed by John Locke and more recently by John Finnis, are grounded in the idea that all human beings have intrinsic purpose and dignity.

According to Locke's primary rights, the right of respect for property can determine how an employee treats the workplace – the use of company materials, telephone, email, more serious cases such as insider trading, which, as we have seen, is often regarded as a form of abuse of property. Natural rights also justify the punishment and removal of an employee or manager should either abuse the rights given to them. In return employees have the right to be protected against abuse by their employers. A raft of legislation today ensures that an employee has a right to fair working conditions, minimum pay for a fair day's work and protection from arbitrary dismissal.

Globalisation, the power of MNCs and the universal nature of human rights, have raised the accountability of business practice beyond local communities and, in keeping with Aquinas' primary precepts, businesses increasingly see their role as maintaining the social order by avoiding the evils of business espionage, offering education and training for their employees and at the highest end of CSR, acting philanthropically in the pursuit of social justice by building and supporting hospitals and schools.

ii) Catholic natural law

Modern Roman Catholic natural law teaching emphasises that business ethics is part of society's striving towards the common good. The underlying principle is expressed in the seventh of the Ten Commandments, 'you shall not steal' (Exodus 20:15). Respect for property, as John Locke also highlighted, is fundamental to the good ordering of society. Without this notion, values of trust, co-operation and enjoyment of the fruits of one's labour are all lost. The *Catechism* comments:

Cross-reference

Read pages 4–5 on Locke and Finnis.

Key quote

'Corporations, especially multinationals, are increasingly judged with regard to their attitude to human rights and how far they respect and protect them.'

ANDREW CRANE AND DIRK MATTEN,
BUSINESS ETHICS, 90

Cross-reference

See page 107 for the four levels of CSR including philanthropy.

Key quote

'Regulating the economy solely by centralized planning perverts the basis of social bonds; regulating it solely by the law of the marketplaces fails social justice, for there are many human needs which cannot be satisfied by the market.'

CATECHISM OF THE CATHOLIC CHURCH, 518

Even if it does not contradict the provisions of civil law, any form of unjustly taking and keeping the property of others is against the seventh commandment: thus, deliberate retention of goods lent or of objects lost; business fraud; paying unjust wages; forcing up prices by taking advantage of the ignorance or hardship of another.

(*Catechism of the Catholic Church*, paragraph 2409, page 515)

Catholic natural law teaching also emphasises the binding nature of promises and the keeping of contracts because 'a significant part of the economic and social life depends on the honouring of contracts between physical or moral persons' (*Catechism*, paragraph 2410) and the strict obligation to pay off debts.

Whilst acknowledging the rights of the individual, Catholic natural law emphasises that each person has a duty to society. It is very critical of any economic or ethical system that promotes individualism and in particular the Adam Smith type of capitalist egoism which is regulated only by the 'invisible hand' of the market place. Catholic natural law teaching on collective responsibility and justice means business ethics involves a range of different players – business managers, representatives of wage-earners (for example, trade unions), public authorities and the state (in the maintenance of human rights). In conclusion, the telos or purpose of business is not only to make a profit but also to maintain the social and natural order:

Those responsible for business enterprises are responsible to society for the economic and ecological effects of their operations. They have an obligation to consider the good of persons and not only the increase in profits. Profits are necessary, however. They make possible the investments that ensure the future of a business and they guarantee employment.

(*Catechism of the Catholic Church*, paragraph 2432, page 520)

iii) Critique of natural law

Natural law offers a comprehensive basis for business ethics, including the role of managers, employees, environment and the necessity of work and economics for the common good. However, unless one is willing to presuppose that everything has an intrinsic purpose or *telos*, then the move from the fact that businesses exist to the notion that they *ought* to do anything (even making a profit) suffers from the facts–values distinction or naturalistic fallacy. However, even if one allows for a basic version of natural law in business ethics there are other problems:

Key question

Is natural law too inflexible to be used as a basis for business ethics?

Cross-reference

Read page 6 on the facts–value distinction.

- **Local customs and values.** A challenge for natural law is to what extent it can accommodate local values and customs. Business ethics in a globalised world increasingly finds that the values operated at home are not always exportable to other territories and cultures. Therefore, if natural law compromises on what it regards as being intrinsically good or bad, then it has accepted moral subjectivism or relativism, which is in direct contradiction to its foundational beliefs.

- **Fair wage**. Natural law calls on all workers to be paid a fair wage according to their contractual duty to a business. However, it offers no way of judging what a fair wage is – should work be judged on skill, effort, time taken? As many businesses depend on the investment of shareholders, should they be paid more than executors and managers? Natural law is too general to be of much help.

- **Too inflexible**. Many consider the absolute nature of natural law makes it inflexible in the real world of business. As we have seen in the Catholic statements above, the term 'strictly' is often applied, but often businesses have to rely on telling part truths (as in the boundary problem raised by insider trading) and trading off some values against others – as in the case of bottled water.

d) Virtue ethics

Virtue ethics in their purist form are neither deontological nor consequential but a combination of both. This makes them an attractive basis for business ethics as their plural outlook enables them to respond to changing circumstance and cultures. Virtue ethics are less concerned with action in itself but the manner in which actions are performed. They believe that a good person will inevitably perform a good action.

We have already seen how Aristotle's distinction between intellectual and moral virtues can be used in modern business practice by developing different types of manager and the skills required to run a business to achieve 'total quality management' (TQM). Ultimately, Aristotle argues, the virtuous life is the one of greatest satisfaction or *eudaimonia*. So, the businessman who deals justly, generously and kindly with his employees is happier in himself and his employees will respond accordingly. As moral virtues are acquired through imitation then other stakeholders will, it is hoped, respond favourably to this business and value it. The business will thrive because it is regarded with respect and an example of the virtuous circle. Virtue business ethics do not work in isolation because, as Aristotle argued, the good individual is also the good citizen. Business ethics therefore do not simply operate internally but aim to support the community or *polis*. Virtue based business ethics project a vision of a harmonious society where business values competition but not at the expense of co-operation, and avoid the vices of business espionage.

But is this idealistic picture really practicable?

Key question

Are virtue ethics too idealistic for business to operate effectively?

Cross-reference

Read pages 108–109 on manager types and TQM.

Key question

Are deceitfulness and dishonesty necessarily bad qualities to have as a leader?

Key people

Niccolò Machiavelli (1469–1527) was born in Florence and became the Secretary to the second Chancery in the Republic of Florence. He was a writer, philosopher and politician. His greatest political work was *Il principe* or *The Prince* (1532).

Key word

Virtù or prowess is used by commentators to avoid confusion with Christian ideas of virtue.

i) Whose virtues?

In **Niccolò Machiavelli's** influential book *The Prince*, he sets out the qualities needed in a great leader, which deliberately question the Christian virtues of compassion, humility, love, mercy and honesty. Sometimes, Machiavelli argues that a leader needs to exercise deceit, cruelty and even extreme violence to achieve a given end. The term Machiavelli uses is the Italian word *virtù*, or prowess, and it is a quality the prince or leader needs if he is to achieve control and ultimately the common good. However, the exercise of *virtù* requires considerable skill and Machiavelli draws a contrast between Cesare Borgia's praiseworthy acts of cruelty and Agathocles' equally bloody and successful acts as a tyrant but lacking in *virtù*. If both men achieved power and control why is Borgia's character to be praised? The answer is that whereas Borgia's actions brought about the common good, Agathocles was only interested in himself.

The point of Machiavelli's argument is that virtues do not exist in isolation but are judged by other values. Machiavelli's argument for extreme cruelty and deceit are shocking because we judge them today against our values such as respect and empathy for others. The problem faced by the virtue ethicist is how he justifies his particular virtues and why these should necessarily be better or worse when achieving a given end. For example, Machiavelli argues that as human beings are essentially untrustworthy, a promise keeper is likely to be worse off than the skilful liar or deceiver:

> *How praiseworthy it is for the prince to keep his word and to live with integrity and not by cunning, everyone knows. Nevertheless, one sees from experience in our times that the princes who have accomplished great deeds are those who have thought little about keeping faith and who have known how cunningly to manipulate men's minds; and in the end they have surpassed those who laid their foundations upon sincerity.*

(Niccolò Machiavelli, *The Prince* XVIII, page 60)

So much of what Machiavelli argues runs contrary to contemporary business ethics, but his views beg the question as to how exactly we justify rationally our business virtues, and why for example, if deceit and dishonesty are in the best interests of the shareholders, they should not be skilfully used.

ii) Virtue ethics are incompatible with business

We began this section by arguing that business managers could embody the virtues that society commends in their daily running of their firms. But Alasdair MacIntyre in his quest to recover virtue ethics for contemporary society isolates one of the key figures as being entirely the wrong model for virtuous living. This figure is the 'bureaucratic manager'. The bureaucratic manager has become the

Key question

Have we placed too much emphasis on businesses to set moral standards?

Key quote

'Characters have one notable dimension. They are, so to speak, the moral representatives of their culture and they are so because of the way in which moral and metaphysical ideas and theories assume through them an embodied existence in the social world.'

ALASDAIR MACINTYRE, *AFTER VIRTUE*, 28

Key quote

'"The love of money" we know, "is the root of all evil"; but not the thing itself. The fault does not lie in the money, but in them that use it.'

JOHN WESLEY, *FORTY-FOUR SERMONS* (FOURTH EDITION 1797), SERMON 44

representative 'character', as MacIntyre terms it, of certain values that society admires because he occupies the vacuum created through the abandonment in the belief of natural law and Christianity, the framework where virtuous living once took place.

Since the late-nineteenth century, industrialised society has admired the values represented by the bureaucratic manager: efficiency, manipulating systems, controlling resources and so on. But the business character is not deep down concerned with people or society in any proper moral sense.

So, MacIntyre concludes that as virtue ethics is about developing genuine human traits, then dependency on businesses as a model of moral behaviour is entirely wrong and incompatible with a view of virtue that has humanity (even God) as its foundation rather than systems and efficiency.

e) Revealed ethics

Christian ethics offer a number of different insights into business ethics. We have already seen that the Protestant work ethic supports a capitalist view of the market. In an influential sermon entitled 'The Use of Money', John Wesley (1703–1791) argued that money in itself is not evil but what matters is how we use it. His sermon says of money: 'gain all you can … save all you can … give all you can'. As stewards of the material world (for example, Deuteronomy 26), humans work as stewards and co-creators to generate wealth and to use it to support their families and communities. However, there is divided opinion as to whether the creation of wealth is to occur in a free and competitive market or whether business is a co-operative and communal activity which should avoid capitalism.

i) Christian business ethics in a capitalist world

Those who argue for Christian business ethics in the capitalist world do so based on the fact that Jesus' teaching often uses examples from the market place to illustrate his vision of the Kingdom of God. The Kingdom of God, or God's rule, is not just a state at the end of the world or life after death but the organisation of society in relationship to God now.

There are various themes in Jesus' teaching on the Kingdom that illustrate how the material world should be used in terms of business:

- **Using one's talents**. In the Parable of the Talents (Matthew 25:14–30) Jesus' example of the use of money illustrates that understanding the practicalities of the marketplace requires skill and wisdom. The master gives each of his servants talents (a talent being more than the fifteen years' wages of a labourer) to invest. The first two servants invest their money and make a profit but the third servant buries his talent because he is scared he will lose it and he fears that his master will punish him. But, whereas the first two servants are commended because they have acted wisely in the market place, the third servant is condemned for failing to use his talent wisely. The parable is also about using one's God-given talents in the Kingdom of God, but it also suggests, as John Wesley taught, that Christianity holds that there is nothing intrinsically wrong with business and making a profit, and that although this means taking risks at times, it is part of human nature to work.

- **Generosity**. Jesus' teaching frequently reminds his followers that generosity in this world will be measured by greater abundance in the Kingdom. Using the metaphor of a measure (that is, a measuring bowl) Jesus says that the 'measure you give will be the measure you get, and still more will be given you' (Mark 3:24), and in the Parable of the Rich Fool (Luke 12:16–21) the rich farmer is condemned for hoarding grain and so failing to use his profits for himself and for others. At the heart of generosity is the question of justice. In business ethical terms, managers have a duty to treat their employees, as well as other stakeholders, fairly as people by using their profit for the good of others. As Wesley's third commandment stated, 'give all you can', but not just in material terms, but in terms of relationships and trust.

- **Honesty and conscience**. Jesus' teaching continued the notion at the heart of Old Testament teaching about maintaining the covenant relationship as established in the Law and the Prophets. The Ten Commandments state that in order for the God–human relationship to work there has to be complete honesty in human relationships. Stealing (Exodus 20:15), the eighth commandment, is fundamentally wrong, yet as we have seen in business ethical terms, many employees 'steal' from the work place but excuse it as a perk of the job. For a business to live in a covenant relationship means having a responsibility to all those in the community. This poses major questions of conscience for MNCs in a globalised world in their use of cheap labour in LEDCs and concern for the environment.

ii) Liberation theology and warnings against capitalism

Cross-reference

See pages 109–110 on employees ethics.

Not all Christian traditions are as supportive of capitalism as the views expressed above. The worst side of capitalism is its individualism and competitiveness which exploits the weak and depersonalises those in the workplace. Liberation theology is one such tradition that shares some of Marx's suspicion of capitalism and uses some of his socio-analytical methods to develop a view of materialism which is radical but also Christian.

At the heart of liberation theology is a reworking of the biblical notion of justice and in particular for those who have been exploited,

Key question

How radical was Jesus' teaching on materialism?

Key quotes

'We affirm the need for conversion on the part of the whole Church to a preferential option for the poor, an option aimed at their integral liberation.'

PUEBLA FINAL STATEMENT NUMBER 1134

'But let justice roll down like waters, and righteousness like an ever flowing stream.'

AMOS 5:24

Key words

Development has a wide range of meanings but refers to the process of improving the quality of human live by raising living standards through an increase in incomes, levels of food production, medical services and education.

Dependency is the state where poorer countries come to depend economically on richer countries in order to survive.

Key people

Gustavo Gutiérrez (b. 1928) is a Peruvian Catholic priest and theologian who lives and works with the poor in Lima. His book *A Theology of Liberation* (1971) was foundational in the development of liberation theology.

Key quote

'I was hungry and you gave me food, I was thirsty and you gave me drink, I was a stranger and you welcomed me, I was naked and you clothed me, I was sick and you visited me, I was in prison and you came to me.'

JESUS' PARABLE OF THE SHEEP AND THE GOATS (MATTHEW 25:35–36)

marginalised and dehumanised by society – that includes the Church. This is often referred to as a 'preferential option for the poor'. The use of 'preference' means giving priority to the poor and 'option' refers to acting in committed solidarity with the poor and dispossessed.

In particular, the liberation theologians are motivated by the eighth century BC Old Testament prophets such as Amos, Isaiah and Micah, whose outspoken message against Israel's leaders and property owners resonates today in a world where rich countries, societies and businesses continue to use their power towards their own ends. Amos describes the hypocrisy of so-called religious people who, at the same time, 'trample upon the poor' (5:11) and who are prepared to short-change the poor because they own the means of production and have the power to 'deal deceitfully with false balances' (8:5). Amos understands that a truly religious society is one that places justice first. In a material world that can be understood in business terms as every transaction, treatment of employees and stakeholders is one of practical application of covenant love.

- **Development.** The founding father of liberation theology **Gustavo Gutiérrez** argues that although Western capitalist countries support the notion of development they do so in the belief that free markets increase people's freedom to choose by enlarging the range of their choices, such as a greater variety of consumer goods and services. But Gutiérrez argues that developmentalism has been particularly destructive in giving more power to the rich, and leads to **dependency**, that in order for rich countries/companies to invest in LEDCs the poor have to support capitalism, but they will never have the business power to trade equally in the marketplace. Dependency reinforces the view that poverty is an unfortunate but predictable by-product of capitalism. Gutiérrez argues that for genuine development to occur there will have to be a radical change in business consciousness:

Attempts to bring about the changes within the existing order have proven futile. Only a radical break from the status quo that is, a profound transformation of the private property system, access to power of the exploited class, and a social revolution that would break this dependence and allow for the change to a new society.

(Gustavo Gutiérrez, *Theology of Liberation*, page 65)

- **Praxis.** Liberation theologians offer a complete reversal to Wesley's business ethic. The aim is not to 'earn all you can' but to work for justice first. Action, or praxis, should precede all business policies and indeed all theology. In Jesus' great parable of judgement (Matthew 25:31–46) those who are condemned are those who failed to side with the exploited, the poor and the marginalised.

Summary diagram

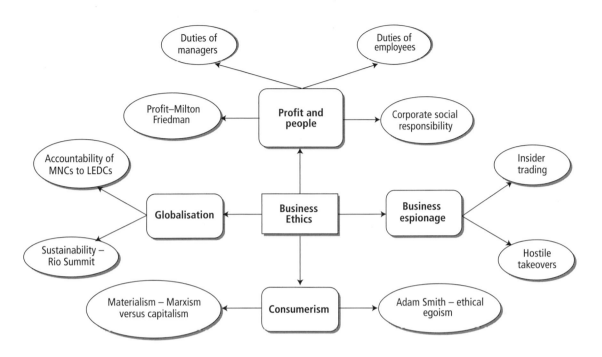

Study guide

By the end of this chapter you should have considered the relationship between personal moral values and those which belong specifically to the world of business. You should be able to consider how consequential and deontological ethics approach the issue of profit and people, and in particular whether virtue ethics offer any insight into the skills of managing a business. Finally, you should understand what is meant by globalisation and its implications for the way in which businesses operate in a global market.

Essay questions

1a Explain what is meant by globalisation.

1b 'In a globalised world business ethics is impossible.' Discuss.

The essay might begin by pointing out that globalisation is a contemporary notion with a variety of meanings. Each of these meanings should be outlined and explained: deregulated trade, effects of cultures on different parts of the planet, 'deterritorisation' and power of communication.

The evaluation might begin by pointing out that business ethics reflect local customs and values. It might be argued from an utilitarian point of view that if global effects really had to be calculated, then trade would become impossible. Moral effects might be considered by MNCs only if they are considered to have cost benefit. On the other hand, globalisation might not be a problem for natural law business ethics because despite cultural differences basic human values remain the same.

Further essay questions

2 'Christian business ethics must reject capitalism.' Discuss.

3 To what extent is business espionage morally justifiable?

4 Assess the view that businesses must always place duties to their customers first.

Revision checklist

Can you define:

■ corporate social responsibility (CSR)
■ stakeholder and shareholder
■ fiduciary relationship
■ globalisation
■ sustainable development.

Can you explain:

■ the views of Adam Smith and ethical egoism
■ the difference between Marxist and capitalist views of materialism
■ the Protestant work ethic
■ Milton Friedman's argument on profit and social issues
■ what is meant by total quality management (TQM)
■ utilitarian cost–benefit analysis.

Can you give arguments for and against:

■ being a 'whistleblower' employee
■ insider trading
■ hostile takeover
■ virtue ethics as a basis for business ethics.

Chapter checklist

This chapter considers the relationship between those who embrace technology and those who are suspicious of it. These positions are developed further in the context of the internet and whether this technology offers a more democratic society or a liberated anarchy or neither. The technology of surveillance is then considered and its implications for privacy, knowledge and power. The chapter concludes by looking at various normative ethical responses to technology.

1 Inventions and new technology

Case study
Modern Times

The film *Modern Times* (1936) shows Charlie Chaplin trying to work faster than the conveyor belt in order to get a break. Some view this iconic film as a criticism of capitalist societies where technology may have increased efficiency and profit but not greater quality of human life.

a) Technophobia and technophilia

Technology might be defined as:

> *the application of organised knowledge to practical tasks by ordered systems of people and machines.*
>
>   (Ian Barbour, *Ethics in an Age of Technology*, page 3)

Ian Barbour argues (*Ethics in an Age of Technology*, page 4) that the advantage of his definition is that:

- **organised knowledge** includes technologies based on practical experience as well as scientific theories
- **practical tasks** include material goods as well as services (such as computers, communications, and biotechnologies)
- **ordered systems of people and machines** reflect the social as well as the hardware aspects of technology.

It is the final part of the definition which points to the ethical dimension of technology. Some embrace technology for the enormous benefits it offers humans whilst others are deeply suspicious of its potentials and claim that it will in some way cheapen human existence.

i) Technophilia

Technological optimists, or technophiles as **Neil Postman** calls them, rejoice in human inventiveness for its own sake, for the sheer excitement of what it might bring, even the thrill of a brave new world. Technology is seen as the great liberator from existing conditions and offers the prospect of new experiences, greater leisure time, greater choice and greater ease of doing things.

Optimists argue that technology has offered some of the following benefits:

- **Higher living standards** through drugs, medicines, nutrition, sanitation and release from the grind of the laborious work of the past.
- **Opportunity and choice** through ease of mobility and transport which have in turn permitted the overthrow of restrictive traditions. Birth control, notably the contraceptive pill and safer means of abortion, have permitted a greater range of sexual expression and regulated family size.
- **Leisure** is now no longer a privilege of the rich landed gentry, but as a result of labour saving technology, machines have freed the masses to enjoy themselves beyond the materialism of day-to-day work.
- **Communications** via travel (train, flight, car, etc.) and information technology (email, internet, mobile phone, etc.) have given humans a hugely increased means of global interaction and

Key people

Ian Barbour (b. 1923) is Bean Professor Emeritus of Science, Technology and Society at Carleton College, Minnesota, USA. He is one of the most influential theologians today in the area of science and religion.

Key people

Neil Postman (1931–2003) was an American author of popular and academic books on the media and culture. Two of his influential books are *Amusing Ourselves to Death* (1985) and *Technopoly* (1992). Postman argues that technology should always be placed after human needs rather than dictate them. His criticism of the technophiles is that they lack knowledge of the history of technology which would enable them to be more critical of inventions.

Key quote

Technophiles 'gaze on technology as a lover does on his beloved, seeing it as without blemish and entertaining no apprehension for the future. They are therefore dangerous and are to be approached cautiously.'

NEIL POSTMAN, *TECHNOPOLY*, 5

Cross-reference

The prospect of global democracy is discussed on pages 136–137.

experience of human diversity, and perhaps the prospect of a truly democratic global community.

Technophiles argue that technophobes have a tendency to over romanticise the past before technology took hold of society. They remind the technophobe that in the past, society was often more brutal, class divided and monotonous. Many technophiles argue that technology will eventually release humans from class and political divisions as future societies will depend on knowledge from the technology experts who will not have a political agenda.

Finally, many technophiles argue that technology offers humans an opportunity to use their God-given power of reason to transform the world and free themselves from the tyranny of nature. **Teilhard de Chardin** was one of the most outspoken advocates for the use of technology for human flourishing. He said humans should 'seize the tiller' of nature and to steer it on a better course rather than allowing nature its own limited purpose.

ii) Technophobia

Technological pessimists or technophobes are those who fear that technology, if left to its own devices, will eventually destroy human relationships and the environment. Barbour suggests the following areas which preoccupy the technophobe:

- **Uniformity and mass society.** Just as Charlie Chaplin felt that he had become a cog in the machine of production, mass production reduces individuality and undermines culture. As technological production relies on conformity in order to be effective, anyone who fails to conform is marginalised.
- **Narrow criteria of efficiency.** As technology bases itself on rational and efficient organisation it values specialisation, speed and maximum output. These qualities are rated greater than humans and make the worker subservient to the machine.
- **Impersonality and manipulation.** Technology has subtly changed our view of society and who we are. The technology of surveillance has made us feel more like objects than people.
- **Uncontrollability.** Technology has taken on a life of its own and, like a runaway car, it has gained so much momentum that we are unable to stop it. The French philosopher **Jacques Ellul** argues that there is a technological determinism, where technology appears to breed more technology with unpredictable consequences that humans cannot control.
- **Alienation of the worker.** Marx in particular argued that technology in a competitive environment of capitalism does not liberate workers as the technophiles suggest, but alienates them from real, creative work.

Key people

Teilhard de Chardin (1881-1955) was a French theologian and scientist. His most influential book *Le Phénomène humain* (1955) argued that the universe is constantly developing greater degrees of complexity moving towards higher levels of consciousness.

Key question

Are some people right to fear technology?

Key people

Jacques Ellul (1912–1994) was professor at the University of Bordeaux. As a philosopher, sociologist and theologian he warned against the tyranny of technology and its inevitable destruction of human spirituality. He argued that only Christianity offers a possible challenge to the sinfulness of technology, but even then the future would ultimately only be in God's control.

The underlying theme of technophobia is that, left to its own devices, technology will undermine human relationships and replace spiritual values with material needs. Finally, there are those who, whilst they share the pessimists' concerns, do not think that technology will in itself destroy society. Neil Postman's rallying call is that society must avoid the blindness of the technophile by constantly questioning the underlying purposes of new technology. What society needs are more technology resistance fighters:

> *A resistance fighter understands that technology must never be accepted as part of the natural order of things, that every technology – from an IQ test to an automobile to a television set to a computer – is a product of a particular economic and political context and carries with it a program, an agenda, and a philosophy that may or may not be life-enhancing and that therefore requites scrutiny, criticism, and control. In short, a technological resistance fighter maintains an epistemological and psychic distance from any technology, so that it always appears somewhat strange, never inevitable, never natural.*
>
> (Neil Postman, *Technopoly*, page 185)

iii) Does technology liberate?

Technophobes observe that new technology creates different problems of its own. The use of email does not seem to have reduced paper consumption in offices. The speed and ease of sending an email leads to a tyranny that expects an immediate response, which is impossible if using paper mail ('snail mail').

Email and internet offered a revolutionary prospect of being able to work from home and thereby reducing traffic, the expense of maintaining an office and time getting to work. But the reality is that people like face-to-face working and find life glued to a computer emotionally and physically unsatisfactory. The home office exists, but it has not offered the technological liberation that many imagined.

Likewise, since Henry Ford (1863–1947) developed a motor car that was cheap and affordable by the masses, the prospect of quick and easy travel meant that people could work further from home, visit friends and relatives with ease and travel in ways hardly envisaged before. But with the rise of cars on the road, more and larger roads have been built, which has encouraged car manufacturers to develop more powerful and efficient cars. So, as the volume of cars on the road has increased travel times have not improved proportionately. It still takes the same time to travel in London as it did a hundred years ago.

However, in response to these criticisms, the optimist and technophile suggest that the pessimist has committed at least two philosophical errors.

- **Fallacy of division.** Technophiles point out that technophobes commit a very common philosophical mistake of inferring that what is true of a few cases must be true of the whole. The fact is that technology covers a very wide range of applications from the tin opener to a space station. It would, for example, be illogical to condemn the humble tin opener because of one's misgivings about the computer.
- **Correlation confusion.** Technophobes argue that technology is the cause of many social problems. Whilst it is possible to show that this might be the case in some circumstances, there may be better causal explanations. For example, it is not technology alone that causes society to malfunction but human character traits (such as selfishness, greed and competitiveness).

Finally, the technophile suggests that being aware of the way in which technology can be misappropriated also enables society to redirect it to better ends. Technology should operate within society's key values – justice, protection of the weak, liberty of expression and so on.

iv) Are humans naturally inventive?

Whilst it is true that many technologies fail to liberate us from certain chores by creating new ones, nevertheless, technology has offered many new experiences of the world that were unavailable in the past. The technophile makes an important observation: humans are naturally inventive and enjoy making new things. Technological inventions are not always about creating new and more useful things, but sometimes no more than exercises of the imagination and inventiveness for their own sake. At the trivial end of technology, the 'gadget' or 'gizmo' often do no more than amuse or offer a different way of doing a common task, and it is difficult to see how such things could be considered harmful.

b) Judging the value of technology

The previous discussion has raised the question: how precisely can we judge the value of new or novel technological inventions?

i) Technology as an end itself

Because we are naturally inventive, for the technophile all technology is intrinsically good. The technophile therefore argues that there should be few controls over technological inventions and development. Some have termed this as the **Promethean** position, which celebrates human desire for greater technological knowledge and mastery of nature itself. For example, the rapid development of micro-electronics used to produce cheap and powerful computers, combined with the imagination of computer programmers has created what many regard as one of the most revolutionary of all

Key quote

'Further, we must press ahead in the name of human adventure. Without experimentation and change our existence would be a dull business.'
SAMUEL FLORMAN, *BLAMING TECHNOLOGY*
193

Cross-reference

For more specific detail on the value of technology from the various normative ethical positions read pages 148–154.

Key word

Promethean means using human intelligence to further our own existence. The idea is based on the Greek myth where Prometheus stole fire from Zeus for humans to use.

Key word

Technopoly is defined by Postman as the belief 'that the primary, if not only goal of human labor and thought is efficiency; that technical calculation is in all respects superior to human judgement' (*Technopoly*, page 51).

Key word

Surplus value or wealth. For Marx wealth indicates that the worker must have been exploited by those who own the means of production.

Key quote

'The rate of surplus value is therefore an exact expression for the degree of exploitation of labour-power by capital, or of the labourer by the capitalist.'

KARL MARX, *CAPITAL* 1, PART III, CHAPTER 9

modern technologies, the world wide web. Postman terms this **technopoly** – a world supposedly enhanced by technology.

Nevertheless, even the technophile realises that if technology is intrinsically good it can still be used for bad ends. For example, a knife's intrinsic purpose is to cut – we use it to eat, to protect ourselves, for surgery, to sharpen pencils and so on, but it can also be used to kill, to threaten and to damage property. This suggests that even if technology has intrinsic worth, it has also to be judged within the context of wider social values.

ii) Technology as a means to an end

The consequential instrumental value of technology does not adopt the technophile's view but judges the value of technology by what it achieves. Innovations are not in themselves either good or bad, but the question the instrumentalist asks is: do we need it? The utilitarian argument adopted by Postman, for example, is that we must be careful not to be seduced by the excitement of the new, but consider critically whether the adoption of a new piece of technology is really going to enhance our future happiness.

Postman argues that new technology can make us buy things we do not really need and create needs that we did not previously have. Postman's argument echoes Mill's famous criticism of Bentham's version of utilitarianism. Whereas Bentham considered that all pleasures are equally good if they produce happiness, Mill, argued that some pleasures have higher and nobler intellectual ends. In other words, the hedonistic utilitarian argument fails to be sufficiently critical of the kinds of ends that will be for the *greater good* of society in the long term. Postman's and Mill's consequentialism warns against rushing into the use of technology without first giving it careful reflection.

Marx's consequential view adds a note of suspicion that technology also fuels a capitalist society's desire for more but at the expense of human existence. For example, improved technology can increase production and create cheaper goods. But who really benefits? In Marx's analysis, efficiency creates **surplus value** or wealth. Whilst some of the surplus value may be passed back to the consumer by making products cheaper, it also makes those who own the means of production richer and more powerful.

The point which Marx and Postman both make in their different ways is that unless we have a very clear idea of what kind of society we want, we can find ourselves allowing technology to be our master, rather than the slave of our needs and wants.

iii) Technology as social worth

The middle path between the intrinsic and instrumental value of technology views expressed above is that technology has to be

Key people

Gordon Graham is Regius Professor of Moral Philosophy at the University of Aberdeen. Among his publications are *Philosophy of the Arts* (2000), *The Internet* (1999) and *The Shape of the Past* (1997).

Key quote

To regard technology as essentially purposeful, then, is to make the mistake of supposing that usefulness is valuable in and for itself.'

GORDON GRAHAM, *THE INTERNET*, 49

Key thought

An example of a new invention which was not the result of an immediate desire is the use of keyhole surgery, originally developed to reduce blood loss but whose unexpected consequences included greatly increased recovery times and therefore shorter residence in hospital.

Key quote

'Technology is truly valuable if it raises the prospect of a better world. A more democratic world would be a better one.'

GORDON GRAHAM, *THE INTERNET*, 61

Key quote

'What we call Man's power over Nature turns out to be a power exercised by some men over other men with Nature as its instrument.'

C.S. LEWIS, *THE ABOLITION OF MAN*, 69

Key question

Does technology empower humans?

viewed in the context of existing social values. The position that **Gordon Graham** adopts is a form of moral objectivism, which does not begin with instrumental questions about whether technology will make life easier or more efficient, nor does it regard technology to be intrinsically valuable, but rather it is to be judged against objective moral values. Graham argues:

- The Promethean argument avoids philosophical rational reflection because it avoids moral reflection altogether. This is clearly not the way we usually consider matters in society and gives an intrinsic moral status to technology's usefulness, which Graham argues is false for the reason we have already considered in the example of the knife.
- The instrumental argument is weak because distinguishing between ends and means is, in practice, far from clear. Furthermore, in a perfect world, technology would have no instrumental value and all inventions would cease – but that is both unrealistic and unhelpful. Besides which, new inventions can have unexpected consequences that are not driven by preceding desires or reason. However, the ends/means distinction can be helpful to clarify what it is we desire (ends) and whether it is worthwhile at any particular time (means).

Graham's proposal is that technology is to be judged by the way in which it enhances the well-being of society in the context of well-established objective social values. This must be a democratic process in which new technology should be assessed according to values such as toleration, reduction of harm to others and compromise of desires.

c) Michel Foucault: technology and power

Michel Foucault's influence on contemporary philosophical, ethical and sociological thinking has been considerable, especially in the analysis of technology and its means of controlling society.

i) Power and discourse

Foucault's argument focuses on the way in which discourses and practices develop. A discourse is more than just the language but the ideas and structures of the world that it presumes to reflect.

Practices are the way in which humans react to the world. Sexual drive, for example, creates different kinds of sexual relationships and the need to develop tools for everyday existence creates technologies.

But often these practices can be taken over and controlled by humans to give them power. The reasons for this are psychological, political and circumstance, but the way in which power is exerted is through a new discourse that controls the practice. It is often very

Cross-reference

See pages 42–43 on Foucault and sexuality.

Key word

Will to knowledge in Foucault's philosophy is a two-fold process of knowing things as they are and knowing how humans have created ideas about them.

Key word

Panopticon means 'the all seeing eye'.

Key quote

'Prison became the general form of punishment, replacing torture. The body no longer has to be made; it must be trained and retrained, its time measured out fully and used; its forces must be continuously applied to labour.'
MICHEL FOUCAULT, *THE PUNITIVE SOCIETY*, IN MICHEL FOUCAULT, *ETHICS*, 55

hard to think outside a discourse, and besides, those who maintain the discourse – the 'experts' such as the scientist or politician – have a vested interest in maintaining a discourse.

The only way the non-expert can attempt to question a discourse and its practices maintained by the expert is to show how it has been constructed. Once exposed, discourses and practices are revealed to be subjective and can therefore permit other alternative discourses.

Once this has been done we are on the right track in the process of the **will to knowledge**. Having knowledge is the means of liberating oneself from the dominate destructive discourses and their practices. So, if we follow Foucault, we should be suspicious of a discourse that thinks in terms of an 'age of technology', as if this is the defining point of human history, and in addition we should be suspicious of the considerable power this gives scientists, inventors or even governments as invincible experts.

ii) 'The Age of Panopticism'

As an example of the dangers of technology Foucault gives the example of the **panopticon**. The panopticon was the invention of the philosopher **Jeremy Bentham**, which, he argued, would revolutionise the prison system and create a happier society. He suggested a new kind of building created in a circular shape, where an outer gallery with small windows facing inwards towards the prisoners' cells in the centre of the building would enable the wardens to constantly monitor the inmates but without being seen directly by the prisoners. Bentham imagined a time when only a very few prison wardens would be needed as the prisoners would assume they were being watched and learn to reform themselves. As an utilitarian reformer Bentham considered the panopticon to be a most efficient and rational use of technology as a means to achieving the greatest happiness of the greatest number.

But Foucault argues that 'the age of panopticism' gave rise to a new technological discourse of power and efficiency, which has had a detrimental effect on many everyday practices.

- The new technology reinforced punishment as part of an industrial process of production and efficiency. As a result, a whole set of new 'illegalities' had to be invented to protect and maintain the machinery of society.
- The new technology developed a new discourse that saw ordinary people in terms of the 'apparatuses of production', to be controlled, moved, hired and fired by technological values of efficiency, regularity and cost effectiveness.
- The panopticon demonstrates how technological discourse is not really concerned with people, but with bodies who can be trained, retrained and their value calculated.

Key question

Who really controls technology today?

iii) Controlling technology

An important question that Foucault raises is who controls technologies today. There are obvious players. First, governments have a key role in funding research and regulating industry for health and safety purposes. Second, scientists and engineers control technology because it is in the nature of science to want to develop new ideas. Third, citizens acts as consumers and if necessary can voice their opinions through public enquiries.

But Foucault's analysis encourages us to look further at the nature of their discourses. Governments have their own political agendas; scientists and engineers do not work independently, but often rely on government backing and funding, and in the academic world may also be controlled by the need to publish research; and businesses have a vested interest in maintaining citizens as consumers of new technology.

2 The internet and society

a) The information age

Perhaps no other technological advance has changed the world quite so much as the internet. What began as a military system to pass on classified information, was then developed by universities to give easy access to scholarly material and has become, via the development of cheap and powerful home computers, the world wide web (the 'web') and internet service providers (ISPs) – a powerful means of communication for the masses. The internet epitomises what many have called the 'information age'.

Unlike television or radio, with comparatively little knowledge or skill, almost anyone can advertise their products and broadcast their ideas by creating a simple web page. The web enables people to join groups and exchange views (for example, MSN Messenger, Facebook, Twitter, etc.), buy and sell goods, download films, read books and access knowledge in countless different ways.

In addition, the internet has made email commonplace in today's society. Email enables almost instant, cheap, global communication that does not require the receiver to be present when a message is sent. Unlike a conventional letter or paper memo, email can disseminate information to a whole institution within seconds.

The internet has spawned its own international language and offered access to ideas and information that not so many years ago would have required considerable patience, time and money to acquire.

Key question

Could the internet help solve some of the problems the democracy?

b) Internet as an aid to true democracy

Besides its everyday uses, Gordon Graham asks whether the internet's power could contribute politically to a more democratic world.

> *Although the use and popularity of the internet is advancing with unprecedented speed, we are still on the very edge of its development. Among the dreams that might be entertained for it, and are actively entertained in some quarters, is that of a world of far greater freedom of expression and democratic control than anything which human history has yet contrived.*

(Gordon Graham, *The Internet*, page 62)

In order to know whether this dream is possible, the issue first to be considered is what democracy is and what its weaknesses are.

Democracy usually refers to the right of the people to rule themselves; as Abraham Lincoln famously put it, democracy is the 'Government of the people, by the people, for the people'. In a direct democracy the people would literally rule themselves, but as there are many practical reasons why this would not work, indirect democracy works by allowing the people to elect representatives to express their will in government. This establishes the second principle of democracy, 'Let all those who are subject to the law make the law'. In a perfect democracy the representative would know and be able to transmit the will of those he represents and dispassionately be able to resolve their needs with those who represent other constituencies.

However, in practice, there are a number of modifications and challenges to the representative democracy model:

- **Knowledge and exclusion**. Not every citizen is given the power to elect representatives because votes are only given to those who have the capacity to understand the issues. Children and the mentally disabled are excluded because the modified principle is 'those who are *sufficiently* able to make the law, make the law'. But if this is true then many adults who vote do so largely from ignorance and are hardly sufficiently well informed about the law and the current issues to make an informed decision.
- **Numbers and distribution**. Democracy allows each person to have one vote to count no more or less than anyone else's vote. Many argue that this hard and fast rule does little to encourage individuals to become part of the democratic process. First, should not the better informed citizen's vote count for more? Second, as a representative is elected depending on a majority of votes, it does not matter whether he or she wins by one vote or a thousand. This suggests that not every vote counts equally. The maximising majority principle can have the effect of making

people feel that their vote has little effective value. Third, the principle of majority rule democracy fits uneasily with the notion of human rights that protect the interests of minorities.

These criticisms highlight that for representational democracy to work properly there needs to be effective communication and information. Technology has, since the printing press, certainly helped to resolve the problem of lack of knowledge and ignorance. More recently, television and radio have enabled party political broadcasts to be brought into the living rooms of ordinary people. But the power of the internet offers an even greater level of information that could tackle the deficiencies of the present system even more:

- The web allows easy access to pressure groups, discussion groups, current feelings of ordinary people (via blogs etc.). This might encourage people to feel that every vote does count because they are not alone in their views and they are acting in solidarity with others.
- Unlike television and radio, which selects what it wishes to broadcast at any particular time, the internet is a store of information that allows the ordinary person to select and compare information.

The internet also provides instant feedback to governments about the mood and feelings of those they represent. As it may not require a new election to alter government policy, people do have a much more active role in the making of law.

But can the internet really plug the deficiencies of democracy as we have outlined? First, the argument suggests that people will use the internet in a responsible, discerning and critical manner. Who is to say that these are not the same people who made it their business to be informed about public issues without the internet? Second, critics suggest that the internet fuels prejudice and false information. Whereas television is open to public scrutiny and can therefore more reliably challenge the views of individuals, the internet is far too complex to be controlled and simply allows people to carry on believing what they wish.

c) The internet, anarchy and freedom

If the internet does not support democracy then might it be the basis of a radical political alternative – **anarchy**? There are two ways of understanding anarchy: positive and negative.

The positive meaning of anarchy envisages communities that are self-governing without the interference and control of a central government reducing their freedom. Positive anarchy, in general, considers that humans are by nature willing to recognise that we

Key question

Does the internet open up the possibility for real human freedom?

Key word

Anarchy means literally without a ruler or government.

Key people

Pierre-Joseph Proudhon (1809–1865) was a French journalist, political activist and social theorist. At a time of social revolution in Europe his anarchist idea of society based on co-operation rather than central political authority was highly influential.

Key quote

'... though this be a state of liberty, yet it is not a state of licence.'

JOHN LOCKE, *TWO TREATISES ON CIVIL GOVERNMENT*, SECOND TREATISE, II.6

Key quote

'Every thing will wear a different look to your illuminated vision: new sentiments will engender new ideas within you; religion, morality, poetry, art, language will appear before you in nobler and fairer forms.'

PIERRE-JOSEPH PROUDHON, *QU'EST-CE QUE LA PROPRIÉTÉ?*

have different interests which can all be equally respected. Society is therefore to be thought of as a web of relationships existing freely and uncoerced. As the influential anarchist **Pierre-Joseph Proudhon** stated:

Free association, liberty – whose sole function is to maintain equality in the means of production and equivalence in exchanges – is the only possible, the only just, the only true form of society.

(Pierre-Joseph Proudhon, *Qu'est-ce que la Propriété?* (1840), in George Woodcock, *The Anarchist Reader*, page 71)

The negative meaning of anarchy is a state of lawlessness and chaos where social structures have collapsed and liberty, as John Locke commented, has become 'licence' to do whatever one wishes with none of the mutual respect expressed in Proudhon's phrase 'the equivalence in exchange'.

The question is whether the internet supports anarchy in its positive or negative sense.

i) Knowledge

The internet does not recognise international boundaries, disregards almost all political coercion of governments and is open to all people, regardless of their race or creed, to exchange information. In Proudhon's vision of anarchic society the corrupt state will wither away to reveal purer forms of knowledge and experience of the world. Could the internet fulfil Proudhon's vision? A problem with the internet is that the information it contains may be totally spurious. Anyone can place data or express their views on a webpage, so there are none of the usual controls that a reputable publisher would have to go through. It is also very difficult to know whether an internet persona is actually who they say they are. Therefore, whereas Proudhon imagined that anarchy would be characterised by true knowledge and empower the people to see the world 'in fairer forms', the internet could do quite the reverse.

ii) Freedom

Positive anarchy offers people liberty and freedom. Proudhon defines liberty as the fulfilment of desires (to associate with whoever) free from external hindrances. The weakness with Proudhon's notion is if priority is given to the fulfilment of desires, then the state of anarchy that follows is not positive co-operation, which he envisages, but licence to do anything – the negation of freedom.

However, Kant reminds us that we are only truly free when we act in solidarity with all people. In other words, the internet could be used critically by considering what others think so as to act in a fully informed manner.

But as reasonable as this may sound, Kant's version of human agency fails to account for the fact that for many the internet is not a public world of real people but a fantasy world with different or no rules. The way some people behave on the internet is not dictated by reason or by the usual standards people treat others in everyday life. The concern then is whether the negative anarchy developed on the internet might somehow begin to spill out into society itself causing it to become fragmented and dysfunctional.

d) Cybercrime

Cybercrime, or computer crime, is committed when a computer or network is the tool, target or place of a crime. Crimes which can be committed in this way are: theft, forgery, fraud, etc.

Computer crime includes illegal access to someone's computer, such as:

- **Data interception** – to obtain information by hacking a password or illegally using a network connection or intercepting a wireless connection.
- **Data interference** – damaging, suppressing or altering data (perhaps via viruses or malware).
- **Systems interference** – by interfering and altering the functioning of a computer, through damaging a program, transmitting or inputting data without permission.
- **Misuse of devices** – identity fraud or identity theft (perhaps by 'phishing').

Cybercrime using the internet might cover many of the crimes mentioned above but also includes:

- **Pornography** – and in particular child pornography and child grooming (for paedophile groups or prostitution).
- **Copyright infringement** – in particular, free music sharing websites, and sites allowing free access to books.
- **Terrorism** – or cyberterrorism is when a terrorist threatens or coerces a government or organisation to promote his political, religious or social beliefs by launching a computer based attack against their computers and network (through viruses, malware, identity theft, etc.). Cyberterrorism might alternatively use the internet as a means of propaganda.

i) Controlling and policing the internet

Policing the internet is particularly problematic because shutting down a website outside a particular jurisdiction requires the co-operation of another government or jurisdiction. Even then a website can move to another ISP.

However, organised public pressure can have desired effects on other crimes. The free music sharing company Napster was forced

> **Key word**
>
> **Phishing** is the process of obtaining sensitive information, such as passwords or bank details, through an official looking electronic form (often an email or website), from a victim with the intent of using that information to steal or commit some other crime.

to close down in 2001, prompted by litigation initiated by the heavy metal band Metallica, and at present the Authors' Licensing and Collecting Society is campaigning against Google's book service which allows people to read large sections of books online free of charge.

ii) Cyber-rape

Key question

Is cyber-rape a crime?

In all these cases the crimes committed infringe laws in the real world. However, there are another class of cybercrimes where the distinction between actual civil society and the cyber world is less clear. For example, in the following case reported in 1993, a player in an online multiplayer text-based world used his computer skills to 'force' one of the women players to have sex with him in front of the other players. As Graeme Kirkpatrick comments:

> On the face of it, this is an ethical non-event, since it only involves text messages on a screen. However, for the victim the strong feelings involved were real.

(Graeme Kirkpatrick, *Technology and Social Power*, page 98)

Feminist commentators, on the other hand, have argued that the cyber personality was still a character which the real person had invested in with time and care. The crime committed was a violation of her power, and that, rather than the actual act of sex, was what made it rape. However, many consider that as the woman player could have turned off her computer or chosen not to participate in the game, there was no actual crime.

Nevertheless, this case illustrates the increasingly complex nature of how we relate to technology, how it should be controlled and how we think of ourselves as people.

3 Surveillance society

a) Definition and examples
i) Surveillance is two-faced

Key people

David Lyon is professor of sociology at Queen's University, Ontario, Canada. He has written extensively on the area of surveillance and technology including *The Electronic Eye* (1994) and *Surveillance Society* (2001).

Case study

Surveillance comes from French, meaning 'to watch over'. This, as **David Lyon** observes, suggests a positive and negative dimension to surveillance. On the positive side, watching over someone is associated with wanting to care and protect; negatively it suggests constraint, control and invasion of privacy. This double aspect of surveillance presents modern society with a constant dilemma: society has always had a duty

to look after its citizens and protect them from harm but the sophistication of modern technology means that we are far less in control of our lives than we imagine. Not only can information about our private lives be distributed around the world in an instant, but as we are the *object* of surveillance, many worry that this slowly depersonalises human relationships.

Lyon defines surveillance as:

any collection of processing of personal data, whether identifiable or not, for the purposes of influencing or managing those whose data have been garnered.

(David Lyon, *Surveillance Society*, page 2)

ii) Examples of surveillance today

The definition of surveillance given above covers a very wide range of technologies. Such examples include:

- **Email**. Email is quick, flexible and has become an instant means of communication from one side of the globe to the other. On the other hand, international **ECHELON** screens emails for key words and scrutinises detail of email on the pretext of national security. But as this is done without anyone's consent and without knowing what kind of information is being gathered, people's personal lives appear to be considered less valuable than the information gathered.

- **Security cameras**. The use of security cameras has suddenly become a common aspect of villages, towns, businesses and institutions since the late-twentieth century. We rely on them to help the police and security services to protect us against attack, robbery and antisocial behaviour. Often their very presence deters bad behaviour. But does this lull us into a false sense of security and does it make us less responsible as citizens by passing on problems to those we assume are monitoring what is going on?

- **ID cards**. A common feature in schools, universities, the armed forces and in many countries is for citizens to use an identity card. The card, with its embedded microchip or electronic data strip, allows access to buildings, rooms, vehicles and information for those have legitimate use. Increasingly ID cards use **biometrics**. Biometrics is a record of our unique biological features such as finger prints or the eye's retina. The card contains

Key word

Biometrics literally means biological measures and is the means to record and recognise unique human features in two ways: physiological (e.g. face, DNA, finger prints) and behaviour (e.g. voice, posture, mannerisms).

Key words

Dataveillance is the collection of data about people and commodities.

Cyberveillance is the collection of data about people and commodities but stored and transmitted electronically.

Key thought

New technology in the context of surveillance refers to the use of computers and telecommunications (via fibre-optic cables and satellites) rather than older methods of direct observation and paper records.

these features encrypted digitally, which are then matched or verified when a person's finger or retina is scanned. But is the detail on these cards increasingly invasive of one's personal life and open to identity theft?

- **Internet.** The internet and the world wide web provide an extraordinary resource for information, ease and choice of shopping, games, communication, and so on. But there are subtle forms of surveillance that websites use to find out more about their users. A cookie, for example, is a simple piece of code sent by a website onto the user's computer, which enables the website to recognise who the user is when they access that website again.

iii) Dataveillance and cyberveillance

Surveillance therefore falls into two categories: **dataveillance** and **cyberveillance**. It is possibly data collection that causes the greatest ethical concerns. Dataveillance has been used for thousands of years. From ancient times, societies have collected data about it citizens and commodities. Birth, baptism, marriage and death certificates have been an aspect of societies for hundreds of years, but what makes the situation different today is that data is stored and transmitted electronically. The question is what, if any, difference the **new technology** makes to our lives. Some fear that the ease and speed of passing information electronically and globally is not only reducing our right to privacy and personal identity but a major challenge to the nation state's control of its citizens.

b) Co-ordination, risk, privacy and power

In his analysis of the sociological effects on society, Lyon outlines four main areas for consideration (*Surveillance Society*, pages 5–8): co-ordination, risk, privacy and power.

i) Co-ordination

Co-ordination is the way in which social relationships have been gradually reshaped through electronic technologies. New technology can ensure people are where they ought to be, and it can arrange and rearrange appointments via email. But, as Lyon says:

> *At the same time, corporations' awareness of the whereabouts and day-to-day activities of both workers and customers has never been more complete.*

> (David Lyon, *Surveillance Society*, page 5)

The power of computers means that shops can use surveillance cameras to map shoppers' movements in the store and, with the aid of electronic check-out tills, computers can gather information about customer purchases. This information can be used to alter the nature of the stock, place desirable objects at strategic places and subtly control what we do.

ii) Risk

Surveillance is also used to manage and minimise risk. Information gathered about the market enables businesses to calculate trends and to make sound investments, calculate costs and assess probable futures. But equally, knowledge of a person's mental and physical health, criminal record and credit ratings can all be used by companies wishing to reduce risks. We find our lives controlled by knowledge that may or may not be true, but which often we are powerless to alter.

iii) Privacy

Privacy for most people is a far more contentious issue than the co-ordination and risk aspects of surveillance. But, as Lyon points out, privacy is an ambiguous and multifaceted notion. Privacy is not only culturally determined but depends on what an individual perceives to be personal.

One problem is knowing when the private sphere ends and the public domain begins. For example, an employer might have a legitimate claim to monitor his employees' use of computers to ensure that they are being used for business purposes and appropriate domestic use. But this knowledge can also be used to find out more about the private life of an employee without them knowing.

But for the question of surveillance to be evaluated with regard to privacy we have to consider why privacy should be considered valuable and weigh this up against the needs of the state/community or national/local security.

- **Liberty and privacy.** Mill's influential definition of liberty regards autonomy and the ability to decide what is in one's own best interests as the most important human attribute. By extension his liberal principle establishes the notion that the state may not interfere within the private sphere unless it is to protect the individual against harm. Knowledge of the individual is justified, therefore, only insofar as it is necessary for the individual's welfare.
- **Totalitarianism and privacy.** By contrast to Mill, the totalitarian communist view that rejects the private ownership of property equally dismisses the view that the individual has private rights over his body. Hence, in communist Russia in 1902, Lenin said, 'we recognise nothing private. Our morality is entirely subordinate to the interests of the class struggle of the proletariat'.

Both views express different ideas about what it means to own oneself. It is true that surveillance technology today challenges the libertarian notion of privacy. On the other hand, Marxist type communism warns of the dangers of a free-for-all market where

Key question

Is privacy an important human value?

Key quote

'This is one reason why privacy is significant: it serves to mobilize opinion regarding surveillance risks.'

DAVID LYON, *SURVEILLANCE SOCIETY*, 7

Key quote

'Over himself, over his own body and mind, the individual is sovereign'.

J.S. MILL, *ON LIBERTY*, (1859)

Cross-reference

Read page 104 on Adam Smith.

Key quote

'The concept of privacy is inadequate to cover what is at stake in the debate over contemporary surveillance. At worst, the dominant framework for privacy debate – self-possessing, autonomous individualism – leaves us with a world of privilege where self-protection is available to those who can negotiate it.'

DAVID LYON, *THE ELECTRONIC EYE*, 196

Key thought

Big Brother was the computer with the ability to see into people's homes in George Orwell's novel *Nineteen Eighty-Four* (1948), that depicted a future dystopia in which surveillance was used to maintain law and order.

Key word

Trade-off is when a person is prepared to gain greater services or commodities by giving up other minor interests.

there is no control and where, as Adam Smith suggested, market forces control themselves. This alternative has the contrary effect of turning privacy into a commodity that can be costed and paid for. For example, some have suggested that companies who take up one's time making unsolicited phone calls advertising their services should pay compensation. If privacy is about personal identity then the surveillance debate is about how we control the kind of people we want to be.

iv) Power

Surveillance might not be on Orwell's '**Big Brother**' scale but the final aspect of surveillance is the issue of power. Once knowledge is acquired in these more subtle modern ways, how is the data to be used? Lyon argues that ordinary citizens have unconsciously allowed and supported a far more invasive infringement of their ordinary lives than they might imagine. Data has always been gathered about people, but now many websites ask for information about one's interests, age and income, which can be passed onto other businesses (it takes a conscious choice for a person to have himself removed from a list). Many people are happy for this information to be given as a **trade-off** for better products or services. But as with the Big Brother world, it comes at a cost. Whereas trade and communication were done largely face to face in the recent past, one of the trade-offs nowadays is a loss of personal autonomy and a gradual dehumanising of relationships.

c) Data storage and leakage

Capitalist societies have an ever greater need for personal knowledge, and the computer's power has made storage, retrieval and analysis of huge quantities of data increasingly easy and has, for example, improved patient care and doctor efficiency. A patient no longer has to have his or her medical notes sent from one doctor to another when they change their GP, because it is now held electronically on the central National Health Service computer. This is potentially life saving and efficient.

Or, again, the Police National Computer (PNC) in Britain was one of the first systems established in 1974 to register car licence plates as a means of speeding up the identity of car theft and associated crimes. Later, with the addition of the National Automated Fingerprint Identification System, the police are now able to build up profiles of typical crimes and compare unsolved crimes through the 'comparative case analysis system'. This is greatly aided by biometric information which can help identify unknown individuals.

Key words

The **Leaky container phenomenon** describes the way in which careless use of data can cause great harm.

Law of unintended consequences are the negative unforeseen side effects resulting from other good consequences.

Key thought

In 1981 the police carried out 30 million checks on the PNC. Twenty-two million of these were vehicle checks and eight million name checks. This can give access to further information. Most checks were on people who had committed no crime. Is this a misuse of surveillance technology?

However, both examples illustrate different aspects of what Lyon has termed the **leaky container phenomenon**. The leaky container argument is not the same as cybercrime (see page 139), in which computers are broken into or hacked and secure and sensitive information (such as medical records) are stolen, but simply cases of carelessness whereby someone has left a computer disk or storage device on a train, which is an example of the **law of unintended consequences**. In the PNC example, an unintended consequence has been that in order for there to be enough information to make the system work, the ordinary policeman on his beat is being asked to log and collate more and more data about the local scene whether directly relevant or not. This requires greater surveillance and greater risk of personal information being stored without consent, and controversially the taking of DNA samples as biometric data even of those who have committed no offences.

There are other unintended consequences when surveillance 'leaks' from its isolated specialised use to more invasive widespread data gathering especially in the workplace. For example:

> *Camera systems installed for the purpose of preventing shoplifting in stores can become a general managerial tool, for instance. At the same time they may become more covert. In some British retail stores closed circuit television cameras that were intended to keep an eye on light-fingered customers are also used to check on the internal threat of theft. But this is not all. The same cameras pick up other details of worker performance, such a compliance with till procedures or refund and exchange procedures, as well as emotional labour – how 'friendly' and 'helpful' staff appear. This shows again how surveillance may spill out of one container and into another by virtue of extending a common technological system.*

(David Lyon, *Surveillance Society*, page 42)

d) Law and rights

In Europe and in the UK the key legal issue is **data protection**, whilst in the USA the central issue is **privacy**. Whereas in the USA citizens have to use existing privacy laws, in the UK and Europe surveillance is regulated centrally through specific data laws and regulating agencies.

i) The Lindop Report

The **Lindop Report on Data Protection** (1978) investigated the private and pubic use of computer systems and set out the following guidelines:

Key words

Data protection has been variously interpreted. For some it refers to the privacy of data subjects for other it is the protection of the processing and application of data.

Privacy describes the state of freedom from intrusion or unwanted attention of others.

Key quote

'Everyone has the right to respect for his private and family life, his home and his correspondence.'

ARTICLE 8, *THE EUROPEAN CONVENTION ON HUMAN RIGHTS*, (1963)

Key question

Is a data protection law sufficient to protect the privacy of individuals?

Key word

Data is defined in the Data Protection Act in several ways. One version is the process of information being passed 'automatically in response to instructions given for that purpose'.

- That 'the right people (and only the right people) have the right to access personal information for right purposes (and only the right purposes)'.
- To establish the principles such as accuracy, lawful obtaining of information and legitimate use of personal information, which may circulate beyond the data subject's control.
- To 'provide a framework for finding a balance between the interests of the individual and those of the data users and community at large'.
- To provide an independent regulatory authority (which can therefore check on government use of computers and data).

ii) 1984 Data Protection Act

The aims of the Data Protection Act (1984) are:

- To regulate the use of automatically processed information relating to individuals and the provision of services relating to such data.
- To cover **data** about living and identifiable individuals.

The Act does not directly affirm a person's right to privacy but it provides three rights for individuals which are: 1) the subject access right to personal data; 2) the compensation right due to harm caused by damage or distress; and 3) the correction and erasure right to prevent and remove data. Some of the key principles are that personal data:

- Shall not be used or disclosed in any manner incompatible with the specified purpose or purposes.
- Must be relevant and not excessive in relation to the specified purpose or purposes.
- Must be accurate and kept up to date and not stored longer than is necessary.
- That data subjects are entitled to be informed about the existence of personal data about themselves, to have access to such data, and where appropriate, to have such data corrected or erased.
- Shall not be transferred to a country outside the European Union unless that country or territory ensures an adequate protection for the rights and freedoms of data subjects in relation to the processing of personal data.

(Based on www.opsi.gov.uk/acts/acts1998)

However, many question whether data protection and privacy law is able to keep up with the rapid changes in new technology, which enable global surveillance to operate well outside the nation state's jurisdiction.

e) The future of surveillance

In the discussions above various themes have emerged, which surveillance and its use of the new technologies has created. First, it has questioned what it means to be a person with an individual identity. Second, it has challenged what kind of society we wish to live in and the role of the national state. Third, it challenges the individual to take a more active role in the use of surveillance. Some argue that if we are not vigilant then we will allow powerful technology to fall into the hands of non-elected non-democratic groups and agencies.

i) Challenge to personal identity

Cyberveillance is increasingly used by employers through the use of Google, Facebook and blogs to build up profiles and check applications of prospective employees. But how accurate and how much do these correspond to real people? It is possible that data versions of ourselves might be very accurate in some respects and can be used to corroborate the information given by the applicant. On the other hand, cyberspace offers various versions of ourselves (from our earlier lives or from distorted site compilations), some of which bear very little resemblance to who we are now.

Some critics are worried that cyberveillance turns autonomous people into deskilled passive consumers as they become manipulated by data held on computers. Even the phrase 'data subjects' marks a subtle but significant shift away from being actual subjects.

ii) Challenge to society and the nation state

Many argue that due to the new technology the dataveillance society, as depicted by Orwell's 'Big Brother', has long been superseded. In the modern (and some would argue postmodern) world there is no central Big Brother-type authority gathering information, but a complex networking of interested parties exchanging and building up information through many technologies worldwide.

- Increasingly, as data gathered by surveillance lies outside government control, the very notion of the nation state is challenged. This could lead to an attractive view of a globalised world but many fear that if there is no regulation of data, sensitive information can be used by foreign governments and extreme political and religious groups in ways that will destabilise democracy and the kind of freedoms Western democracies presently enjoy.
- Dataveillance reinforces social divisions, class, race and sexual stereotypes. Lyon argues that as analysis of data is often done by categorising into social/racial types, eligibility and access can be

determined by excluding and including data subjects according to type. Spam email is just one example of the way in which products and services can be targeted at particular types of people.

iii) Challenge to active citizenship

Lyon and others argue that we need to re-embody the self in the surveillance society but without the individualism fostered by Mill's views of privacy. As people are inherently social beings then the challenges to surveillance societies are:

- For citizens to become much better informed about what surveillance is and how they should be involved in its process. They need to reverse some processes so that voluntary self-disclosure of personal data becomes the norm and not the other way round.
- For citizens to welcome all types of people into society and not to exclude them based on electronically controlled data knowledge. They should be more suspicious and questioning of the utilitarian/capitalist approaches to surveillance, which are driven by the 'statistical' person. That means having a human value-driven view of surveillance that is based on peace (not violence), love (not control) and forgiveness (not suspicion).

4 Normative ethical responses to technology and society

a) Utilitarianism

Key question

How does utilitarianism judge whether a technology is worthwhile?

Despite all the various forms of utilitarianism its great strength is that it judges the value of anything by whether it satisfies the greatest needs of the greatest number. Utilitarians do not necessarily share the technophile's view of technology, partly because it lacks a rational and critical means of assessment. Technology is not good if its ends are bad or evil, however efficient it might. So, for example, the gas chambers used by Hitler in his concentration camps might have been very efficient in exterminating Jews, but as mass murder of this kind is not for the greater good, the technology cannot be condoned.

i) Cost–benefit analysis

Key word

See page 116 for definition of cost–benefit analysis.

Efficiency is therefore not a necessary condition of the utilitarian assessment of technology. Some suggest that utilitarianism's strength for society and industry is through its **cost–benefit analysis**. In Benthamite terms the value of a possible technology is measured by balancing what it costs to research and make against the benefits of what it will create. This commonsense approach is a great strength of utilitarianism. However, both elements are problematic.

- **How are costs to be defined?** All of the following might be a way of defining a cost: money, labour, time taken in the development of the idea, long-term time to sustain and develop the technology, the time/money of other technologies on which this technology depends
- **What counts as benefit?** A benefit might be defined as an additional comfort, something which raises the general standard of living, satisfying a small number of people a lot (rather than a lot of people a very little), culturally enriching, or stimulating the imagination.

Cost–benefit analysis indicates what, in the debate between Bentham and Mill, has always been a utilitarian problem; namely that Bentham treated all pleasures as being equal, whereas Mill argued that a benefit should be of a higher intellectual imaginative level.

ii) Unintended consequences and risk assessment

Any consequential system has to deal with the fact that we cannot always judge long-term let alone short-term outcomes. This is not necessarily a bad thing. As we have seen, there might be unforeseen beneficial side effects of technology, just as much as there might be risks. Some risks might be treated as 'trade-offs'. The Lindop Report on data protection is founded on the principle that in exchange for the protection of individual interests (for example, promptness of welfare payments) then a person would have to be willing to forfeit some of their privacy. But as Ian Barbour notes, many technological trade-offs are 'multi-dimensional' and might include unforeseen factors such as negative impact on the environment.

iii) Slippery slopes and competent judges

On the other hand, unintended consequences may undermine our sense of integrity in what Lyon termed 'leaky containers' in surveillance. In response to the act utilitarian Promethean attitude and failure to deal with these kind of **slippery slopes**, the rule utilitarian argues that technology must be regulated by what Mill termed the competent judges. But who should these be? It could be the technical experts. But technological experts do not have the wider picture of society that a government has and so the control of technology should probably be part of the political process. However, once this occurs, the flexibility of utilitarianism appears to have been greatly diminished.

b) Revealed ethics

i) Creation and human sin

Christian responses to the use of creation to develop technology fall into three categories:

Key quote

'I have suggested that God works through the continuing evolutionary process and through our lives today. Human beings are endowed with intelligence and creativity. We can be coworkers with God in the fulfilment of God's purposes. As coworkers we can co-operate with God in the continuing creation in nature and history.'

IAN BARBOUR *NATURE, HUMAN NATURE AND GOD*, 70

Key quote

'If we say we have no sin, we deceive ourselves, and the truth is not in us.'

1 JOHN 1:8

Key quote

'The Word became flesh and dwelt amongst us, full of grace and truth.'

JOHN 1:14

Cross-reference

Read page 138 on knowledge and the internet.

Key quote

'The Lord spoke to Moses … "Take a census of all the congregation of the people of Israel".'

NUMBERS 1:1–2

Key quote

'One might say surveillance in the non-modern context is either intense but unsystematic or systematic but remote. By contrast, most surveillance today is both systematic and intense.'

DAVID LYON, *THE ELECTRONIC EYE*, 164

- The **technophile** or optimist argues that technology is no different from any other resource that the creation has to offer. Some (for example, de Chardin) consider that humans have a God-given gift to use their talents and develop the world's potentials in new, unrestrained and creative ways. Information technology, for example, opens up a new stage in the development of the human spirit.
- The **contextualist** (for example, Barbour) argues that humans have a duty to act as stewards of God's creation developing it in co-operation with God's will. Used with critical care technology can be for the good of society.
- The **technophobe** or pessimist (for example, Ellul) considers humans to be too sinful ever to stand sufficiently outside technology to develop it for entirely good ends. However, being aware of the fallen nature of humankind at least offers the critical insight lacking in non-religious ethics, which can therefore check the development of technology.

ii) Incarnation and persons

As already discussed, one of the criticisms of information technology and surveillance is that face-to-face relationships can so easily be displaced by regarding humans as data subjects. The biblical view of humans is that being created in the image of God, humans are not data vessels but animate spirit-filled creatures. The incarnation of God in the person of Jesus reminds humans of their unique spiritual nature. Therefore any technology which is treated as an end in itself is a form of idol worship and hinders authentic human relationships. Some aspects of the internet fall into this category.

There is no specific biblical view of technology but we might consider how the use of the census in the Old Testament is similar to surveillance today. In the ancient world the census was used to make the Jews work harder and support the king (for example, Numbers 1–4). The difference today is the varied means and capacity by which data can be collected. This is all the more reason why Christians as members of society have a duty to ensure that it is used for what it is intended to do; to look after, not to exploit, individuals.

iii) Justice and the Kingdom of God

The Bible has constant reminders about the misuse of power, especially the dangers in the institution of the king and the rulers of society as to how they use their authority to exploit the means of production. King Ahab, for example, famously cheated Naboth out of his vineyard (1 Kings 21). The message of the prophets that is reinforced by Jesus in his teaching on the Kingdom of God is that justice demands that the use of the earth's resources is to feed the poor and ensure that the weak are not exploited. But although

Key quote

'The Lord enters into judgment with the elders and princes of his people: "It is you who have devoured the vineyard, the spoil of the poor is in your houses. What do you mean by crushing my people, by grinding the face of the poor?" says the Lord GOD of hosts.'

ISAIAH 3:14–15

modern animal and plant technology holds out great prospects to fulfil this duty, the Christian contextualist, in particular, is aware that the advantages of these technologies are often weighted heavily towards capitalist Western countries. Technology is not sufficient in itself to bring about justice but what is needed is a change of attitude of Western powers who own the means of production. In Christian terms this is *metanoia*, the Greek word often translated as 'repentance' but better rendered as 'a radical change of mind' and situation.

c) Kantian ethics

For the Kantian, the purpose of human history and its development is for humans to live according to their nature, which is two-fold: to be rational and to be sociable. But everything else exists as objects not subjects. The purpose and value of an object is not to be found in itself but in our use of it. The crucial difference, Kant argues, is that whereas we can reflect and consider our state of mind, all other things lack self-awareness and human intuition. It would therefore be a fundamental error to attribute intuition to things and to remove it from humans.

i) Technology as a servant of reason

This distinction recognises that technology belongs to the world of objects which function as a means to achieving a given end and no more. Technology is acceptable so long as it is the servant of human reason never the master. This suggests a very limited function for technology. As Kant is deeply suspicious of any action performed out of desire rather than reason, then it must be presumed that the technophile's love of technology for its own sake is to be strongly resisted. But many would consider that Kant has failed to acknowledge that achieving aesthetic satisfaction is also part of our nature. We might argue that just as nature can give us pleasure, so might television, and other technological gadgets.

ii) People as subjects of society

Key question

Have the new technologies made the world a freer place to live in?

Cross-reference

Read page 145 on Lyon's analysis of surveillance.

Nevertheless, Kant's contribution in the present debate about the use of technology highlights a point we have already observed through diverse thinkers such as Marx, Foucault, Lyon and Postman – that unless we take seriously Kant's second version of the categorical imperative to treat people 'never merely as a means but always as an end', then the seductiveness of technology sets up a new social condition which treats people as objects. Technology then becomes the value-giving subject treating humans as 'data consumers' and 'data subjects' rather than human subjects. Lyon fears that surveillance technology has almost made the individual subject invisible.

The rapid advances in surveillance and human genetic engineering appear to have developed with almost no consideration of the kind of society in which humans have genuine relationships.

Kant's kingdom of ends imagines a state where humans act freely as law givers and law abiders in mutual respect. The question is whether technologies such as the internet, computers and surveillance have made the world a freer place, with greater autonomy of the individual. Some argue that surveillance, for example, has not served its purpose by making us a safer more harmonious global society but has had the adverse effect by making people more concerned with privacy and individual consumer rights rather than with universal duty. Finally, the anarchic aspect of the internet might be considered to be in complete contrast to the Kantian utopian view of society, where people act in accordance with each other's will to achieve a state of 'perpetual peace'.

d) Natural law

Although the natural law ethicist might agree with those who consider that humans are naturally inventive and that human imagination has achieve some extraordinary technologies, they also consider that reason dictates that all human activities are assessed and evaluated. As Gordon Graham argued, the Promethean view which permits humans to pursue the 'human adventure' unchecked ignores philosophical investigation. Natural law ethicists argue that simply because we can do something does not mean that it is right; the place of natural law philosophy is to ask whether ultimately technology enables humans to flourish.

Natural law ethicists are not technophobes. They agree that technophobes frequently commit the fallacy of division — a few dangerous pieces of technology does not condemn all technology. Likewise it is not technology in itself that is either good or bad, but the way in which we use it that determines its value. The natural law ethicist does not share the technophile's enthusiasm for technology for its own sake. These two points are fundamental in the Catholic Church natural law teaching on technology.

i) Power and society

Although the aims of Foucault and natural law ethics are in many ways very different, natural law ethicists are indebted to Foucault's analysis which often reveals the way in which technology has not been used for the common good but to gain power and control. Lyon's analysis of new surveillance technology illustrates just how far surveillance has penetrated the deeper structures of society for good, but also in a more sinister 'Big Brother' way. Whilst natural law ethicists argue that society needs to be controlled through the application of law and punishment, a 'panopticon' society fails to acknowledge that a just and moral society is one that respects the natural rights of privacy, personal identity and autonomy of individual citizens.

Cross-reference

Read pages 136–139 on the internet as anarchy or democracy.

Key question

To what extent do natural law ethicists think that technology is good?

Cross-reference

See page 133.

Key quote

'Science and technology are ordered to man, from whom they take their origin and development; hence they find in the person and in his moral values, both evidence of their purpose and awareness of their limits.'

CATECHISM OF THE CATHOLIC CHURCH, 493

Cross-reference

See page 131 on the fallacy of division.

Cross-reference

See page 134 on Bentham's panopticon.

ii) An ordered society

One of Aquinas' natural primary precepts is to live in an ordered society. The question as we have considered above is whether the internet makes this more or less possible? Natural law, though, suggests that the internet cannot be allowed to develop uncontrolled and without regulation. At its best it offers a very powerful version of democracy and sociability, but equally, uncontrolled it could lead to an anarchic society which abandons many of the norms of moral behaviour according to natural law (in particular sexual behaviour). For example, natural law ethicists consider that the intention of an act is to be judged just as much as the outcome. So, as the case of cyber-rape illustrates, it is morally wrong not just because of its intentions (even though it is proportionally less bad than actual rape) but also because of the damage this might cause to other forms of moral behaviour in society.

iii) Limits and justice

Most forms of natural law would disagree that the only aim of technology is efficiency if for no other reason than the purpose of an ordered society is also to educate, preserve and protect life, and form sexually appropriate relationships. A critical assessment of technology sets some boundaries which, according to natural law, cannot be passed. For example, technology that makes abortion or euthanasia more efficient or safer can never be justified because it involves deliberately killing innocent lives and is therefore intrinsically wrong. Likewise, cybercrime is to be treated in the same way as any other crime which infringes natural rights and society's welfare.

e) Virtue ethics

The Aristotelian **golden mean** might provide a very good starting in the consideration of technology from the virtue ethicist point of view. Between the Promethean excess of the technophile which appears to allow free reign of technology and the deficient, restrictive and pessimistic view of the technophile, use of the golden mean offers a practical, sensible way ahead. Furthermore, Aristotle's distinction between the two kinds of virtue – intellectual and moral – offers a subtle way of considering the use technology for its own (intellectual) sake and within the community (moral).

i) Intellectual virtues and technology

Modern day technology is a spectacular expression of Aristotle's description of the intellectual virtues of human technical and artistic skills, the acquiring and application of scientific knowledge, and ingenuity and intuition in the use of this knowledge. As virtue means

Cross-references

See pages 136–137 on the internet as a source of democracy.

See page 140 on Cyber-rape

Key question

What virtues does the active citizen need today in a technological society?

Key word

Golden mean is the middle way between the vices of excess and deficiency.

'excellence', the scientist and technician are encouraged to create the very best that they can. However, the notion of the very best also implies accountability to the community. This is expressed in the key intellectual virtue, wisdom or *phronesis*, the skill of being able to balance technical intellectual virtues with the needs of others. In other words, the virtue ethicist not only requires the scientist and technician to exercise professional integrity in the way they develop their inventions and acquire their knowledge, but they also have to balance what they know with the moral needs of society.

ii) Community and moral virtues

One of the most problematic aspects of modern virtue ethics, as MacIntyre argues, is the lack of community with a sense of its narrative past. Without a clear understanding of community, it then becomes very difficult to know where the boundaries are within which scientists and technicians operate.

Much depends on how one understands the nature of community. In our discussion of the internet, the positive view of anarchy suggested the development of new world wide communities, brought together via new information technology. For some, such as Foucault, the development of a multi-discourse plural society is a welcome means of challenging the controlling power of society's self-appointed experts, where each group develops its own virtues. But for others, the anarchic view of society does not offer the stability and security of democracy. MacIntyre and many modern virtue ethicists have argued strongly for the need to resist further fragmentation of society. This requires people to be much more active citizens and to be better informed about what technology really does; if knowledge is power, then this is a crucial intellectual virtue in the technological age.

Finally, once knowledge is acquired, the good citizen requires the moral skills of application. Those who use their knowledge on behalf of others by revealing bad industrial practices, cover-ups by corporations and the misuse of power in government, and who are motivated by Aristotelian virtues of courage, truthfulness and righteous indignation, illustrate how the virtues may still play an essential part in democratic societies today.

Key quote

'For even if the good of the community coincides with that of the individual, it is clearly greater and more perfect thing to achieve and preserve that of a community.'
ARISTOTLE, *ETHICS*, 1094A22 (PENGUIN EDITION, 64)

Cross-reference

Read pages 133–135 on Foucault.

Key quote

'The social obstacles derive from the way in which modernity partitions each human life into a variety of segments, each with its own norms and modes of behaviour. So work is divided from leisure, private life from public, the corporate from the personal.'
ALISDAIR MACINTYRE, *AFTER VIRTUE*, 204

Key thought

Consider again the issues raised by surveillance. Quite how much do the public know about these technologies?

Summary diagram

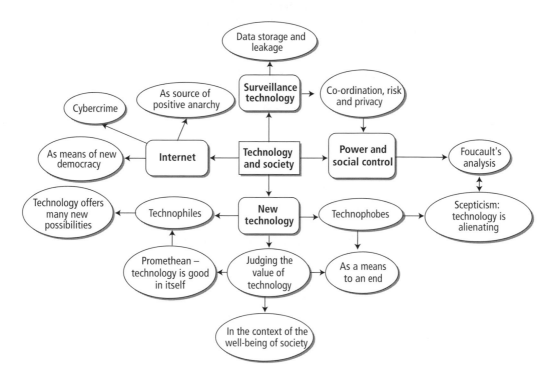

Study guide

By the end of this chapter you should have considered why some people think there should be moral constraints on the development of technology and why others argue that as humans are naturally inventive there should be no restraints. You should be able to provide examples of new and novel inventions and argue whether the internet and surveillance are merely developments of older technologies or raise new and important issues for today's society.

Essay questions

1 'There should be no constraints on the development of technology.' Discuss.

The argument might begin by distinguishing between those who attribute intrinsic value to technology and those who consider its value to be instrumental. The view of the Promethean technophile might first be explored as opening up the vast potentials of the world. Examples of technological successes should be outlined. Postman's critique might then be summarised and the dangers of power (Foucault), exploitation of humans (Elul) and the environment explored. The essay might then focus on one area of technology, for example, surveillance, and assess the arguments set up so far.

Further essay questions

2 a   Explain what is meant by cybercrime.
2 b   'Cybercrime is morally different from the same crime committed in the real world.' Discuss.

3 Assess the view that surveillance undermines the value of privacy.

4 To what extent is the internet compatible with Kantian ethics?

Revision checklist

Can you give definitions of:

- technophobe
- technophile
- Promethean
- panopticon
- cybercrime
- surveillance and dataveillance.

Can you explain:

- the arguments why technology is a source of liberation
- the cause correlation confusion as applied to technology and social problems
- Foucault's argument about technology and power.

Can you give arguments for and against:

- the internet as a means of democracy
- the internet as a source of knowledge and freedom
- surveillance and the leaky container argument.

ENVIRONMENTAL ETHICS

Chapter checklist ✓

This chapter considers the major concerns about the environment and evaluates these against various theories about the value of the environment – from shallow to deep ecology. The particular issue of how non-human animals should be treated is reviewed before considering the views of the environmental sceptics. The chapter concludes by looking at various normative ethical responses to the environment.

1 Environmental issues

Case study
A farmer's dilemma

Consider the following hypothetical situation. A farmer in the UK decides to increase the yield of his wheat crop by giving a high dosage of nitrogen fertilizers. This, in turn, leads to a greater multiplication of pests which attack this crop. The wheat is more vulnerable to disease as it is genetically uniform. This is the consequence of artificial breeding to produce high-yield varieties which take out the natural variability within a wild strain. If he tried to grow a wild strain the yields would be much poorer, but it would be less subject to disease. He decides to spray the crop with pesticides in order to keep the yields high. The market pressure to produce cheap wheat is high since there are other competing sources from Canada and the USA. The public demand for cheaper food keeps the prices down with a low profit margin. Unfortunately, the high level of nitrates originating from the fertilizers runs into the river water nearby and means that it is no longer acceptable for human consumption. Also pesticides have killed a large number of fish so that local fishermen go out of business.

(Celia Deane-Drummond, *A Handbook of Theology and Ecology*, pages 68–69)

This case illustrates the range of environmental issues which have come to dominate modern thinking. How is one to balance the business interests of the farmer against damage to the environment? Whose interests should be considered: the farmer, the fishermen, the consumers, future generations, non-human animals, the earth itself? To what extent is the farmer's non-environmentally friendly use of chemicals indirectly destroying the livelihoods of poor farmers in less economically developed countries?

Cross-reference

See pages 176–177 on the Copenhagen summit.

Key word

Global community is the view that as the world is interconnected (through transport and communication) it should therefore be treated as a whole not as separate nation states.

From the late-twentieth century onwards, politics, academic study and everyday language have become increasingly dominated by the idea that many aspects of the environment are in crisis. Some have argued that the immensity of the crisis is so large that it makes the threat of nuclear war insignificant by comparison. A great deal of this fear is due to the threat that global warming poses to our way of life and to the very existence of the planet itself. There are those who doubt the extremity of climate change and who consider that the language of crisis is over-exaggerated. But even if this is true it has had the effect of making us reconsider how we treat the environment and our place in the natural order.

As the Copenhagen Climate Change Summit (December 2009) demonstrated, by the largest ever gathering of nation states, environmental issues have become part of the agenda of international politics. As a global issue it has called on heads of state to think of themselves as belonging to a **global community**. But just how will this work? For any community to work requires agreed shared values and common goals. If this is difficult to establish at a local level it is questionable whether this will ever be possible at a global level. Environmental ethics, therefore, are more than just the way we determine our treatment of nature but also the ways and means all humanity work together.

The Copenhagen Summit failed to reach complete political agreement sufficient to implement far-ranging controls over carbon dioxide (CO_2) and other greenhouse gas emissions, but for many this only highlighted further the pressing need to reform international institutions to deal with some of the issues outlined below.

a) Climate change

The trapping of heat by greenhouse gases has led to weather change, rises in sea level, threats to the infrastructure of coasts and changes in the quality of freshwater supplies. The **greenhouse effect** has come about through the burning of fossil fuels, the destruction of the rain forest, use of nitrogenous fertiliser and the release of methane and **CFCs** into the atmosphere. A major source of methane is cattle. Some have even suggested that the effects on global warming could be solved if we stopped using cattle for meat.

Key quote

'Never again should we let a global deal to move towards a greener future be held to ransom by only a handful of countries. One of the frustrations for me was the lack of a global body with the sole responsibility for environmental stewardship.'

GORDON BROWN (UK PRIME MINISTER), *THE TIMES*, 21 DECEMBER 2009

Key word

The **greenhouse effect** is when certain gases in the atmosphere (notably carbon dioxide, methane and nitrous oxide) trap heat from the Earth and stop it from escaping thereby causing a rise in the Earth's temperature.

Key thought

CFC or chlorofluorocarbon is the gas thought to damage the ozone layer in the Earth's atmosphere.

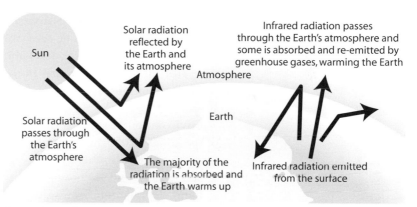

The greenhouse effect

The ozone layer has been depleted through the release of CFCs into the atmosphere. An increase in the level of nitrous oxide in the atmosphere has led to an increase in skin cancer, damage to the protein of living things, mutations in the environment and harm to sensitive organisms that in turn has affected the food chain.

b) Production

Natural resources have been greatly reduced due to greater technological demands and the rise in the global population. It is projected that all coal, oil and gas reserves will have run out by 2636, or even earlier if consumption increases at the current rate. Countries have become economically dependent on the use of fossil fuels; as a result powerful industrial countries have a vested interest in maintaining their current levels of consumption.

Alternative power sources are not without their environmental problems. Wind and solar power are possible but both need large capital outlay; output is variable and only a fraction of what is needed is produced. Wind farms are unsightly, take up a large amount of land, cause noise pollution and can harm wildlife. Use of hydroelectric power is another possibility but this causes the displacement of people and wildlife as land is submerged upstream of hydroelectric dams. Nuclear power is a third option but radioactive waste is expensive to dispose of and if it leaks can result in years of environmental mutations and death.

c) Conservation and pollution

Pollution has increased as a result of a rise in the world's population and the use of man-made fertilisers and increased industrialisation has led to an increase in acid rain. Release of fumes from vehicle exhausts and industrial processes have produced great quantities of sulphur and nitrogen oxides and carbon monoxide. This has led to an increase in asthma and lung problems in humans.

There has also been an increase in the pollution of land and the water-cycle through industrial waste; pollution of rivers and seas has occurred alongside this. The sea has been used increasingly as a dumping ground for waste, and rubbish in landfill sites may result in toxic run-off. Finally, there has been an increase in nuclear pollution through the disposal of waste radioactive material in the ground or at sea.

Environmental stress is the reduction of biodiversity due to loss of species. By 2050, half of already existing species could be extinct. Stress to the environment is also caused by monoculture farming which requires greater use of fertilisers and pesticides.

Land degradation occurs due to the over-use of intensive farming methods. Top soil can take 200–120,000 years to develop but only a few months to destroy. For example, Mesopotamia (modern Iraq) was very fertile 4,000 years ago but now much of it is desert.

d) Population

The rate of human population growth places huge demands on the environment in terms of a greater need for food and energy. The extent of the present ecological crisis can be seen by comparing the rate of population growth from the past and today. For example, in 1650 the world population was approximately 500 million and population growth was 0.3 per cent or a doubling of population every 240 years. Today, the world population is 6.8 billion (an increase of 83 million since 2008); since the 1970s growth has been calculated at 2.15 per cent or a doubling of population every 30 years. In the developed world the birth rate has dropped (on average a family has 1.8 children) but mortality rates are much lower and so there is an aging population. In developing countries population growth is far greater than in developed countries but as the mortality rate is higher there is a greater need to have larger families.

Larger populations have forced greater use of technology through the use of genetically modified (GM) crops, intensive farming, fishing and energy sources (fossil fuels and nuclear energy), all of which have put greater demands on the natural world.

2 Valuing the environment

Key question

On what basis do we decide how the environment is to be valued?

Key words

Humanocentric ethics consider that humans alone are the source of moral values.

Geocentric ethics are those which consider all aspects of the world/nature to be morally relevant.

Key people

René Descartes (1596–1650) was born in France, studied science, theology and philosophy in Paris and taught in Holland. He published several works including *A Discourse on Method* (1637) and *Meditations* (1641).

Environmental ethics depend on the value or ontological status of the environment itself. There are broadly three views: instrumental ecological value; inherent ecological value; and intrinsic ecological value. In practice there is a sliding scale from those who hold the view that the environment has no intrinsic value and is only valuable if it is useful, to those who consider that nature has its own 'deep' value quite independent of whether it serves any human purpose.

Put another way: shallow ecologists argue that environmental ethics are **humanocentric** as it is only human beings who make value judgements about what is right and wrong, whilst deep ecologists consider that environmental ethics are **geocentric** because, although humans have a major part to play in the way in which the world is used, our response is determined by the environment's intrinsic or inherent value.

a) Instrumental value: shallow ecology

All shallow ecologists share the basic dualistic notion that there is an ontological distinction between value-giving creatures and the rest of nature. It therefore follows that only those who are capable of value-giving are in a position to decide how the rest of nature should be treated. An extreme example is **Descartes**' argument that as only humans are conscious, then all animals are mere machines, lacking souls and the ability to feel anything. Essential to Descartes' argument is that as 'brutes', animals lack the ability to communicate through language and cannot therefore have a rational soul.

> *And this proves not only that the brutes have less reason than man, but they have none at all: for we see that very little is required to enable a person to speak … it is incredible that the most perfect ape or parrot of its species, should not in this be equal to the most stupid infant of its kind, or at the least to one that was crack-brained, unless the souls of brutes were of a nature wholly different from ours.*
>
> (René Descartes, *A Discourse on Method*, Part V)

i) Utilitarian value

For many utilitarians, Protagoras' saying that 'man is the measure of all things' implies that only humans are able to decide what is valuable according to the standard utilitarian maxim of the 'greatest

Cross-reference

Read pages 178–179 for more detailed discussion of utilitarian ethics and the environment.

good of the greatest number'. So, for example, as deforestation has bad long-term consequences for humans, then it is in our best interests to have policies that curb those who exploit forests for their wood, even if that means reducing their livelihoods. The heart of utilitarianism is self-interest. The utilitarian who campaigns against a motorway being placed in an area of great beauty does not do so for any intrinsic value of trees, flora or wildlife but for the aesthetic pleasure which these things give him and which would be lost if the project were to go ahead.

However, not all utilitarians hold such a sharp human/nature dualism. For example, Peter Singer argues that there are non-human animals who have interests in the way they are treated. Jeremy Bentham himself had suggested that the second part of the utilitarian maxim, 'the greatest number', should include all creatures capable of feeling pleasure or pain. Therefore, when the preference utilitarian makes his calculation about the motorway being cut through the countryside, his concern cannot be entirely humanocentric but also **biocentric**, and must give equal consideration to the preferences of all those who are capable of having an interest.

ii) Kantian value

However, not all instrumentalists are utilitarians. Some philosophers such as Kant follow Descartes' argument and take an instrumental view of nature because only other humans are rationally capable of becoming part of the moral community. Kant's dualism between rational and non-rational nature means that the use and treatment of the environment is essentially instrumental and non-moral. However, Kant did not advocate that non-human animals should be caused unnecessary harm simply because they lack rationality. Kant argued that cruel and malicious behaviour diminishes humanity as these are qualities which by analogy we would want to apply ourselves.

> *Any action whereby we may torment animals, or let them suffer distress, or otherwise treat them without love, is demeaning to ourselves. It is inhuman, and contains an analogy of violation of the duty to ourselves, since we would not, after all, treat ourselves with cruelty.*
>
> (Immanuel Kant, *Lectures on Ethics*, page 434)

Therefore, we have good reason to protect the welfare of non-human animals in much the same way as we protect our own infants before they become rational enough to become autonomous members of the moral community.

Cross-reference

Read pages 168–169 on Bentham's and Singer's argument.

Key word

Biocentric ethics are those which value non-human animals (and some would also argue plants) in themselves.

Cross-reference

Read page 180 below for more detailed discussion of Kantian ethics and the environment.

Key quote

'Any action whereby we may torment animals, or let them suffer distress, or otherwise treat them without love, is demeaning to ourselves.'

IMMANUEL KANT, *LECTURES ON ETHICS*, 434

iii) Critique

The strength of the utilitarian environmental ethic is that it takes self-interest seriously. Would many people, for example, be interested in reducing CO_2 emissions if global warming had no direct effect on our welfare? Or would we seek to develop alternative forms of energy if the cost of conventional energy sources were to become more and more expensive and resources scarcer?

But for many, the shallow ecologists' approach to nature is not enough. History has demonstrated that a dualistic view of minds and matter is insufficient to develop a satisfactory environmental ethic. The effects of Descartes' mind–body dualism can be seen in the Enlightenment's promotion of reason over matter and the growth of technology to tame nature. Since the eighteenth century, the effects of improved medicine and farming techniques on population growth and sophisticated technology on transport and pollution are just a few of the very visible effects of the dominance of the humanocentric values.

b) Inherent value: relational ecology

If the failure of the shallow ecological position is that it gives too much power to humans then an alternative is the relational view of nature held by many Christian environmental ethicists. For these **theocentric** ethicists, God gives value to nature by setting up its potentials and by being constantly involved in its processes until it reaches its completion. In other words, the world is good because God values it. If nature is **inherently good** then humans also have a duty to treat it with respect because they have a special relationship with it – they are not the ones who decide what it is worth. Relational ecology rejects the deep ecologists' claim that nature is intrinsically good because that would imply that its value is mysterious and independent from God.

i) The Christian idea of creation and covenant

There are four broad principles which form the basis of most Christian ecological views.

The first principle is that the creation is good (Genesis 1:10). It is good because God has created every aspect of it to be purposeful and fruitful (Genesis 1:22), and even the smallest birds and plants are sustained by his constant presence (Matthew 10:29).

The second principle is that as humans are created in the image of God they also have the duty to maintain and sustain the earth in the same manner in which God creates. Genesis presents this duty in two ways. First, it means to have **dominion** (Genesis 1:26) over all living creatures and to 'subdue the earth' (Genesis 1:28). Dominion, or *radah* in Hebrew, expresses man's kingly rule over the world in the same way as God is king of the universe and

Key words

Theocentric ethics believes that something is good because God values it.

Inherent good means that one of the characteristics of the world is that it is has value.

Dominion means to rule over.

Cross-reference

Read pages 180–182 for more detailed discussion of Christian ethics and the environment.

Key quote

'A jubilee shall be the fiftieth year to you; in it you shall neither sow, nor reap what grows of itself, nor gather the grapes from the undressed vines.'

LEVITICUS 25:11

commands obedience. Second, human duty is described to be as a **steward** of creation, to look after it as God's caretakers on earth.

The third principle is that God's relationship with humans is a **covenant**. The covenant describes the duties humans have towards God in order to receive his love and forgiveness. One key aspect of the covenant is land. The covenants made with Abraham, Moses and David all contain the idea of a promised land in which God and his people will live again in peace and harmony with nature. However, the land is never to be owned absolutely by the Israelites, as the **Law of Jubilee** (Leviticus 25:8–55) states, and those who possess it have a duty to treat those who live on it justly and generously and every fifty years allow it to lie fallow so that the land might be replenished.

The fourth principle is that the restoration of the world after the fall of humans and the coming of the Kingdom of God will occur once humans have repaired the damage they have done to it. In Hebrew this is called *tikkun olam*. St Paul describes (Romans 8:18–23) how human sin has caused the whole universe to 'groan', waiting for humans to restore the time when humans and the natural world lived in harmony as in the Garden of Eden (Genesis 2).

ii) Critique

One of the most influential critiques of the Judeo-Christian view of the environment is **Lynn Townsend White's** lecture *The Historical Roots of our Ecological Crisis* (1966). White argues that the present environmental crisis is due to the Christian command to have dominion over the earth. He argues that for two thousand years as Christian missionaries have converted people from the ancient nature religions they have done so by directing attention away from the sacredness of nature to the God who has dominion over nature. White argues that the ecological crisis will continue as long as we continue to hold the broadly Christian axiom that nature is there to serve human needs. Even so, White acknowledges that there are elements of Christian theology which respect nature. These are represented in particular by **Saint Francis of Assisi** who treated all nature equally, worthy of God's faith, hope and love. But despite Saint Francis' efforts his influence on Christianity was not sufficient to alter the way in which it has gone on to exploit the natural world.

c) Intrinsic value: deep ecology

Deep ecologists argue that *all* things in the universe have their own intrinsic value and are interconnected with one another. This **holistic** view is based on an ontological monism that rejects the matter–reason dualism of the instrumentalists and the matter–spirit distinction of relationists, and instead considers all matter in some sense to be spiritual or alive. It is for this reason that deep ecologists

Key word

Holism is the notion that as everything is interconnected then no one thing is superior in value to anything else.

Key people

Arne Naess (1912–2009) was one of Norway's best known philosophers and developed his deep ecology as a keen mountaineer. He lived for most of his life in an isolated hut in the Norwegian mountains. His philosophy was influenced by Spinoza, Gandhi and Buddha.

Key thought

Naess argued that a world population of 100 million (about a sixtieth of the present figure) would be compatible with quality of life, but 11 or 12 billion (the numbers predicted for the end of the twenty-second century) would be more than the world could endure.

Key people

James Lovelock is an inventor, scientist and author. He was made a Fellow of the Royal Society in 1974. He has worked with NASA and his inventions have been used in their planetary exploration programmes. He has developed his Gaia Theory (originally called the Gaia Hypothesis) in many books notably *The Ages of Gaia* (1988 and 1995) and *The Vanishing Face of Gaia* (2009).

Key word

Gaia refers to the ancient Greek goddess of the earth.

Key word

Homeostasis means to maintain a balance or equilibrium.

generally reject the need for God as the one who values nature as this view sets up a hierarchy of value and gives more power to some than to others.

i) Ecosophy

Arne Naess argues that there are two things that are considerable morally. The first is the biosphere as a whole and the second is the large ecosystems that constitute it. The extinction of a species may not be bad in itself but it may be in relation to the larger goal of maintaining the biosphere or ecosystem. Ecosophy is the 'realisation of the Self'; that humans are not superior because they are conscious beings but have their place in the ecosphere. Naess was critical of Christian teaching on stewardship and regarded it arrogant to give humans a morally superior place in the universe.

An 'everything ethic' also suggests that non-living things, which lack consciousness and even basic biological organisation, must be considered morally significant because the natural order has intrinsic value. It is our duty to keep it healthy. An action such as mining, by smashing up rocks and disturbing geological structures should not be valued in relation to the task of mining effectively or satisfying a human need, but rather it must be considered in relation the intrinsic value of the rocks.

In order to preserve biodiversity Naess suggests that humans should reduce population growth, abandon the notion of economic growth, conserve diversity and live in small self-reliant communities.

ii) Eco-holism

One of the most influential holistic environmental theories was developed by **James Lovelock** in the 1970s. He called it the **Gaia Theory**. As a scientist and engineer he was acutely aware of the interconnectedness of all matter and he therefore argued that it was wrong to consider the earth as inert but that it is in some way alive – however odd that may sound to the scientist. Lovelock argued that:

- Gaia is a super-organism much like a bees' nest where life describes all aspects of the social interactions of things to one another. Gaia is not to be confused with the biosphere (the collection of individual organisms) which is part of Gaia but not all of Gaia.
- Gaia is the regulating principle of the earth without which the unstable nature of the atmosphere would certainly collapse and life would be impossible. Life (not just human life) appears to be the greatest product of Gaia.
- However, Gaia is emphatically non-teleological and seeks only for **homeostasis**.

Key quote

'Just as the shell is part of a snail, so the rocks, the air, the oceans are part of Gaia ... Gaia, as a planet sized entity, has properties that are not necessarily discernible by just knowing individual species or populations or organisms living together.'

JAMES LOVELOCK, *THE AGES OF GAIA*, 19

Cross-reference

Read *The Ages of Gaia*, Chapter 3 on Daisyworld.

Key quote

'The idea that the Earth is alive is at the outer bounds of scientific credibility.'

JAMES LOVELOCK, *THE AGES OF GAIA*, 3

• Homeostasis is illustrated in the **Daisyworld** thought exercise. Daisyworld consists of white and black daisies. Black daisies absorb heat and they flourish in lower temperatures whereas white daisies reflect heat and flourish at higher temperatures. Therefore as the temperature of the world increases more white daisies grow and as they reflect heat thereby lowering the temperature this encourages more black daisies to grow and flourish. But as the black daisies absorb heat this increases the temperature of the world, which encourages the white daisies to increase and the black daisies die out. This process carries on without stopping and illustrates that overall the world is in a state of equilibrium or homeostasis.

Gaia has been used in many different ways. The notion can lead to a moral imperative that humans need to co-operate not only with each other but with all of nature. The homeostatic view of nature does not mean that Gaia will necessarily correct our exploitation of the environment. As Lovelock says:

> The truth is almost diametrically opposite. Gaia, as I see her, is no doting mother tolerant of misdemeanours, nor is she some fragile and delicate damsel in danger from brutal mankind. She is stern and tough, always keeping the world warm and comfortable for those who obey the rules, but ruthless in her destruction of those who transgress. Her unconscious goal is a planet fit for life. If humans stand in the way of this, we shall be eliminated with as little pity as would be shown by the micro-brain of an intercontinental ballistic nuclear missile in full flight to its target.
>
> (James Lovelock, *The Ages of Gaia: A Biography of Our Living Earth*, page 199)

The Gaia theory suggests that it is misleading to think of a separate 'environmental ethics', as everything we choose to do is in the context of the environment.

iii) Critique

There are two major criticisms of Naess' ecosophy. The first is irrationalism. As it is not possible to demonstrate that the ecosystem is morally considerable or that matter is equally valuable, then we have only Naess's word for it. This does not appear to offer a philosophically persuasive foundation on which to build an ethical system. This leads to a second practical objection. As humans are in a position of making morally significant decisions about nature, how are they to decide whose needs are greater at any particular moment given that all matter is equally valuable?

Some ecologists question Lovelock's claim that ecosystems display long-term stability. Other scientists dislike the idea that the sum of the parts appears to be greater than the parts themselves. Gaia is an emergent property – but is it an *actual* property? What does it mean to say that the planet is alive and in what sense does Gaia enable the world to evolve if it is maintaining a homeostatic equilibrium? The Gaia conditions for one organism may not be appropriate for another which thus implies that genetic adaption occurs independently from Gaia. The Daisyworld thought exercise assumes stability, but it may not be so. It is possible to conjecture a world that destabilises the process rather than achieving homeostasis and which therefore does not aim to support life.

Some support a weak version of Gaia that stresses the interconnectedness of things and places us within this process.

3 Animals

Key question

Is it always wrong for humans to use animals for entertainment?

Case study
Killing animals for fun

Each Labor Day from 1934 to 1998, a live animal shooting festival took place in the small town of Hegins, Pennsylvania (USA), before the event was banned. Participants travelled from around the globe to take part. In the annual event, some 5,000 pigeons were released from traps, one by one, only to become targets for participants. Most of the birds who were shot – more than three-quarters, according to investigators for The Fund for Animals *– were wounded but not immediately killed. Some would be left on the shooting fields as each contestant completed his or her round of shooting, while some would escape to nearby woods to die slowly from their wounds. After each round was completed, young children collected injured birds and killed them by stomping on them, ripping off their heads, smashing them against the sides of barrels, or tossing them into barrels to suffocate among other dying or dead pigeons. The shooters and children did not carry out these activities in secrecy. Thousands of spectators paid admission to sit in bleachers, eat, drink beer, and roar their approval for the shooters and children.*

(David DeGrazia, *Animal Rights: A Very Short Introduction*, page 12)

Many people find the scene described above deeply disturbing. Perhaps it is because that it reflects badly on human nature and maybe as animals ourselves we know what it means to suffer, and to allow such unnecessary cruelty is simply a contradiction of our own morality. Finally, for the moral ecologist, animals have intrinsic rights which we have a duty to respect and to disregard these rights is to threaten the ecosystem itself.

Key people

Peter Singer (b.1946) is a philosopher specialising in medical ethics and animal rights and liberation. He was director of the Centre for Human Bioethics, Monash University, Australia and co-founder, and for many years, President, of The Great Ape Project, an international effort to obtain basic rights for chimpanzees, gorillas and orangutans.

Key words

Sentience is the capacity to experience pain and pleasure.

Morally considerable describes any sentient being whose interests must form part of human moral decision making.

Key quote

'The question is not, Can they reason? not, Can they talk? but, Can they suffer?'

JEREMY BENTHAM, *AN INTRODUCTION TO THE PRINCIPLES OF MORALS AND LEGISLATION*, CHAPTER XVII PARAGRAPH 4

Key words

Equal consideration is the principle that all like things must be considered alike.

Speciesism is the discrimination against animal species by human beings based on an assumption of human superiority.

Key quote

'We must take care when we compare the interests of different species. In some situations a member of one species will suffer more than a member of another species.'

PETER SINGER, *PRACTICAL ETHICS*, 59

a) Animal welfare

Advocates of animal welfare, such as **Peter Singer**, argue that just as it is wrong, from a utilitarian point of view, to deliberately cause suffering to a human being, it must be equally wrong to do so to *any* **sentient** creature (that is any non-human animal which has the capacity to suffer). The humane principle, as it is often referred to, was posed by Bentham in the question 'Can they suffer?'. So, for Singer and others, a sentient non-human animal is **morally considerable** if it has interests, and if so then these must be included in any moral decision or calculation.

i) The principle of equal consideration

Peter Singer was one of the first to advocate that the failure to apply the principle of **equal consideration** to non-human sentient animals as much as to humans leads to an essentially contradictory morality. Singer's argument rests on the following ideas:

- **Speciesism.** All species which are sentient have an interest not to suffer. It is therefore illogical and prejudicial to prefer one species over another and therefore give priority to humans.
- **Equality of interests.** Having interests is the only criterion which determines whether something is morally considerable (not intelligence or consciousness for example). Interests may be measured and calculated as in any utilitarian system according to their strength and intensity.
- **Greater and lesser interests.** Equal consideration does not mean that *all* animals are intrinsically equal. The ability to suffer varies from those simpler animals which have only very basic interests perhaps amounting to no more than mere survival, to those animals which can form basic plans and have a sense of a future, to those which have intelligence and are able to reflect on their state of mind. A coherent animal welfare system has to be able to distinguish greater and lesser interests when it comes to making decisions between animals, not based on species but individuals' capacity to suffer.
- **Vegetarianism.** Singer argues that although, in theory, one could eat animals if they were well looked after and slaughtered painlessly, on balance the suffering caused to animals outweighs the pleasure we gain in eating them. For that reason there are compelling reasons for most people to become vegetarians.

ii) Argument from marginal cases

A test for speciesism is the argument from marginal cases. A marginal case is one where a human being lacks characteristically human capacities. So, Singer argues, if it came to saving thousands of people through animal experimentation, then experimenting on an 'orphaned human with severe and irreversible brain damage' would be more justified than using healthy 'apes, monkeys, dogs, cats and even mice and rats':

> *There seems to be no morally relevant characteristic that such humans have that non-human animals lack. Experimenters, then, show bias in favour of their own species whenever they carry out experiments on non-human animals for purposes that they would not think justified when using human beings at an equal or lower level of sentience, awareness, sensitivity and so on.*

(Peter Singer, *Practical Ethics*, page 68)

iii) Negative rights

Read pages 5–6 on utilitarianism and rights.

Although utilitarians do not believe in moral rights many advocate legal rights to achieve the greatest happiness of the greatest number. This positive rights position means that for Singer and other utilitarians, all sentient animals have the legal right not to suffer unnecessary pain (negative rights). Those who argue from a contract based notion of rights say that animals are not entitled to rights because they are unable to reciprocate rights with duties. Singer points out that as contract type rights already make exceptions for children and incapacitated humans who are unable to enter morally into the contract, then there is already good reason to extend rights to animals.

b) Animal rights

Those who advocate animal rights consider that the animal welfare position outlined above does not take animals as subjects in their own right seriously enough. In the end, as we have seen from the utilitarian point of view, if human needs outweigh animal suffering (such as the cure for Aids) then human welfare prevails. But a more thorough-going biocentric approach to animal welfare argues that animals need not be human persons in order for them to be treated as subjects with *moral* and not just legal rights. But for this to happen we need to change a mindset that still regards non-human animals as human property.

i) Analogy with slavery and racism

Read page 90 for Singer's analysis of racism and equality of interests.

The situation is analogous to slavery and racism. The suffering of slaves was considered morally acceptable as long they were regarded as the property and had no rights. The argument wasn't that slaves were not capable of suffering. What changed the situation was when slaves were given the basic right of equal consideration as any other human being that their unjust and unnecessary suffering was outlawed. So, by analogy, if we wish to apply the humane principle consistently and coherently then we must give non-human animals the moral right of equal consideration as a *minimum*.

Key question

Would it be wrong to carry out scientific experiments on a severely brain damaged human child?

Cross-reference

Read pages 5–6 on utilitarianism and rights.

Key thought

According to research, two-thirds of Americans and 94 per cent of Britons think that animals should be protected from cruelty and suffering.

Key question

To what extent do we regard animals as human property?

Cross-reference

Read page 90 for Singer's analysis of racism and equality of interests.

Key people

Gary Francione is professor of law and philosophy at Rutgers University, USA and has written *Animals, Property and the Law* (1995).

Key quote

'When it comes to other animals, we humans exhibit what can best be described as moral schizophrenia … We claim to regard animals as having morally significant interests, but our behaviour is to the contrary.'

GARY FRANCIONE, *ANIMAL RIGHTS*, 108 AND 110

Key question

As a matter of animal rights what human uses of animal should be made illegal?

Key thought

Seventy-five per cent of racehorses are slaughtered each year.

Cross-reference

Read page 174 for some objections to giving animals moral rights.

ii) Equal consideration as a basic animal right

Failure to give animals rights, argues **Gary Francione** is to create a situation of social 'moral schizophrenia'. Moral schizophrenia occurs because, although popular opinion indicates that animals should never be subject to suffering and though animal welfare laws do not permit undue animal suffering, in practice animals endure levels of cruelty which would never be permitted on human beings. Francione argues that animals do not need to be considered people (in the same way that humans are people) or even moral agents for this to be an intrinsic wrong. Although many of Singer's arguments above are correct, all animals need to be regarded as non-human subjects with intrinsic worth, if equal consideration is to be justly achieved.

iii) Unnecessary animal suffering

Making equal consideration of non-human animal rights, of course, does not mean the end of all animal suffering. Animals will continue to suffer much in the same ways as humans expect to endure some suffering. The issue is what human actions cause animals to suffer unnecessarily and which as matter of contract rights we have a duty to stop.

- **Food**. Each year eight billion animals are killed in the US food industry – that is 16,000 per minute. We do not need to eat animals to survive and if the only reason is that we enjoy the taste of eating their flesh then the considerable suffering of animals through intensive factory farming and fishing cannot be justified.
- **Hunting and entertainment**. Two hundred million animals are killed per year in the USA alone. Animals, as in the pigeon shoot case study, are often tortured for fun. Racing dogs and horses are used for entertainment and are often shot when they cease to be useful. Animals are made to perform unnaturally in circuses and on television shows or kept caged in zoos. So, just as no civilised society that takes rights seriously would treat humans in this way, there is no rational basis for treating animals differently.
- **Experimentation**. Equally unacceptable is the considerable pain and indignity suffered by animals through scientific research for human advancement and welfare. The principle of equal consideration reasons that just as we don't permit experimentation on very mentally disabled people, young or old (or merely small babies), because they lack certain cognitive facilities then the same prohibition must apply to non-human animals.

iv) More than basic rights for non-human subjects

Biocentric animal ethics consider that although animals are not human persons, they are morally considerable as subjects. There are

Key people

Tom Regan was professor of philosophy at North Carolina State University specialising in animal rights. His book *The Case for Animal Rights* (1983 and 2004) has strongly influenced the animal liberation movement.

Cross-reference

Read pages 7–8 on Dworkin's idea of rights as trumps.

some who go further than Fancione's basic right that all animals should be protected from unnecessary suffering. **Tom Regan** advocates a 'strong animal rights' notion that those subjects who are more sophisticated are entitled to a greater range of *moral* rights such as freedom from boredom, freedom of movement and the right to life even if implementing these rights 'trumps' human needs. But all animal rights proponents agree that humans are in a privileged position which gives them a duty to implement and enforce animal rights.

c) Animal environmentalism

However, for deep ecologists the value given to animals by biocentric relational ecologists fails to do justice to animal life as a whole. Animals are morally considerable for the simple reason that they are alive. Therefore animal life is to be protected because it is part of the ecosystem and essential to the flourishing of the whole environment. In practical terms this means preserving the natural habitats for wild animals in particular, such as rivers, vegetation and rocks.

Animal environmentalists value biodiversity and given the choice between preserving the life of a domestic animal against an endangered species, would preserve the endangered species.

4 Environmental scepticism

Key word

Environmentalism is the political and ideological belief that the environment should be protected from harmful human activities.

Despite the increasing awareness of environmental issues and in particular the effects of climate change, there are many who consider that the present popularity of **environmentalism** has to be treated with caution or even scepticism. It is, of course, quite right to question whether something is right merely because it is the consensus view; on investigation it may well turn out to be far from true and mask other motives. Doubt or scepticism is a necessary process in any philosophical analysis.

Key question

Can we prove that human activities have caused global warming?

a) Cause–correlation confusion

The crux of the climate change and global warming argument is that it is caused by human production of greenhouse gases through rapidly growing technology and industry. However, there are scientists who doubt that there is such a direct link. Their argument distinguishes between an actual cause and what appears to be a cause but is in fact only a **correlation**.

Key word

Correlation describes the strength of the statistical relationship between two variables.

For example, suppose it is noted that everyone who goes to the pub develops lung cancer. Pub-going and lung cancer would be said to be perfectly correlated. We might therefore conclude that drinking *causes* lung cancer. However, the actual cause of lung cancer is smoking and it just happens that most people who go to pubs also smoke. Therefore, although there is clearly an extremely strong correlation between pub-going and cancer, pub-going in itself is not the cause of cancer.

There are a number of scientists who argue that carbon dioxide levels are not the direct cause for climate change. Their argument is that extreme climate change has always been a characteristic of the world, independent of humans. For example, the Medieval Warm Period (approximately 1000–1400) was followed by the Little Ice Age (approximately 1400–1850). After the Little Ice Age the global temperature began to rise well before CO_2 gases were observed to have increased. So, whilst it is true that since the Industrial Revolution there has been considerable population growth, pollution and increase in greenhouse gases, and these all appear to correlate with global warming, they are not necessarily its cause.

b) Suspicion

Environmental sceptics also question the motives of environmentalists. Hermeneutics of suspicion consider the deeper cultural, historical and psychological reasons that form an idea. Nietzsche, Marx and Freud, the three 'masters of suspicion' have each contributed their own tools of suspicion. Nietzsche proposed that beliefs are often maintained by those who depend on them for their power and identity; Marx extended this by asking who stands to benefit materially; and Freud looked to the deeper psychological motivations such as fear and attachment.

All these suspicions form the basis of the journalist Christopher Booker's analysis of global warming. Booker's argument does not reject concern for the environment but argues that it is not the most important moral concern of the twenty-first century. He rejects the apocalyptic language that spells out global disaster and he considers that many of the arguments use fear and guilt rather than reason.

Booker's argument might be summarised in terms of suspicion as follows:

Cross-reference

Christopher Booker *The Real Global Warming Disaster* (2009).

- **Psychological suspicion.** Environmentalism has adopted the language of fear by exaggerating the degree of the problem. For example, announcements about global warming are often made during heatwaves when the evidence appears to be at its most incontrovertible. Humans often need to focus their existence on threat and since the decline of the communist Eastern bloc countries in the 1980s, the threat of world nuclear war has been replaced by the threat of environmental melt down. Pressure groups such as Greenpeace and Friends of the Earth, which were formed to campaign against nuclear weapons, have now found a related cause that relies on living off fear.

Cross-reference

See page 177 on the Rio Earth Summit.

- **Cultural suspicion**. Environmentalism has been the means for implementing other cultural/political goals. For example, the Earth Summit at Rio was really about the rich–poor divide and the problems of development and distribution of wealth. The environmental issue was a convenient means of reinforcing a more basic human concern. In other words, we have to ask who has a vested interest in keeping the environmental idea at the forefront of the political agenda.

- **Historical suspicion**. One group who stand to benefit are scientists. Booker and others argue that many scientists have suddenly found themselves in positions of power and influence because their work on climate and environment has made them invaluable experts for governments and pressure groups. However, how neutral can a scientist be when there is a lot to lose professionally by being ridiculed by other scientists who subscribe to the consensus view? So, for example, Mann *et al.*'s so-called 'hockey stick graph', which indicates the rapid rise in global warming since 1900, has become so well accepted that it is almost impossible for any scientist to doubt it unless he wishes to be branded an anti-environmentalist.

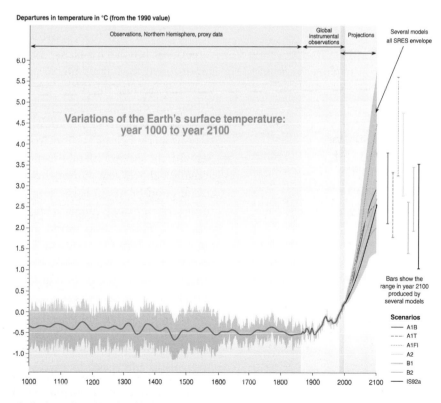

The 'hockey stick graph' produced by Michael Mann, Raymond Bradley and Malcolm Hughes in 1999 shows northern hemisphere temperatures over the past millennium. The graph was featured prominently in the 2001 United Nations Intergovernmental Panel on Climate Change *Third Assessment Report*, as supporting the consensus view of climate scientists that there has been a relatively sharp rise in global temperatures since 1900.

c) Non-human rights

As we have seen in Chapter 1, the idea of what a right is, how it is derived and how it is implemented is far from obvious. For the environmental sceptic, giving non-human entities rights confuses the idea of rights and undermines the very idea of a moral community.

If, as Article 29 of the Universal Declaration of Human Rights states, rights and freedoms are always to be understood as duties to the community there is no obligation to extend these to the whole of the non-human community. The sceptic does not take issue with shallow ecologists but rather with relational and deep ecologists because they assume that somehow the environment is capable of responding to the rights that have been given to it.

Giving rights to non-human entities is unsatisfactory for two reasons:

Key word

Sentimental fallacy (or pathetic fallacy) makes the false assumption that because something appears to behave in a human-like way it must have human-like qualities.

Cross-reference

Read pages 10–11 on Hohfeld's rights and duties relationship.

Cross-reference

Read pages 7–8 on Dworkin and rights.

Key quote

'If dogs have rights, punishment is what they must expect when they disregard their duties.'
ROGER SCRUTON, *ANIMAL RIGHTS AND ANIMAL WRONGS*, 67

- First, the argument that the environment has rights suffers from the **sentimental fallacy**, which confers on non-humans beings human-like qualities and values. We can see this if we apply Hohfeld's notion of rights and liberties. For example, I might legislate, using Hohfeld's idea of a 'immunity right', that trees have a right not to be cut down. This does not oblige the tree to do anything in return by way of duty. But if the tree dropped a branch which smashed my neighbour's car then, according to Hohfeld's 'power rights' category, it is liable for blame. But in reality, blame is not apportioned to the tree but to me for failing to maintain the tree's branches, because the tree is my property. This suggests that although we might protect the environment using rights language, these are not rights in any meaningful *moral* sense, as rights can only properly belong to humans.

- Second, the environmental sceptic doubts that the environmentalist actually believes that all non-humans are capable of intending moral good or moral harm. For example, if we follow Dworkin's theory of rights we might acknowledge that, although we all have a right to equal consideration, a legal system does not sanction my right to freedom of speech and at the same time give me the right to censure others from free speech. To be part of the moral community means that one understands this. But can non-human animals do this? Sceptics such as Roger Scruton think not. Others concede that this could be true for a very few species of higher mammals who might be considered to be persons, but it is stretching things too far to imagine, as the deep ecologist does, that bugs, plants and rocks do anything other than exist.

d) The rights of future generations

Environmental sceptics question the argument used by environmentalists that the present generation has a duty to future

Key question

Do future generations have a right which obliges us to treat the environment with care?

Key quote

'The practical difficulties of representing future generations again speaks of thinning out of rights and provides a practical argument against expecting representatives now living to advocate the straightforward rights of future beings.'

BERTRAM BANDMAN, *DO FUTURE GENERATIONS HAVE THE RIGHT TO BREATHE CLEAN AIR?*, 98

Cross-reference

Read page 10 on claims rights and liberty rights.

Key word

The **fallacy of affirming the consequent** occurs when it is falsely assumed that because a premise is true then the conclusion must also true. This often occurs because the premise or antecedent *may* imply the consequent (what follows) but is not necessarily so. The fallacy or mistake is caused depending on how the word 'if' is used.

generations to protect the environment because unborn generations have a right to live in an environment which will enable them to flourish.

i) 'Thinning out' and confusion of rights

Some environmental sceptics argue that having duties to all generations as yet unborn imposes such impossibly vast duties that they cannot in all practical senses be kept. This has the effect of 'thinning out' rights by reducing their significance. A particularly good example of thinning out can be seen in contract-based rights because the contract is almost entirely one-way: from present generation to future generations but not vice-versa. It follows that as future generations do not yet exist they cannot exercise any duties and if this is so it makes any rights they might theoretically possess so insignificant that they become almost meaningless.

Thinning out is also caused by the confusion inherent in giving future generations rights. For example, some environmentalists have argued that we have a duty to preserve the countryside from the expansion of cities because our forebears preserved it for us and therefore future generations have a right to have it preserved for them. But this argument fails to distinguish between different types of right by confusing a 'claims right' with a 'liberty right'. The present generation may argue that acting according to a liberty right gives them the option of preserving the countryside but without obligation to future generations. There are no claim rights that future generations can make which obliges the present generation to act on their behalf.

ii) Fallacy of affirming the consequent

The environmental sceptic also considers that it is a fallacy to argue that as future generations have an interest that the environment should be looked after then it necessarily becomes their right. The fallacy is committed because it wrongly assumes that anything which has interests must also have rights. Whilst it is possible that a being with interests might have rights, there are many beings with interests which are not sentient and therefore cannot have human rights. Furthermore, as future generations are not yet sentient, then it is impossible to know what their interests as rights are in order to protect or implement them. The whole argument rests on the non sequitur that wrongly infers rights from interests. The fallacy might be expressed as follows:

> *If x has rights then x has interests*
> *x has interests*
> *so, x has rights*

5 Earth summits and protocols

There have been many **summits** to discuss environmental matters of global concern. Two recent summits have been those at Kyoto and Copenhagen.

a) Kyoto 1997

The Kyoto summit established The Kyoto Protocol on climate change. It was prompted by the Intergovernmental Panel on Climate Change (IPCC) report that there was a consensus among scientists that the effects of emissions of greenhouse gases on the world's climate would be to warm the Earth by up to 5.8 per cent by the year 2000.

- **COP3.** The Protocol adopted the consensus of the third Conference of the Parties (COP3) in 1997, which legally bound members of the convention to gas emission targets to the post-2000 period.
- **Reduction of greenhouse gases**. The Protocol went beyond the UN Framework Convention on Climate Change by requiring industrialised countries to reduce six key greenhouse gas (together referred to as CO_2 gases) emissions from 1990 levels by an average of 5 per cent over the period 2008–2012
- **Targets for gases**. For developed countries the target reduction of gases would be 20 per cent (if there were to be no cuts in emissions by 2010).
- **'Carbon credits'.** The Convention allowed richer countries to buy and sell emissions credits. A country which had achieved more than its target reduction would be able to trade these to those who have yet to achieve their targets.

b) Copenhagen 2009

The Copenhagen meeting of the United Nations Climate Change Conference (or COP15) comprised 192 countries. Although there was no political consensus, the summit delegates 'took note' of the Copenhagen Accord drawn up by the USA, India, Brazil, South Africa and China. The agreement between developed and developing countries marked a breakthrough not achieved at Kyoto – especially the participation of China and the USA, the two largest producers of greenhouse gases. So, even though the Accord is not legally binding, it marks another stage in the global concern for the environment.

The focus was on climate change based on the IPCC Fourth Assessment Report. The Copenhagen Accord states:

- The desire 'to urgently combat climate change in accordance with the principle of common but differentiated responsibilities and respective capabilities' to keep global temperature rise below

2 degrees Celsius (as from 2009) implies that there must be 'deep cuts in global emissions' as 'required according to science' (paragraphs 1 and 2).

- Signatories of the Kyoto Protocol are to set out proposals for economy–wide emissions reduction targets for 2020 by the year 2010 (paragraph 4) and non-signatories are to adhere to the Protocols according to their domestic situation and to report every two years (paragraph 5).
- The need of 'reducing emission from deforestation and forest degradation' (paragraph 6) will be internationally funded.
- That in 2015 there will be need to review temperature increases and to consider a goal of no more than 1.5 degrees Celsius (paragraph 15).

('Copenhagen Accord', United Nations Framework Convention on Climate Change, 18 December 2009)

c) Globalisation and biopolitics

Globalisation has become a fashionable if not slippery term since the 1970s to describe the way we think about and treat the world. Environmentalists increasingly argue that environmental ethics have to be a **bio-political** issue. As the case study of the farmer at the start of this chapter illustrates, consciousness of globalisation illustrates the complex relationship between environment, society, business and technology. From a business point of view, the environment is one consideration among many when balancing profit against market economics. It is the multinational corporations (MNCs) who, more than any other groups, have the power to affect how natural resources are used in the global market. As Celia Deane-Drummond comments:

> *The market economy tends to ignore the real costs of environmental damage. The process becomes more complicated once the damage is at a site far removed from the site of production, as in the generation of gases which lead to acid rain, for example.*

(Celia Deane-Drummond, *A Handbook in Theology and Ecology*, page 125)

It is one of the many paradoxes that despite global communication, human concerns for the environment do not stretch much outside our own communities.

A good example of this paradox was the Earth summit at Rio de Janiro in 1992. Motivated by the injustices of the rich–poor divide, development and dependency as global environmental problems, the summit developed in its **Agenda 21** a raft of recommendations including: desertification; women and indigenous peoples in sustainable development; protection of the atmosphere and oceans; and basic human needs – health, housing and education.

Key quote

'Developed countries shall provide adequate, predictable and sustainable financial resources, technology and capacity-building to support the implementation of adaptation action in developing countries.'

THE COPENHAGEN ACCORD, PARAGRAPH 3

Cross-reference

Globalisation and MNCs are discussed at greater length on pages 112–114.

Key word

Bio-political refers to the way in which governments and those in power control human activities/technologies and their impact on the environment.

Key word

Agenda 21 is the set of environmental recommendations resulting from the Rio summit.

However, to implement Agenda 21, US$600 billion would be needed to make the changes required by developing countries. But because existing foreign aid from richer countries fell far short of this, these countries were not persuaded to increase their contributions to cover the additional US$125 billion needed. The failure of Rio therefore not only highlights the extent of the North–South divide but the considerable unwillingness of developed countries to sacrifice their lifestyles for world development despite shared concern for the world.

6 Normative ethical responses to the environment

Cross-reference

See pages 161–163 on shallow ecology.

Key question

Is utilitarianism naturally inclined towards environmental scepticism?

a) Utilitarianism

We have already considered several aspects of the utilitarian position on the environment. Utilitarianism as shallow ecology is humanocentric and seeks to maximise the surplus of human happiness over unhappiness – only humans in this version are morally considerable. Nevertheless, even a shallow utilitarian ecology can point to the way in which the natural world can contribute to human happiness by offering an ecologically richer environment, a focus for aesthetic pleasure, or even an outlet for recreational activity.

i) Cost–benefit analysis

At the heart of the utilitarian approach to the environment is a cost–benefit analysis. What has to be weighed up is whether environmental policies have any human benefit. As the environment has no intrinsic value, utilitarians take seriously the objections raised by environmental sceptics especially, for example, cause–correlation confusion over climate change and duties to generations as yet unborn.

Cross-reference

See pages 171–172 on cause correlation confusion and future generations.

Cross-reference

Read pages 168–169 on Peter Singer's preference utilitarianism and non-human life.

ii) Non-human sentient life

However, Peter Singer has encouraged humans to understand the principle of utility not simply in human terms but to include the interests of all sentient beings. This approach seeks to avoid arbitrariness and to identify the different interests of each species and act in the interests of as many as possible. This leads preference utilitarianism to adopting a deeper relational ecology that takes into account the way in which human activity such as clear-cutting forests, damning rivers, quarrying mountains and constructing pipelines are all morally significant factors if they threaten non-human sentient life.

Some critics have pointed out that Singer's argument for vegetarianism is contrary to utilitarian aims. Based on the utilitarian maxim of always acting for the greatest number (of sentient beings), if the vegetarian principle were to be applied then fewer animals would be bred and there would consequently be fewer sentient beings in the world. What matters, from an utilitarian point of view, is the quality of animal welfare not banning eating meat as such.

iii) Biodiversity and deep ecology

Key question

On what grounds might utilitarians support deep ecology?

Some utilitarians have argued for a deeper ecology that does not just take sentient life into account. The principle is that biodiversity is better for the ecosystem (and indirectly for us). This means, for example, that if we had to choose between preserving the life of a pig-nosed turtle over a shrub then the turtle's life is more worthwhile ecologically than the shrub as there are many shrubs and only a few pig-nosed turtles. On the other hand, if protecting a rare plant is better for the ecosystem than a pig–nosed turtle then the plant should be preserved as there are other kinds of turtle.

However, this approach falls short of Naess' ecosophy. The utilitarian justifies the selection of one aspect of the environment over the other and this, by Naess' standards, is actually a decision based on what humans consider to be good or useful. In the end, even the utilitarian deep ecologist is motivated by humanocentric instrumental concerns not by the intrinsic value of the world.

Cross-reference

Read page 165 on Naess' ecosophy.

iv) Calculating systemic value

The greatest challenge to the utilitarian is the way in which ends are calculated. Are these ends short term or long term? Are ends to be calculated according to the immediate situation or, as some environmentalists suggest, to the system as a whole? Many consider that Singer's preference utilitarianism inclusion of animals has already made the job of the utilitarian very difficult.

Nevertheless, some utilitarians argue that calculating ends according to the systems as a whole is possible. All utilitarian calculations involve probabilities and we have to allow that taking informed risks is the best we can do. This may mean that we have to take a decision that we just have to allow some things to die out. For example, pandas have no systemic place in the biosphere and so on cost–benefit analysis we should put our efforts into maintaining more important aspects of the biosphere.

But in practice it is hard to be quite so coldly rational. Humans find pandas aesthetically pleasing and even though it actually makes more rational sense to give priority to microbes which have more systemic value than 'higher' mammals, in the end human emotions have to be taken into account. If *we* like pandas and that increases general human happiness, is that sufficient utilitarian reason to protect them?

Cross-reference

Read page 162 on Kant's attitude to animals.

b) Kantian ethics

As we have seen in Kant's epistemology, as humans are the only value–giving agents then nature and animals have no intrinsic worth; God is only a guarantor of human moral law and does not command nor bestow value. Yet, among environmentalists, Kant's secular humanist ethics are often considered to be one of the major reasons for the environmental crisis. As the categorical imperative applies only to human persons, Kant takes an entirely instrumentalist view of all other aspects of nature.

However this may be an over simplistic view:

- The categorical imperative is also a sign of our humanity. Just as it is wrong to treat people as a means to an end, anyone who treats animals inhumanely for sport or fun is acting according to their base desires rather than to reason. Some contemporary Kantians suggest that although animals should not have moral rights, they should be given legal rights to protect them.
- If the utopia of the kingdom of ends is to be a possibility it requires a world to exist that treats all people with equal respect, and that would not be possible if the environment was not included.

Key question

Has the absence of religion been a cause of today's ecological crisis?

Cross-reference

Read page 164 on Lynn White and Christianity.

c) Revealed ethics

i) Creation and the Eleventh Commandment

Although most scholars consider Lynn White's argument that the present environmental crisis is due to the Christian teaching of dominion as wrong, it has nevertheless prompted a reappraisal of biblical ecology. For example, the World Council of Churches at the Vancouver Assembly (1998) coined the term 'the integrity of creation', which considers the environment to be as morally significant as human rights, peace and nuclear disarmament. 'Integrity' indicates that humans are not separate from creation but part of it, as both are equally dependent on God as Creator.

The shift in modern theology has moved noticeably from a humanocentric to a geocentric view of ethics. In his influential article, Vincent Rossi argued that this shift should be marked by the addition of an eleventh commandment.

Key quote

'The earth is the Lord's and the fullness thereof: thou shall not despoil the earth, nor destroy the life thereon.'

VINCENT ROSSI, *THE ELEVENTH COMMANDMENT: TOWARD AN ETHIC OF ECOLOGY*

> *The natural world must be seen as sacred because it is the abode of God. Man is now acting like a cancer in nature, not because religion has in the past allowed man to abuse nature, but because modern man has abandoned true religion in favour of spiritless humanism.*
>
> (Vincent Rossi, 'The Eleventh Commandment: Toward an Ethic of Ecology' (1979), quoted in Lewis G. Regenstein, *Replenish the Earth*, page 157)

Key quote

'They do not say in the hearts,
"Let us fear the Lord our God,
who gives the rain in its season,
the autumn rain and the spring
rain, and keeps for us the weeks
appointed for the harvest".'

JEREMIAH 5:24

Key word

Exile refers to the events leading
up to 586 BC when the
Babylonians destroyed Jerusalem
and sent its leading classes to
Babylon.

Cross-reference

See page 164 for a definition of
covenant.

Key people

Andrew Linzey is professor of
theology and animal welfare at
Oxford University. He has written
widely on the subject including his
book *Animal Theology* (1994).

Respect for the created order is a constant theme of the Bible – and especially the Hebrew Bible (Old Testament). The prophet Jeremiah in his prophetic vision of the future looks forward to a time when the harmony of Genesis 1 will be restored, when humans, animals and land coexist. He describes the sinfulness of the people of Israel to be like those who ignore the gifts of the seasons. Modern commentators compare Jeremiah's description of sin to the modern world's desire to want more, to exploit natural resources, to build on flood planes, and to ignore the seasons by demanding food whether in or out of season.

ii) Biopolitics and the rejection of God's covenant

Michael Northcott is struck by how closely the message of Israel's prophets corresponds to the present global environmental crisis. Because secular and humanist values in the West have generally privatised religion, Northcott argues that a major biblical tradition has been lost. But none of the prophets understood religion in this way. Their messages of warning were closely linked to the politics of their day. Jeremiah, for example, argued that the **exile** of Israel was a punishment for political complacency. Because they had failed to adhere to the **covenant** they had caused their own geopolitical disaster. Northcott argues that global markets caused by the USA and Europe, capitalism and exploitation of cheap labour in LEDCs are all equivalent to abandoning the covenant. Our complacency is further illustrated by our dependency on technology to solve problems rather than taking responsibility for the world ourselves. He blames the secular post-Enlightenment mindset which has given humans a false sense of their superiority as a major cause for environmental meltdown. The crisis, like the exile, is a sign of creation's and therefore God's judgement on human sinfulness:

> Global warming is the Earth's judgement on the global market empire and on the headless consumption it fosters.

(Michael S. Northcott, 'Biopolitics', in *The Environment*, page 20, Shap Working Party on World Religions in Education, 2008/9)

The message of the prophets is that Christians have a moral and religious duty to be involved in biopolitics and to support the aims of the summits at Rio, Kyoto and Copenhagen.

iii) Non-human animals

Andrew Linzey's outspoken views for an animal theology of liberation also draw attention to an aspect of the Christian salvation which he argues has frequently been overlooked. Traditionally, Christ's death was considered to be exclusively for humans. But, Linzey argues, the restoration of the world includes *all* living things. He refers to Paul's letter to the Colossians, where Paul writes about Christ:

Key question

What does the Bible command about the treatment of non-human animals?

Key quote

'When I bring the clouds over the earth and the bow is seen in the clouds, I will remember my covenant which is between me and you and every living creature of all flesh.'

GENESIS 9:14–15

Key quote

'God said, "Behold I have given you every plant yielding seed which is upon the face of all the earth, and every tree with seed in its fruit; you shall have them as food".'

GENESIS 1:29

Key question

Are biblical ethics compatible with deep ecology?

Cross-reference

Read pages 165–166 on Lovelock's idea of Gaia.

Key question

To what extent does natural law support relational ecology?

He is the image of the invisible God, the first-born of all creation: for in him all things were created, in heaven and on earth.

(Colossians 1:15–16)

If *all* things were created in Him, all living things exist to glorify God and it would therefore be wrong to cause deliberate harm to them. Animals, especially, have a special place because the covenant with Noah (Genesis 9:14–15) is made with humans *and* animals. The restoration of the world through Christ's redemption creates a 'new creation' (Galatians 6:15), which we now understand to include human and non-human animals alike. Even so, humans have a special place in the world and there may be times when animals have to be used in experimentation for the good of all. But Linzey argues that these should be done on a very selective basis and not on the mass scale which presently happens. Likewise he questions the need to eat animals when we can live just as easily as vegetarians – Genesis suggests that before the Fall Adam and Eve were vegetarians. However, others acknowledge that the Bible commands kindness should be shown to animals even when slaughtering them for food, and vegetarianism is therefore an ideal but not a duty.

iv) Gaia and Genesis

There are several reasons why the Bible could be seen to support a Gaia-type deep ecology. Both:

- Consider that humans are part of the biosphere and we must co-operate with it if we and the world are to flourish.
- Illustrate that respect for the environment is one of relationship and respect for the created order not exploitation.
- Demonstrate that failure to respect the cosmos will result in disaster, possibly the destruction of humankind.

However, in other respects Gaia and the Bible are incompatible. Gaia is not involved spiritually in the lives of humans, as the biblical covenant suggests, nor does Gaia offer hope to humans despite their faults, whilst in the Bible God's grace restores the world including humans.

d) Natural law

Even though natural law is often dismissed by scientists and ecologists because they do not see the world in teleological terms, natural law ethicists argue that the shallow ecology of the instrumentalists is flawed in two ways. First, scientists often do speak in broadly teleological terms using such terms as competition, survival and natural selection to describe the purpose of nature. Second, deep ecologists constantly emphasise the interconnected relationship of all matter, in a way which only makes sense if, as natural law ethicists maintain, the environment is either inherently or intrinsically valuable.

i) Relational ecology

Despite some of the weaknesses of Aristotle's and Aquinas' attitude to non-human animals, many find in natural law ethics sound rational basis for modern environmental ethics. As natural law argues that many of its primary precepts are written into the minds of all humans, then its universality cuts across all cultures and provides a starting point for global policies on the environment.

- **God as the value-giving subject**. God, according to Aquinas is the first and final cause of all matter. Aquinas argued therefore that whilst God is the **ubiquitous** source of all value, all matter has its own freedom to fulfil its purpose or not. In this way no aspect of the environment could ever be considered to lack value or even be treated as evil. Even things which may appear to be defective are so because they perform an important function as part of the whole. As Aquinas says:

> *The defect in one thing yields to the good of another, or even to the universal good: for the corruption of one is the generation of another, and through this it is that a species is kept in existence … A lion would cease to live, if there were no slaying of animals.*

> (Thomas Aquinas, *Summa Theologica*, I.22.2)

- **Do good and avoid evil**. The central precept of natural law is that *all* things have a right in the created order to achieve their telos and not to be thwarted in that purpose. The significance of this, as Michael Northcott argues, is that unlike other ethical systems the natural order of the world is also, and equally, a *moral* order, which means it can make demands on humans to treat it well.
- **Goods**. Although all things are inherently good within the created order, not all things are equal. Different things have different ends and therefore different 'goods'. The goods for humans are the five elements of the five primary precepts. Many of these, humans share with other animals such as reproduction and education of the young. But, as only humans have rationality then only they have the goods which lead to knowledge of God and live in ordered and just communities. This gives humans a special place in the world with the responsibility to maintain the harmony of the created order as a principle of justice.

ii) Non-human animals

However, despite the strongly relational aspect of natural law there are some ambiguities about the degree to which non-human animals and the environment should be treated. Some argue that

---

Key word

Ubiquitous means being present everywhere.

Key quote

'Hence this is the first precept of law, that "good is to be done and pursued, and evil is to be avoided". All other precepts of the natural law are based upon this.'
THOMAS AQUINAS, *SUMMA THEOLOGICA*, I.II., 94.2

Cross-reference

Michael S. Northcott *The Environment and Christian Ethics* page 232.

Key quote

'There is in man an inclination to good, according to the nature of his reason, which nature is proper to him: thus man has a natural inclination to know the truth about God, and to live in society.'
THOMAS AQUINAS, *SUMMA THEOLOGICA*, I.II., 94.2

Key question

Are all non-human animals part of the moral community?

Aristotle and Aquinas both acknowledged that some animals have practical reason which is very little different from the kind of rationality a human child might have. Therefore, just as society cares for its young and educates and nurtures them, then it should also give the same consideration of care to some non-human animals. This is not a view shared by all. Anthony Kenny's interpretation of Aquinas concludes that animals cannot be considered to have any form of practical reason as they are unable to express themselves in language and without language they lack the capacity to reflect and analyse their actions. Non-human animals are therefore not part of the moral community.

iii) Deep ecology

In his address to the Athenians, St Paul used a Stoic form of natural law on which he assumed he would find broad agreement. He argued that the world is ordered, life giving and purposeful because it depends on a single God or divine principle for its existence. His conclusion shares something of the deep ecologist's sense of the interconnectedness of all things and our dependency on a unifying Gaia-like principle:

> *Yet, he is not far from each of us, for 'In him we live and move and have our being'.*

> (St Paul, in *Acts of the Apostles*, 17:28)

Although natural law ethicists consider that all aspects of nature are purposeful and have their own potentials to flourish, this does not necessarily support the deep ecological positions of Naess or Lovelock. Even if Lovelock is not entirely right to deny that Gaia is goal-oriented, Gaia's amoral telos is contrary to natural law which gives particular value to human life. In addition, Lovelock's order of creation gives priority to microbes, which were the first life to occupy the biosphere and at which point Gaia appeared; but in natural law it is the other way round – humans are the final product of creation and God, or in Aristotle's thinking the first principle of the universe, has always existed.

e) Virtue ethics
i) Habits and attitudes

Although virtues may be taught many others are acquired through habit and by imitating others. Therefore, how communities treat the environment are visible indicators of the kind of moral habits which affect every aspect of life. For example, although it remains unclear how effective recycling household waste actually is, it establishes the practice of mindfulness rather than profligacy (wastefulness), which can be equally applied to others as well as to other aspects of the environment. Virtues shape consciousness and perhaps of all moral

Key question

Why should Christians care for animals?

theories virtue ethics go further in the environmental debate in making members of society think about themselves in relation to others in society whether local or global, human or non-human.

ii) Dependency and care

In his book *Dependent Rational Animals*, Alisdair MacIntyre argues that today as never before virtues are necessary in shaping our modern communities if they are to flourish. There is, however, one particular aspect of virtue which tends to get overlooked and that is care for the weaker members of society. Although care might be generally associated with Christian virtues, MacIntyre argues that care is an important part of the more ancient Aristotelian tradition. Aristotle argues that we care for children even though they may lack full rational powers because we know that in time they will become part of the moral community. The habit of care might, therefore, also and equally be extended to the sick, the aged and mentally disabled. It follows that by analogy care ought to be extended to other dependent beings even if they lack the kind of rationality which allows them to reciprocate.

So, in the case of dolphins (and other higher mammals) who form communities and are able to reflect on their behaviour, it would be very inconsistent to deny them the care which we offer our own human children. After all, as animals ourselves, we share many common traits. MacIntyre argues that the virtue of care imposes great responsibility on humans to make judgements about animal welfare, but it does not mean we are obliged to treat animals as equals, any more than we treat children as equals.

ii) Sympathy

A slightly different argument is proposed by the humanocentric ethicist **Roger Scruton**. Scruton does not share MacIntyre's proposal that some non-human animals should be considered as part of the moral community and he agrees with the sentimental fallacy which states that simply because we feel we have an emotional attachment to non-human animals (especially higher mammals) that they therefore share any equivalent human rational traits. On the contrary, only humans are capable of making moral choices. However, as moral agents, and as anyone who takes virtue ethics seriously knows, as Kant argued, the way we treat animals reflects on the kind of people we are. He argues that the essential virtue for any flourishing community is sympathy. The person who sympathises with another rejoices in their happiness and pities them in their suffering and so the virtues of pity and joy must also form the basis for our moral duties to animals. As Scruton says, 'these two feelings lie at the root of our moral duties towards animals'.

Key quote

'The care for others that dolphins exhibit plays a crucial part in sustaining their shared lives.'

ALISDAIR MACINTYRE, *DEPENDENT RATIONAL ANIMALS*, 82

Key people

Roger Scruton (b. 1947) philosopher and writer, and was for many years professor of aesthetics at Birkbeck College, London. He takes a conservative view on many areas of ethics. His book *Animal Rights and Wrongs* (1996) supports fox hunting.

Key quote

'Pity and sympathetic joy extend naturally to other species.'

ROGER SCRUTON, *ANIMAL RIGHTS AND WRONGS*, 34

Cross-reference

Read page 174 on the sentimental fallacy.

Pity and sympathetic joy extend naturally to other species. I know that the dog with a broken leg is suffering, in something like the way I would suffer, I know that the same dog, hunting in a lively scent feels a joy that has its equivalent in me. Only a heartless person would feel no distress at the sight of such canine sufferings or pleasure at the sight of such joys.

(Roger Scruton, *Animal Rights and Wrongs*, pages 34–35)

iii) Balance of extremes

Virtue ethics are dependent on situation. What may occupy us today was not a concern of our forebears and that means practical wisdom (phronesis) can only judge appropriate behaviour based on what is current and pertinent to the well-being (eudaimonia) of society. The environment is one such issue. There are many instances where the virtue of prudence might work, in the issues we have considered, in finding the middle path between extremes. For example: between the environmental sceptics and the environmentalists; between the need for governments to tackle climate change and the need to provide for local communities; between the deep ecologist's requirement to respect all of the biosphere and the shallow ecologist's concern for humans alone.

Key question

Is the virtue ethical approach to environmental justice too idealistic?

Summary diagram

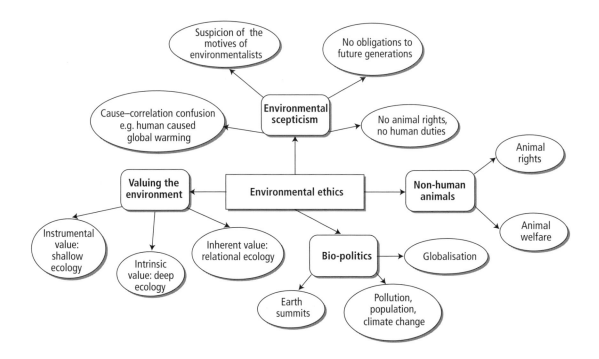

Study guide

By the end of this chapter you should have considered the various theories about how and why we value the environment. You should be able to distinguish between the humanocentric approach which values the environment in terms of its usefulness to humans and the geocentric position which gives inherent or intrinsic value to nature. You should understand these views critically by evaluating them against the various arguments of the environmental sceptics.

Essay questions

1 a *Explain how an utilitarian might assess issues about the environment.*

1 b *'Utilitarianism has a very selfish view of the environment.' Discuss.*

The essay might begin by explaining that most utilitarians have a shallow humanocentric ecological view of the environment. If the aim of utilitarianism is the 'greatest happiness' then an instrumental treatment of nature makes it morally considerable only in so far as it serves human needs. The examples of human created climate change or pollution might be given. The essay might go on to show that many preference utilitarians argue that non-human animals must form part of an environmental ethic as they feel pain and have preferences.

The evaluation might agree that the utilitarian concern for the environment is largely motivated by self-interest and cost–benefit effectiveness. The utilitarian might argue that even deep ecologists are motivated by self preservation (for example, Gaia and human life). On the other hand, some utilitarians are not entirely humanocentric and have a deeper ecological concern for biodiversity.

Further essay questions

2 Assess the view that although animals may be entitled to care they do not have rights.

3 'Deep ecology and Christian teaching on the environment are compatible.' Discuss.

4 'Of all ethical theories natural law provides the most coherent approach to the consideration of the environment.' Discuss.

Revision checklist

Can you give definitions of:

■ the greenhouse effect
■ intrinsic and inherent value
■ Bentham's 'humane principle'
■ environmentalism.

Can you explain:

■ the difference between humanocentric and geocentric consideration of the environment
■ Kant's attitude to animals
■ various interpretations of the Christian dominion argument
■ Lovelock's Daisyworld thought exercise
■ utilitarian cost–benefit analysis of the environment.

Can you give arguments for and against:

■ the principle of equal consideration as applied to animals
■ experiments on animals
■ duties to future generations.

GLOSSARY

absolute other describes how, according to de Beauvoir, women as conscious subjects have been completed ignored by society.

adultery is when a husband or wife has a sexual relationship with someone other than his or her spouse.

Agenda 21 is the set of environmental recommendations resulting from the Rio Earth Summit.

anarchy means literally without a ruler or government.

androcentric means to derive values from the male perspective.

androgynous means having neither conventional masculine or feminine characteristics or blending both characteristics together.

annulment recognises that for various reasons a marriage was never fully implemented and the couple are released from their marital duties to each other.

ars erotica or 'erotic art' is Foucault's term to describe societies who view sexuality in terms of pleasure.

assimilation is the process by which one group takes on the cultural characteristics of a larger group.

bad faith or *mauvaise fois* is the unauthentic life that is not lived freely but according to a stereotype or preconceived image or idea.

baptism is the moment when a person becomes a Christian through repentance and accepting salvation through Jesus Christ.

biocentric ethics are those which value non-human animals (and some would also argue plants) in themselves.

biometrics literally means biological measures and is the means to record and recognise unique human features in two ways: physiological (e.g. face, DNA, finger prints) and behaviour (e.g. voice, posture, mannerisms).

bio-politics refers to the way in which governments and those in power control human activities/technologies and their impact on the environment.

capitalism is the belief that human societies flourish best when operating in a free competitive market motivated by profit. See chapter 5 for a fuller discussion of its meaning.

casuistry in the general sense is the application of moral rules but it is often used negatively to mean over-subtle argument and legal hair splitting.

chastity means to refrain from sex.

civil rights or legal rights are those rights which are based on economic or welfare needs.

civil partnership gives legal rights and protections to a same-sex couple in similar ways as marriage does for a heterosexual couple.

cohabitation contract (or agreement) might, for example, set out who is responsible for childcare, who owns what and how assets will be divided if a couple separate.

cohabitation effect is used to describe the negative psychological effects that cohabitation has on partners and the fact that cohabitation does not lead to long term, stable marriages.

common law marriage or marriage by repute where a couple have lived together as husband and wife but without going through a marriage ceremony or obtaining a marriage contract.

companionate marriage states that the primary purpose of marriage is love or companionship (that is, not necessarily children, property, etc.).

convention is an agreement which is slightly less formal than a treaty.

correlation describes the strength of the statistical relationship between two variables.

cost–benefit analysis calculates whether a product or service is worthwhile in terms of: labour, materials, time taken, short-/long-term success or failure.

covenant in the Judeo-Christian tradition is the promise made by God with humans that in exchange for worship and obedience, God will protect and provide for his people.

cyberveillance is the collection of data about people and commodities which is stored and transmitted electronically.

data is defined in the Data Protection Act in several ways. One version is the process of information being passed 'automatically in response to instructions given for that purpose'.

data protection has been variously interpreted. For some it refers to the privacy of data subjects for other it is the protection of the processing and application of data.

dataveillance is the collection of data about people and commodities.

deontological moral systems are those based on duties and rules.

dependency is the state where poorer countries come to depend economically on richer countries in order to survive.

development has a wide range of meanings but refers to the process of improving the quality of human live by raising living standards through an increase in incomes, levels of food production, medical services and education.

difference in its sexual sense means accepting a wide range of sexualities. In its philosophical usage *différence* is the endless play of existence that seeks to disrupt any dominant ideology (such as heterosexuality).

diriment impediments diriment means to invalidate or nullify; impediment is a legal obstruction. A diriment impediment refers to a legal reason why a marriage is null or invalid.

discourse is any written or spoken communication but Foucault understands discourse to be the way in which language symbols and practices are put together in a particular way.

dominion means to rule over.

ECHELON is an electronic system that screens and monitors communication systems (telephone, email, satellite, etc.). It is used by five countries (including the UK and USA) for information gathering security purposes.

enlightenment refers primarily to the eighteenth-century thinkers such as Hume and Kant who argued that knowledge could only be obtained through human reason and observation, and not through divine revelation or other authorities.

environmentalism is the political and ideological belief that the environment should be protected from harmful human activities.

equal consideration is the principle that all like things must be considered alike.

essentialists believe that there are intrinsic qualities, for example essentialists claim that there are definable masculine and feminine characteristics.

ethical egoism is the belief that morality is entirely based on self-interest.

ethnic refers to a group who share a national, linguistic, religious and moral heritage, whether they live in the country of origin or not.

exile refers to the events leading up to 586 BC when the Babylonians destroyed Jerusalem and sent its leading classes to Babylon.

facts–value distinction considers that the move from saying what something is to what it ought to be is wrong. Fact statements are objective and do not imply value judgements which are subjective and determined by human beliefs or feelings. The distinction is summarised by the phrase: 'is does not imply ought.'

fallacy of affirming the consequent occurs when it is falsely assumed that because a premise is true then the conclusion must also true. This often occurs because the premise or antecedent may imply the consequent (what follows) but is not necessarily so. The fallacy or mistake is caused depending on how the word 'if' is used.

false consciousness is when a person or group of persons holds a belief or view of the world which they believe to be true but is in fact false.

fiduciary relationship is the relationship of trust between the trustee (i.e. managers) and shareholders whom he represents.

Gaia refers to the ancient Greek goddess of the earth.

geocentric ethics are those which consider all aspects of the world/nature to be morally relevant.

global community is the view that as the world is interconnected (through transport and communication) it should therefore be treated as a whole not as separate nation states.

golden mean is the middle way between the vices of excess and deficiency.

goods or the purposes of marriage are traditionally stated as: children, containment of sin (that is, derived from the lust for sex) and faithfulness of the couple to each other.

greenhouse effect is when certain gases in the atmosphere (notably carbon dioxide, methane and nitrous oxide) trap heat from the Earth and stop it from escaping thereby causing a rise in the Earth's temperature.

holism is the notion that as everything is interconnected then no one thing is superior in value to anything else.

holocaust is the general term used to refer to the systematic isolation and subsequent extermination of Jews and others by the Nazis in the Second World War (1939–1945). From 1942 onwards the Nazis chose wholesale extermination rather than deportation.

homeostasis means to maintain a balance or equilibrium.

hostile takeover is when 'an investor, or a group of investors, intends to purchase a majority stake in a corporation (often secretly) against the wishes of its board' Crane and Matten *Business Ethics* page 193.

humanocentric ethics consider that humans alone are the source of moral values.

inalienable means that rights cannot be transferred or taken away.

incarnation in Christian theology is the belief that God took on human form in the person of Jesus.

indissoluble means marriage cannot be undone or 'dissolved' through divorce. **Inherent good** means that one of the characteristics of the world is that it is has value.

instrumental value is achieved by outcome. A right, for example, from the utilitarian perspective, has instrumental value if it brings about the greatest happiness or welfare.

intersexual describes those who have an extra sex chromosome (for example, XXY) and whose sex is therefore neither fully male or female. About two per cent of the population are intersexual.

IUD or intrauterine device is a small piece of plastic or copper inserted into the womb that acts as a contraceptive.

Kingdom of God is the term used by Jesus to describe a new social order based on an intimate, personal relationship with God now or in the future.

Law of Jubilee in ancient Israel decreed that every 50 years the land was to not be farmed so it could be replenished.

leaky container phenomenon describes the way in which careless use of data can cause great harm

LGBT is the acronym for lesbian (women attracted to women), gay (men attracted to men), bisexual (attracted to men and women or being both heterosexual and homosexual) and transgendered (where a person's biological sex does not match their perceived gender identity).

master-slave relationship is an analogy which Hegel used to describe the way in which history and human consciousness have developed through a process of conflict and struggle.

migration means moving from one country or area to another.

mitigation means alleviation and in law is used to refer to factors which can be used to justify a lesser punishment.

modernity describes the present trend in culture which values reason, democracy, science, capitalism and so on.

monogamy means being married to one person at a time or having a sexual relationship with only one person.

morally considerable describes any sentient being whose interests must form part of human moral decision making.

multinational corporations (MNCs) or transnational corporations are businesses which trade, produce and offer services in more than one country. Often their income or revenue is greater than the gross domestic product (GDP) of some countries.

natural law theorists believe ethics are not derived from human custom but independently from nature.

new racism is a term used by sociologists to describe the way racism is practised by ordinary people as opposed to those who self-consciously develop a theory of race.

new technology in the context of surveillance refers to the use of computers and telecommunications (via fibre-optic cables and satellites) rather than older methods of direct observation and paper records.

open marriage is where both partners agree to allow extramarital relationships without being considered unfaithful.

organisational culture refers to the collective moral and social values which are derived from a business' organisation, system and structure.

panopticon means 'the all seeing eye'.

paternalism means literally to 'act in a fatherly way' and justifies overriding a person's or people's autonomy if it is for their own good.

patriarchal refers to the values and structures of society which are derived from the male point of view.

phenotype is the visible characteristic of an organism as the result of its genetic makeup and its relationship with the environment.

phishing is the process of obtaining sensitive information, such as passwords or bank details, through an official looking electronic form (often an email or website), from a victim with the intent of using that information to steal or commit some other crime.

phronesis is the Greek word used by Aristotle and others meaning practical wisdom or the ability to make sound moral judgements.

porneia is from the Greek translation of the Hebrew *erwat dabar* from the book of Deuteronomy 24:1. In English it is often taken to mean 'indecency' or 'improper'.

pornography is any form of sexually explicit medium (such as film, photographs and literature) which is intended to cause sexual arousal.

positive and negative liberty negative liberty is freedom from interference from others. Positive liberty is the active involvement of citizens in the control of state.

positivism is the view that rights are decided by humans on what is observed to work well for society. They are not found in nature or commanded by God.

premarital sex is where two unmarried people have sex before marriage.

prenuptial agreement is a contract drawn up before marriage outlining how assets will be distributed should there be divorce.

prima facie duties were developed as an idea by W.D. Ross (1877–1971) to mean that some duties can be overridden by a stronger moral duty. Prima facie means literally 'on first appearance'.

privacy describes the state of freedom from intrusion or unwanted attention of others.

Promethean means using human intelligence to further our own existence. The idea is based on the Greek myth where Prometheus stole fire from Zeus for humans to use.

promiscuity means casual and indiscriminate sexual intercourse with many partners.

prostitution means offering sexual services and/or sexual intercourse in exchange for money.

queering means to challenge all beliefs and structures that seek to fix sexuality as if it is something objective.

race relations refers to the tensions between immigrant people and their host nation.

reconstituted family (or step family) is where children from a previous relationship are brought up by at least one non-biological parent.

rhythm method is the moment just before a woman ovulates where nature provides a moment (or 'rhythm' in nature) when a couple can have sexual intercourse without the probability of having a child.

scapegoating is when a person or people are made to take the blame for others.

scientia sexualis or 'science of sexuality' is Foucault's term to describe the way in which sexual practices have been controlled and formalised by various institutions in Western societies.

sentience is the ability to experience pain and pleasure.

sentimental fallacy (or pathetic fallacy) makes the false assumption that because something appears to behave in a human-like way it must have human-like qualities.

separation in marriage may take two forms. Divorce, when the marriage is dissolved (*a vincula*); or judicial separation (*a mensa et thoro*) when each are released from their duties as husband and wife.

sexism is the discrimination of women by men (and sometimes the other way round) based on cultural or stereotypical prejudices.

sexuality refers to sexual identity.

slippery slope is not so much an argument as an observation that people often weaken a principle or rule, which then creates a generally undesirable state of affairs.

social contract is an agreement made between individuals and a governing power, where individual liberties are given up in exchange for general social well-being.

social evolutionism (sometimes also called Social Darwinism) developed in the eighteenth and nineteenth centuries and broadly held the view that human civilizations have progressed from basic hunter-gatherers to complex and sophisticated societies.

speciesism is the discrimination against animal species by human beings based on an assumption of human superiority.

stakeholders are all those affected (harmed or benefitted) by the aims and activities of a business.

stereotype is a simplified generalisation about a group which may or may not be based on fact.

steward means to look after something on behalf of someone else.

subspecies describes humans (or plant or animal) who have distinctive appearances but who can still interbreed.

summit is a top level diplomatic conference between heads of governments or their representatives to discuss matters of great importance.

sustainable development is a term coined by the World Commission on Environmental Development in 1987. 'Development' is the aim to improve human living conditions and dignity.

technopoly is defined by Postman as the belief 'that the primary, if not only goal of human labor and thought is efficiency; that technical calculation is in all respects superior to human judgement'

theocentric ethics believes that something is good because God values it.

total quality management (TQM) is a style of management which encourages co-operative, not authoritarian, management style throughout the whole process of production.

trade-off is when a person is prepared to gain greater services or commodities by giving up other minor interests.

treaty is a formal contract and agreement.

trump means to override other considerations.

ubiquitous means being present everywhere.

unintended consequences are the negative unforeseen side effects resulting from other good consequences.

unitive sex means for loving purposes.

utilitarianism argues that an action is good if it produces the greatest happiness of the greatest number.

virtù is Machievelli's idea of prowess as used by commentators to avoid confusion with Christian ideas of virtue.

will to knowledge in Foucault's philosophy is a two-fold process of knowing things as they are and knowing how humans have created ideas about them.

will to power according to Nietzsche is the instinctive basic drive which is the source of all human activities and

xenophobia is the fear of foreigners.

FURTHER READING

Amnesty International *When the State Kills.* Amnesty International, 1989.

Aristotle *Ethics* (Editors: Thompson, Tredennick and Barnes). Penguin, 1976.

Baker, Ernest *Social Contract: Essays by Locke, Hume, Rousseau.* OUP, 1971.

Bandman, Bertram 'Do Future Generations Have a Right to Clean Air? A Note,' in *Political Theory*, Volume 10, Number 1, (February, 1982).

Barbour, Ian *Ethics in an Age of Technology.* SCM Press, 1992.

Beauvoir, Simone de *The Second Sex* (Translator: H.M. Parshley). Vintage, 1997.

Blasius, Mark and Phelan, Shane (editors) *We are Everywhere: Historical Sourcebook in Gay and Lesbian Politics.* Routledge, 1977.

Booker, Christopher *The Real Global Warming Disaster.* Continuum, 2009.

Bulmer, Marton and Soloms, John (editors) *Racism.* OUP, 1999.

Carmichael, Liz *Friendship.* T&T Clark, 2004.

Catholic Church *Catechism of the Catholic Church.* Geoffrey Chapman, 1994.

Clapham, Andrew *Human Rights: A Very Short Introduction.* OUP, 2007.

Cone, James *A Black Theology of Liberation.* Orbis,1986, 1990.

Cone, James *God of the Oppressed.* Orbis, 1975, 1997.

Countryman, William *Dirt, Greed and Sex.* XPress Reprints, 1996.

Crane, Andrew and Matten, Dirk *Business Ethics.* OUP, 2004.

Davies, Jon and Loughlin, Gerard (editors) *Sex These Days.* Sheffield Academic Press, 1997.

Deane-Drummond, Celia *A Handbook of Theology and Ecology.* SCM Press, 1996.

DeGrazia, David *Animal Rights: A Very Short Introduction.* OUP, 2002.

Descartes, René *A Discourse on Method* (Translator: John Veitch). Dent, 1986.

Dominian, Jack and Montefiore, Hugh *God, Sex and Love.* SCM Press, 1989.

Douglass, Frederick *Narrative of the Life of Frederick Douglass, an American Slave.* Penguin, 1986.

Fiorenza, Elisabeth Schüssler *In Memory of Her* (2nd edition). SCM Press, 1994.

Fischer, Ernst *Marx in His Own Words.* Penguin, 1970.

Fletcher, Joseph *Situation Ethics.* Westminster: John Knox Press, 1966.

Florman, Samuel *Blaming Technology.* St Marin's Press, 1981.

Foucault, Michel *Ethics* (Editor: Paul Rainbow). Penguin, 2000.

Foucault, Michel *The History of Sexuality: The Will to Knowledge.* Penguin, 1998.

Gilligan, Carol *In a Different Voice.* Harvard University Press, 1982, 1993.

Graham, Gordon *The Internet: a Philosophical Inquiry.* Routledge, 1999.

Gutierrez, Gustavo *Theology of Liberation.* SCM Press, 2001.

Julian of Norwich *Revelations of Divine Love* (Translator: Clifton Wolters). Penguin, 1966.

Kant, Immanuel *Toward Perpetual Peace* and Other Writings on Politics, Peace, and History (Editor: Pauline Kleingeld; Translator: David L. Colclasure). Yale University Press, 2006.

Kant, Immanuel *The Grounding for the Metaphysics of Morals* (Translator: James W. Elington). Hackett, 1981.

Kant, Immanuel *Lectures on Ethics* (Editors: Peter Heath and J.B. Schneewind). CUP, 1997.

King, Martin Luther Jr *A Knock At Midnight: The Great Sermons of Martin Luther King, Jr* (Editors: Clayborne Carson and Peter Holloran). Abacus, 2000.

Kirkpatrick, Graeme *Technology and Social Power.* Palgrave Macmillan, 2008.

Lovelock, James *The Ages of Gaia: A Biography of Our Living Earth* (2nd edition). OUP, 1995.

Lyon, David *Surveillance Society.* Open University, 2001.

Lyon, David *The Electronic Eye: The Rise of Surveillance Society.* Polity Press, 1994.

Machiavelli, Niccolò *The Prince.* OUP, 2008.

MacIntyre, Alasdair *After Virtue* (2nd edition). Duckworth, 1985.

MacIntyre, Alasdair *Dependent Rational Animals.* Duckworth, 1999.

Macourt, Malcolm (editor) *Towards a Theology of Gay Liberation.* SCM Press, 1977.

Marx, Karl *Capital* (Editor: David McLennan). OUP, 1995.

Mill, John Stuart *Utilitarianism* (Editor: Mary Warnock). Fount, 1962.

Mill, John Stuart *On Liberty* (Edited: Gertrude Himmelfarb). Penguin, 1974

Northcott, Michael S. *The Environment and Christian Ethics.* CUP, 1996.

Oakland, John and Morris, Peter *Pocket Guide to TQM.* Butterworth-Heinemann, 1988.

Rattansi, Ali *Racism: A Very Short Introduction.* OUP, 2007.

Regenstein, Lewis G. *Replenish the Earth.* SCM Press, 1991.

Rudy, Kathy *Sex and the Church.* Beacon Press, 1997.

Scruton, Roger *Animal Rights and Animal Wrongs.* Demos, 1996.

Simmonds, N.E. *Central Issues in Jurisprudence: Justice, Law and Rights.* Sweet and Maxwell, 1986.

Singer, Peter *Practical Ethics.* CUP, 1979.

Singer, Peter (editor) *Ethics.* OUP, 1994.

Singer, Peter (editor) *Companion to Ethics.* Blackwell, 1993.

Singer, Peter (editor) *Applied Ethics.* OUP, 1986.

Smart, J.C.C. and Williams, Bernard *Utilitarianism: For and Against.* CUP, 1973.

Steger, Manfred B. *Globalisation: A Very Short Introduction.* OUP, 2009.

Sunstein, Cass R. and Nussbaum, Martha C. (editors) *Animal Rights.* OUP, 2004.

Thompson, Mel *Ethical Theory* (3rd edition). Hodder Education, 2008.

Vardy, Peter *Business Morality.* Marshall Pickering, 1989.

Warnock, Mary *An Intelligent Person's Guide to Ethics.* Duckworth, 1998.

Wesley, John *Forty-Four Sermons* (4th edition). Epworth, 1944.

Wilcockson, Michael *Issues of Life and Death* (2nd edition). Hodder Education, 2009.

Wilcockson, Michael *Medical Ethics.* Hodder Education, 2008.

Wilcockson, Michael *Sex and Relationships.* Hodder and Stoughton, 2000.

Woodcock, George *The Anarchist Reader.* Fontana, 1977.

On-line resources for this book and others in the series

New books and websites are appearing all the time.
Keep up-to-date and share your own suggestions with other students and teachers.

For suggestions for further reading, comments from the authors of the *Access to Religion and Philosophy* series and further advice for students and teachers, **log on to the** *Access to Religion and Philosophy* **website at**:

www.philosophyandethics.com

INDEX